"Covering everything from Aristotle to zombies to *Breaking Bad*, Carol Owens and Stephanie Swales have written a masterpiece unlocking the secrets of ambivalence. In *Psychoanalysing Ambivalence with Freud and Lacan*, they demonstrate that ambivalence is perhaps the central category in social relations. The need for this book is especially urgent today, in an era characterised by its various ways of refusing ambivalence, which are, Owens and Swales make clear, ways of refusing the price of interacting with others altogether. *Psychoanalysing Ambivalence with Freud and Lacan* speaks to the contemporary political catastrophe better than any book I've read."

–Todd McGowan, Professor, University of Vermont, USA

GW00673328

Psychoanalysing Ambivalence with Freud and Lacan

Taking a deep dive into contemporary Western culture, this book suggests we are all fundamentally ambivalent beings. A great deal has been written about how to love – to be kinder, more empathic, a better person, and so on. But trying to love without dealing with our ambivalence, with our hatred, is often a recipe for failure. Any attempt, therefore, to love our neighbour as ourselves – or even, for that matter, to love ourselves – must recognise that we love where we hate and we hate where we love.

Psychoanalysis, beginning with Freud, has claimed that to be in two minds about something or someone is characteristic of human subjectivity. Owens and Swales trace the concept of ambivalence through its various iterations in Freudian and Lacanian psychoanalysis in order to question how the contemporary subject deals with its ambivalence. They argue that experiences of ambivalence are, in present-day cultural life, increasingly excised or foreclosed, and that this foreclosure has symptomatic effects at the individual as well as social level. Owens and Swales examine ambivalence as it is at work in mourning, in matters of sexuality, and in our enjoyment under neoliberalism and capitalism. Above all, the authors consider how today's ambivalent subject relates to the racially, religiously, culturally, or sexually different neighbour as a result of the current societal dictate of complete tolerance of the other. In this vein, Owens and Swales argue that ambivalence about one's own jouissance is at the very roots of xenophobia.

Peppered with relevant and stimulating examples from clinical work, film, television, politics, and everyday life, *Psychoanalysing Ambivalence* breathes new life into an old concept and will appeal to any reader, academic, or clinician with an interest in psychoanalytic ideas.

Carol Owens, Ph.D., is a psychoanalyst and psychoanalytic scholar in Dublin, Ireland. She edited *The Letter: Perspectives in Lacanian Psychoanalysis* (2003–2008), *Lacanian Psychoanalysis with Babies, Children and Adolescents: Further Notes on the Child* (with Stephanie Farrelly Quinn, Routledge, 2017) and *Studying Lacan's Seminars IV and V: From Lack to Desire* (with Nadezhda Almqvist, Routledge, 2019). She is the series editor for the newly established Routledge series, *Studying Lacan's Seminars*.

Stephanie Swales, Ph.D., is an Assistant Professor of Psychology at the University of Dallas, USA, a practicing psychoanalyst, a licensed clinical psychologist, and a clinical supervisor located in Dallas, Texas. Her first book, *Perversion: A Lacanian Psychoanalytic Approach to the Subject*, was published by Routledge in 2012.

Psychoanalysing Ambivalence with Freud and Lacan

On and Off the Couch

Stephanie Swales and
Carol Owens

Routledge
Taylor & Francis Group

LONDON AND NEW YORK

First published 2020
by Routledge
2 Park Square, Milton Park, Abingdon, Oxon, OX14 4RN

and by Routledge
52 Vanderbilt Avenue, New York, NY 10017

Routledge is an imprint of the Taylor & Francis Group, an informa business

© 2020 Stephanie Swales and Carol Owens

British Library Cataloguing-in-Publication Data
A catalogue record for this book is available from the British Library

Library of Congress Cataloging-in-Publication Data
A catalog record has been requested for this book

ISBN: 978-1-138-32844-0 (hbk)
ISBN: 978-1-138-32845-7 (pbk)
ISBN: 978-0-429-44865-2 (ebk)

Typeset in Times New Roman
by Swales & Willis, Exeter, Devon, UK

MIX
Paper from
responsible sources
FSC
www.fsc.org   FSC™ C013985

Printed in the United Kingdom
by Henry Ling Limited

Carol dedicates this book to Carles, for 25 years of love, hate, and bitter-sweet ambivalence: *que em caldria agrair-te tant temps que fa que t'estimo ...*

Stephanie dedicates this book to Michael, for all the things you are, *je t'aime.*

Contents

Acknowledgements

This book is the result of a labour of love, even though it is a book about ambivalence. It comes about because of our close and committed friendship, and our mutual passion for psychoanalysis. We met at an Affiliated Psychoanalytic Workgroups conference in Toronto in the Autumn of 2014 and almost immediately began to correspond about ambivalence as it emerged for us in our clinical cases, from films and TV shows we had seen or heard about. So began a friendship and work partnership that spans six time zones, taking place over thousands of emails, hundreds of skype calls, yoga classes all over North America, and hikes wherever and whenever we can. Bits and pieces of the work have brought us as far away from our own homes as Reykjavik, Massachusetts, Vancouver, New Jersey, Colorado Springs, and Boston. We always have fun, even when exhausted, and we quite often raise a few eyebrows – as much for our perceived connectedness, as for our theme. At its most absurd, we are taken for each other, pure semblants; often, we are called upon to explain "how it works", how "we work"; what seems inexplicable to colleagues is that we can write in a way that allows us to work happily and harmoniously together in a world which also requires us to compete with each other (for a share of fame, academic regard, or status). This very tension is one that we devote much time to exploring within these pages. It is because we believe in ambivalence, avowed, that we are as committed to working out its vicissitudes in how it may play its part in our own relationship as we are in the various tropes we have chosen to write about. As such, the order of our names as they appear on this book cover represents nothing other than the toss of a coin; heads, we both win.

There are a number of people who deserve our gratitude. First, we thank Kate Hawes, Senior Publisher at Routledge, who has believed in our project from the start. We also thank Charles Bath and wish him our best in his future endeavours. We consider ourselves extremely fortunate in having had Elliot Morsia (our principal editor at Routledge) working with us on this book and thank him profusely for his efforts. Over the past couple of years we have presented aspects of the work to various groups and benefitted hugely from feedback we have received. In particular, we are grateful to the Dallas Society for

Psychoanalytic Psychology and to Rolf Flor and the members of the Boston Lacan Study Group. We also want to thank Manya Steinkoler and Vanessa Sinclair for giving us a first published outing for our work on zombies, and we thank Molly Anne Rothenberg for her careful reading of our zombie chapter for Manya and Vanessa's book. In addition, we are indebted to a number of individuals whose careful readings of a draft version of this manuscript and their accompanying comments provided immensely helpful assistance that enabled us to bring the book to its final form. We thank Todd McGowan for his enthusiastic careful reading of the manuscript following an exhausting work period for himself (when surely reading a manuscript on ambivalence would have summoned up a fair bit of ambivalence)! We thank Sheldon George for similarly finding time in between deadlines to provide his most valued comments on our discussions of xenophobia and race and for gifting us with a certain nomination of our jouissance. We thank Kareen Malone, Roseanne Florence, and Michael Tillman for their careful readings of the manuscript.

We also thank our patients for granting us permission to use snippets and vignettes from our work together.

We want to thank Òscar Pujol Owens for inviting us to think about zombies and in particular for getting us to watch *The Walking Dead*. The rest, as they say, Òscar, is history.

Stephanie would like to thank her husband Michael for his unending support, intellectual curiosity, and ready supply of puns. She would also like to thank the University of Dallas for providing a summer stipend that assisted with the book's completion and her colleagues in the psychology department there for their encouragement and interest in this book project.

Carol thanks Carles, Tomàs, and Òscar for being the best family in the world (without whom …). She thanks number one best friend Roseanne Florence for suffering endless discursions on zombies, vampires, Lacan, and Trump over the past couple of years whilst watering or planting in our allotment. Finally, Carol also thanks Olga Cox Cameron and Ian Parker for being steadfast, interested, and enthusiastic interlocutors.

Some of the contents of our book were previously published in different forms.

An assortment of material from Chapters 1–3 appeared in V. Sinclair, and M. Steinkoler, (2019), *On psychoanalysis and violence: Contemporary Lacanian perspectives*, New York: Routledge, (as a book chapter entitled "Why the zombies ate my neighbors: Whither ambivalence?").

The discussion of bulimia and humour in Chapter 6 appeared in P. Gherovici and M. Steinkoler (2016), *Lacan, psychoanalysis, and comedy*, New York: CUNY (as part of a book chapter by C. Owens, entitled "Not in the humor: Bulimic dreams").

Some material in Chapter 6 appeared in C. Owens, "Having a Riot 1968/ 2011 (Which lack, what act?)", *Lacunae*, 3 (2), 2014, pp. 59–68, and "'Sex-folly-ation': Don Juan's desire and the jouissance of the nymphomaniac," *Lacunae*, 10, May 2015, pp. 139–150.

The lines from *"Advent"* by Patrick Kavanagh in Chapter 6 are reprinted from *Collected Poems*, edited by Antoinette Quinn (Allen Lane, 2004), by kind permission of the Trustees of the Estate of the late Katherine B. Kavanagh, through the Jonathan Williams Literary Agency.

About the authors

Carol Owens, Ph.D. is a psychoanalyst and clinical supervisor in private practice in North Dublin, Ireland. She is the founder of the Dublin Lacan study group. She was editor of the journal *The Letter: Perspectives on Lacanian Psychoanalysis* from 2003–2007. She is co-editor of *Lacanian Psychoanalysis with Babies, Children and Adolescents* (with Stephanie Farrelly-Quinn), published by Routledge in 2017. She is co-editor of *Studying Seminars IV and V: From Lack to Desire* (with Nadezhda Almqvist), published by Routledge in 2018. She is the series editor at Routledge for the series, *Studying Lacan's Seminars*. She has published articles and book chapters in the field of Lacanian psychoanalysis, and at its junctures with critical psychology, queer theory, film theory, cultural studies, and critical management theory.

Stephanie Swales, Ph.D. is an Assistant Professor of Psychology at the University of Dallas, USA, a practicing psychoanalyst, a licensed clinical psychologist, and a clinical supervisor located in Dallas, Texas. She is the founder of the Dallas/ Fort Worth area Lacan Study Group, recently served as the president of the Dallas Society for Psychoanalytic Psychology, and is on the executive board of the Dallas Postgraduate Program in Psychoanalytic Psychotherapy. Her first book, *Perversion: A Lacanian Psychoanalytic Approach to the Subject*, was published by Routledge in 2012. She is also the author of numerous articles and book chapters on the theory and practice of Lacanian psychoanalysis – in some cases as it intersects with critical psychology and cultural studies.

Foreword

About the author

"I love you to death" and "I love you to pieces" are two everyday phrases that perfectly evoke the French psychoanalyst Jacques Lacan's statement from his twentieth seminar that "analysis reminds us that one knows nothing of love without hate" (1999, p. 91). Perhaps ironically, but not surprisingly, someone who says "I love you to death" is most often unaware of the hatred implied in such a statement. Ambivalence – or, *hainamoration* (hateloving), the term Lacan preferred – is the cornerstone of psychoanalysis for the very reason that psychoanalysis posits a subject who is fundamentally split by language. Far from being about "mixed feelings," as Freud explained the concept in his paper *Totem and Taboo*, ambivalence involves the conflict between two equally strong currents that are "localised in the subject's mind in a way that they cannot come up against each other" (Freud, 1913, p. 35); when one current is conscious, the other is unconscious. *To have* an unconscious in these terms therefore, is at one and the same time to be ambivalent.

In Freud's reading of Sophocles' *Oedipus Rex* as well as in his creation of the myth that founds society in *Totem and Taboo* (1913), he identified an unconscious ambivalence at the core of human relationships. In Freud's first take on ambivalence love and hate are divvied up; love for the mother and hate for the father; his second framing operates in order to indicate both love and hate for the same person with one state being conscious while the other is unconscious. Freud's case history of the Rat Man (1909d) marvellously exemplifies the ambivalence at the heart of obsessional neurosis, but at the time of writing up the case the term ambivalence had yet to be coined. Freud embraced it immediately when Eugen Bleuler introduced the term: *ambivalenz*, etymologically linked with the Latin "*ambi*" meaning "both" and "*valentia*" meaning "strength" or "force". Freud made numerous laudatory remarks about the usefulness of the term, and we believe it was "Bleuler's happily chosen term" (1905d, p. 199) that allowed for Freud to theorise the bi-location of love and hate in the mind of the subject and to retroactively found totemic law upon the tensions of the Oedipus complex.

Lacan, however, was not a fan of the term ambivalence (Lacan, 1999, pp. 90–1).

He considered the word "ambivalence", with its denotation of two similar and equal forces, to be a bastardization of the true zone of experience of psychoanalysis. He proposed the neologism *hainamoration*, or hateloving, as a superior alternative (Lacan, 1999, pp. 90–1). So why is *hainamoration* so much better? *Hainamoration* evokes both what Lacan conceived as the symbolic unconscious *and* the real unconscious, which he regarded as essential concepts in order to properly situate the psychoanalytic field. Love, said Lacan, addresses itself to the semblance of being, the place of the object *a* (p. 92); hate, by contrast, does not need discourse to support it since hatred "is addressed to being" (p. 99). Hate, moreover, connected to the being of the other is also immanent in what Lacan theorised as the jealous hatred that springs forth from *jealouissance*, the jouissance one experiences in hating one's neighbour. So it is that Lacan's *hainamoration* breathes new life into an old concept.

We decided to write a book on ambivalence that makes use of both Freud and Lacan's formulations of the concept. We chose ambivalence not only because of its centrality in psychoanalysis and subjectivity but also because it seems to us that nowadays, experiences of ambivalence, and the tensions of those experiences are increasingly foreclosed – a foreclosure that has effects on psyche, which we try to indicate in moments from our clinical practices, and on culture at large which we try to indicate in our scanding of TV and film.

The way we see it, there are two contradictory ideologies which predominate today which together function to disallow the experience of ambivalence. First, there is the dictate –which Freud discussed with much fervour as to its absurdity – to love thy neighbour as thyself. This "love thy neighbour" motif has become woven into the commanded complete tolerance of the other implicated in non-discrimination discourses and policies. Second, however, neoliberalism poses our neighbour or colleague as a rival threatening to steal our object *a* out from under us such that we had better defend our territory with hatred. And so, somehow we are being encouraged to love or to hate. In our book, we aim to investigate the ways in which the contemporary subject relates to ambivalence, and manages the tensions of this existential experience, which is, we argue, increasingly foreclosed.

Despite the inescapability of the operation of ambivalence, there are few places outside of the psychoanalytic clinic where ambivalence is recognised and can be worked through. Whereas Punch and Judy shows and fairytales from the Brothers Grimm once offered such psychical possibilities and locations, children these days are increasingly offered stories which are cleansed of the messiness of ambivalence, in which conflict is easily resolved and is often based on a simple misunderstanding. Naturally, it is our own anxieties and fears related to hostility and hatred projected onto children that mobilise the production of such washed-out stories on the big, and small screens of our times. Adults as well as children have come to rely substantially on TV and film to teach us how to desire, how to enjoy, and how and when to feel ambivalent and how to handle our ambivalence. Prevailing ideologies, including neoliberalism and those promoting tolerance or empathy, find their way to the screen and influence how encounters with difference (of race, gender, sexuality, religion, etc.) are staged. So although TV and film can and do often make a show out of our ambivalence – reflecting our deeper psychical processes and perhaps helping us to understand something of our ambivalence – they also fail to help us manage the tensions of our ambivalence or to work through our ambivalence. In the absence of adequate practices to stage the tensions of ambivalence, there are outcomes at the level of individual psychopathology – outcomes that we delineate by tracing old and new figurations of the father and ways of relating to the object.

In the last two chapters of the book, we show how the concept of ambivalence for us elucidates the operations of racism and xenophobia. Using Lacan's concept of extimacy, we theorise that at the foundation of xenophobia and racism is an extimate ambivalence about one's own jouissance. Via extimacy, we see that what is most intimate in the subject is inextricably connected with the Other (Lacan, 1992, p. 139) – that the Other's jouissance is our own jouissance, rejected into the exterior and perceived in another person or group of people. Perhaps disappointingly for some readers, we do not set out to provide solutions to the problems we address in this book; that would be an odd twist for us to perform given that we want to open up the spaces for thinking and speaking about ambivalence, rather than close them down with "solutions".

The great British psychoanalyst Adam Phillips reminds us that Freud's insistence about our ambivalence, "is also his way of saying that we are never quite as obedient as we seem to be: that where there is devotion there is always protest; that where there is trust there is suspicion; and that where there is self-hatred (guilt) there is self-love" (Phillips, 2015, p. 87). This book is about the fundamental ambivalences at the core of human existence, and because we are psychoanalysts, we take "Freud's insistence about our ambivalence" seriously. What follows in these chapters is the result of that. Because we are great friends and co-workers what follows in these chapters is also the result of this working union, a full-on avowed and tended ambi-valence. How could it be anything else?

References

Freud, S. (1905d). Three essays on the theory of sexuality. In *The standard edition of the complete psychological works of Sigmund Freud* (pp. 123–246). *S.E., VII* (1901–1905).

Freud, S. (1909d). Notes upon a case of Obsessinal Neurosis. In *The standard edition of the complete psychological works of Sigmund Freud. S.E., X* (pp. 138–151).

Freud, S. (1913). Totem and taboo. In *The standard edition of the complete psychological works of Sigmund Freud. S.E., XIII* (pp. 1–164).

Lacan, J. (1992). *The seminar of Jacques Lacan, Book VII: The ethics of psycho-analysis, 1959–1960*. Edited by J.-A. Miller. Translated by D. Porter. New York: W.W. Norton & Co.

Lacan, J. (1999). *On feminine sexuality, the limits of love and knowledge, 1972–1973. Encore: The seminar of Jacques Lacan book XX*. Ed. J.-A. Miller, trans. B. Fink. New York and London: Norton.

Phillips, A. (2015). *Unforbidden pleasures*. London: Penguin Random House.

Chapter I

The tensions of ambivalence

It seems to us that in our contemporary times, experiences of ambivalence and of the tensions of ambivalence are increasingly foreclosed. We are, it appears, no longer expected to be "in" or "of two minds" about anything. Moreover, not only are we not expected to be ambivalent about figures, objects, or places in our lives, but in fact it is as if ambivalence itself has become an unsuitable psychical position or experience. Being ambivalent is increasingly and rather negatively interpreted for what it belies; that is, a less than unitary or singular response to someone or something. But as the great British psychoanalyst and essayist Adam Phillips remarks, we can be ambivalent about anything or anyone; our ambivalence reveals what matters to us, and indeed it is often the way we recognise that someone or something has become significant to us (Phillips, 2015, p. 87).

Our biggest claim in this respect – and one we will come back to a good deal throughout this book – is that although ambivalence is an essentially human lived experience and psychical operation, there are few places outside of the psychoanalytic or psychotherapeutic consulting room currently where such experiences are taken seriously and given the chance to be worked through. This means that for the most part, we rely on other *methods* for the management of our ambivalence, and this is why in this book we write a lot about television shows (TV) and movies. We have, we believe, come to rely heavily on TV and film in order to know how and when to feel ambivalent and what to do about that. But as we rely upon cultural products such as TV and film in this way, we cannot ignore that prevailing ideologies and their complicated relationships with power and politics govern their production and as such instruct us in the ways of our ambivalence with a heavier hand than we might care to imagine. This is, of course, another way to say that some ambivalence is hard at work behind the scenes in the very writing of a show, or in the production of a film.

We want to trace some of the slippery, behind-the-scenes activities of ambivalence, especially as we believe that it has been repressed or excluded from much contemporary discourse, tied as it increasingly is to two prevailing but contradictory ideals. On the one hand there is the ideal that we should all get along with our "neighbours" (fellow workers, peers) even if we cannot stand them; this is of course the "love thy neighbour" full tolerance of the other which is thoroughly implicated in discourses and practices of anti-racism and other types of non-discrimination. On the other hand, under neoliberalism, our neighbour (fellow worker, peer) is also often our biggest competition or rival and it would serve us better to stand on their head for an advantage. These two ideals are commonly distilled and condensed onto situations where encounters with difference (*other* races, ethnicities, genders, classes, sexualities, etc.) are staged. In this way all the fighting (and perhaps much of the loving as well as the hating) takes place on the TV. This of course was not always the case. For it is one thing to see how TV (or film) may "reflect" our deeper, inner, psychical operations and processes, and even does a bit of work on our behalf by helping us to understand our conflictual tensions of ambivalence; however, it is an entirely different thing to understand the seemingly voracious appetite for opportunities to cathect these psychical experiences and seek out the possibility of their cathexes on the small or big screen. We happen to think that the latter fails considerably. For while cultural products unsurprisingly convey, represent, and otherwise indicate the psychical activities of their spectators, they do not, except incidentally, treat them. It seems to us that whilst TV and film show us our ambivalence, they do not help us to manage the tensions of our ambivalence. And we happen to believe – in the best psychoanalytic tradition – that what gets repressed, excluded, or foreclosed pops up elsewhere.

We will jump right in and invite you to reflect a bit on King Henry VIII in this light. The fantastically compelling 2007–2011 TV series "The Tudors" (Hirst) focuses on the infamous political and religious trials and tribulations during the reign of King Henry VIII, arising out of his determination and passion to have a male heir. At the height of his frustration regarding what was referred to as his "great matter" – the euphemism for his wish to marry Anne Boleyn and have her recognised by the Roman Catholic church as his legitimate Queen – he had banished his Spanish Queen Catherine of Aragon from court and martyred Sir Thomas More and Bishop Fisher because they would not sign allegiance to his governance of the church above God. Meanwhile, he continued to have to endure the evidence of diminishing loyalty among his subjects and their audible disdain for his new wife Anne Boleyn, and had to suffer rejection by the French King Francis I of his proposal to have his and Anne's daughter Elizabeth betrothed to his son in marriage. At the very high point of his crisis, in this version of *his*tory, his secretary Thomas Cromwell comes up with an interesting idea. In order to counter the negative effects of the ambivalence among his subjects towards Anne, he suggests writing a series of plays to be performed throughout the kingdom in which the very drama causing all the tension at Court is staged in a humorous manner: the heads of the Catholic Church are depicted as bumbling and foolish, whereas the head of State is depicted as tolerant and benign. Whether or not it is true that

Cromwell ever wrote or staged such plays, what all the historians agree upon was that he was at once architect and engineer of the tides of opinion which he controlled in order to bring about the King's wishes. If indeed he was also the playwright and stage director of the received version of the King's various crises, he merits the attention given to him by historians and writers alike. In recent times, Hilary Mantel's 2009 best-selling, Booker prize-winning *Wolf Hall* is dedicated to following Cromwell's inventiveness and ingenuity in spinning the web which sustained Henry at the epicentre. What is most interesting from our point of view is that the "dramas" of King Henry VIII's life and marriages in all its versions, whether written up as literary fiction (Gregory, 2015; Mantel, 2010, 2015), as history (Wooding, 2015), staged (Anderson, 1948; Shakespeare, 1613/1997), or filmed (1933; 1953; 1966, 1969, 1971, 1998, 2008), for the big screen as well as for the small screen, testify that the now 500-year-old history of his life and his marriages are as interesting for contemporary audiences as they had been in whatever epoch they have been portrayed hitherto. And we note that almost every decade of the twentieth and now twenty-first century have produced at least one film or TV version of Henry VIII's life. But why might this be? What is it that is "put on stage" that is of such interest to contemporary and older audiences alike?

One of the elements that makes Henry's life so fascinating is that regardless of to whom he is married, the figure of the wife in question at first charged (hyper-cathected) with value – libidinal and/or political – later becomes emptied of it. She stands first for what he desires and is the very embodiment of his fantasy (to sire his heir, to consolidate his diplomatic position vis-à-vis the Catholic Church, or France, or indeed, his own kingdom and subjects), but this changes as she is revealed as blocking this desire in some way (whether through her own inability to bear a son/child, or some other factor which comes to the fore). The old ditty that helps school-children remember the destinies of each of his wives – "divorced, beheaded, died, divorced, beheaded, survived" – can be seen as naming the effects of Henry's ambivalence around his wives but also capturing the essence of this history as a sequence. Each marriage fails to bring about the desired outcome and in order for that marriage to be brought to an end, Henry has to undergo and stage a complete reversal of his position that led so strongly to the securing of the marriage in the first place. He moves, and builds a case for moving, from one pole of his ambivalence to another: each wife is emblematic first of his absolute love and passion, and then of his absolute hatred and vitriol (with the exception of his last wife Catherine Parr, only by virtue of the fact that she succeeds him). Even as Head of the church in England, as Head of State, and as having the final word in the Law courts, Henry still had to justify his decision of wanting to end each marriage, and since the times he lived in were penalised by anything other than absolute congruity and agreement with the King's position (whatever that position was at the time, and regardless of the King's own oscillations):

any "difference" in opinion to that position normally ended up on the scaffold, or upon the executioner's block. And here we have a clue as to another element that continues to make Henry's life so fascinating to twentieth and twenty-first century audiences. In a manner picked up by Lewis Carroll in his portrayal of the whimsical and dangerous Queen of Hearts in *Alice in Wonderland* whose throaty cry "off with their heads" signals the occurrence of even a trivial misunderstanding with one of her subjects, so too, did Henry VIII stage over and over his disappointments when his wives – or indeed any of his other subjects – differed from his point of view. The TV drama detailed in horrific realism each and every one of the executions Henry ordered. No expense was spared in capturing the appetite for a "good execution" on the part of his ordinary subjects; the myriad of details surrounding the executions – from the skill and championship of a certain swordsman to the bribing of another for a bungled and therefore most painful execution. These details – no doubt accurately observed from the historical records – fascinate us in the same way that zombie film killings and massacres appear to do. In the time of the Tudors, the conditions for staging the tensions of the King's ambivalence were both legitimated and anchored as custom, ritual, and tradition in the symbolic order of the period: if you fell from the King's love to his hatred, it could only end badly.

In our time (and in most of our places), the public execution has left the stage (notwithstanding the enactment of the death penalty in the presence of witnesses where that act is still practised). We recognise of course that the conditions for staging ambivalence are not the same as they were for our blood-thirsty ancestors. For this we can be indeed thankful. On the other hand, most Millennials know the best way to kill a zombie, and judging by the sheer volume of zombie films in production, our sense is that the appetite for a good execution has not diminished much. We shall speculate further about zombie executions in Chapter 2.

To be clear, our argument is *absolutely not* that we need an execution in order to purge ourselves of our hostile impulses, but rather that as the conditions for staging what we experience as the tensions of ambivalence themselves undergo change from epoch to epoch, the ways in which ambivalence is expressed also changes. And since in our time ambivalence is increasingly foreclosed from the social bond, there is nowhere for the normal, natural antagonism that accompanies human relations to go. So what are these conditions for staging the tensions of ambivalence? How are they constituted differently in each epoch? What can we learn from the variation of these stagings?

The benefits of tragedy

The Tudors were not the only ones who knew how to stage(-manage) their ambivalence. In *Truth and Method* (2004), Gadamer comments that Aristotle, in his scrutiny of the Attic tragedies, was struck by how the representation of the tragic action had a specific effect on the spectator, which he called *catharsis*. The representation worked through the affects of *Eleos* and *Phobos*. *Eleos* and *Phobos* are commonly translated as pity and fear respectively, although Gadamer finds something lost in these translations since in his view Aristotle is referring particularly to the *overwhelming* aspects of these emotions. *Eleos* should rather denote the misery that comes over us in the face of what we call *miserable*, and *Phobos* is the very thing we feel when our blood runs cold, and we shudder. For Aristotle, these "effects" were purifying. Why so? Because being overcome by misery and horror was supposed to involve the spectator as he came to recognise himself in the play and affirm something essential:

> What does the spectator affirm here? Obviously it is the disproportionate, terrible immensity of the consequences that flow from *a guilty deed that is the real claim on the spectator*. The tragic affirmation is the fulfilment of this claim. It has the effect of a genuine communion.
>
> (Gadamer, 2004, p. 128, *our emphasis*)

Aristotle had defined catharsis as the "purging of the spirit of morbid and base ideas or emotions by witnessing the playing out of such emotions or ideas on stage" (Aristotle, 1941/2001, 1458). For Aristotle, the effect of catharsis induced in the spectator of the Attic tragedy established this drama form as a drama of balance, which provided the opportunity for the mind of the spectator to arrive at a state of balance. His proposition from the *Poetics* that tragedy through the arousal of pity and fear brings about a relief of these emotions is usually interpreted as indicating that just as tragedy arouses powerful feelings in the spectator, it also has a salubrious effect: after the storm and climax there comes a sense of release from tension, and of calm (Aristotle, *Poetics*, 1449b). Through witnessing the tragedy and suffering of the protagonist (commiserating with him/her, shuddering at the thoughts of what s/he was going through), such emotions and feelings in the spectator are purged. The purging of emotions therefore creates the conditions for feeling relieved, and the spectator emerges in better moral, ethical, and psychological shape than s/he was in before. However, it is not just any random act which can properly lead to the kind of fear or pity which overwhelms the subject and brings about the conditions for catharsis; in Aristotle's comments regarding the circumstances that strike fear or pity in the spectator he observes that:

> when the tragic incident occurs between those who are near or dear to one another – if, for example, a brother kills, or intends to kill, a brother, a son his father, a mother her son, a son his mother, or any other deed of the kind is done – these are the situations to be looked for by the poet.
>
> (Aristotle, ibid., 1453b)

In other words, the poet who would write the successful cathartic tragedy would do well to reflect something of the ambivalence inherent in the very closest of human bonds.

The German philologist Jacob Bernays' ground-breaking study on Aristotle and catharsis is regarded as having "overturned the dominant moral reading of tragedy" (Billings & Leonard, 2015, p. 8). In his close study of Bernays' essay, James Porter argues that Bernays caused upheaval in the academic world of tragedy because he disputed the established idea of catharsis which hung on the single widely quoted sentence from Aristotle's *Poetics* (Porter, 2015). Bernays disagreed with the notion that catharsis entailed a purification of tragic emotions – a common misreading of Aristotle in his view – claiming that such a misreading had turned the Aristotelian interpretation of tragedy into a "moral house of correction" (Bernays, 1857/2015, p. 4). Initially Bernays underscored the medical meaning of the term elsewhere in Aristotle's work emphasising the purgative aspects of catharsis (i.e., a process that involved a violent bodily discharge such as orgasm, vomiting, evacuating …), while claiming that certain purgative effects although therapeutic are not essentially transformative, nor in the least bit morally so. Later, however, Bernays built what we could call a psycho-social theory of catharsis. He argued that the drama Greek audiences observed on the Euripidean stage offered them an opportunity to share in what he called the suffering "in the face of a collapsing old-world order" and a delicious "fear and shuddering at the prospect of a fast-approaching age" (Bernays, 1857/2015, p. 46). Indeed, he further claims that social life with its "never ending reversals" offers an all too ready supply of "cultural objects" that can create the conditions for the experience of cathartic disturbances, pinned as these objects are to cultural pressures and cultural shifts (Bernays, 1857/2015, p. 46). This view examining the cathartic frenzy in representations of moments of social change and unrest on stage in ancient Greece is one that links very well for us to the arguments zombie film scholars articulate about the rise and rise of the zombie apocalypse film. In these apoca-lyptic scenes scholars find in the zombie its function as a barometer of cultural change and social unrest, as well as indexing something of the fear and anxiety emerging from socio-political conflicts and tensions.

Bernays' 1857 study is therefore seen as paving the way for Nietzsche's recuperation of the notion of ecstatic discharge in his *Birth of Tragedy* (Porter, 2015). In *The Birth of Tragedy*, Nietzsche argued that the Greek subject knew and felt the terror and the horrors of existence, or indeed we could say, the horrors of co-existence, which were represented in the conjunction of the Apollonion and Dionysian motifs and themes of the Attic tragedies (Nietzsche, 2003, pp. 1–2). Nietzsche saw in the Dionysian spectacle the redemptive potential in which "all the stubborn, hostile barriers, which necessity, caprice or 'shameless fashion' have erected between man and man, are broken down. Now, […] each one feels himself not only united, reconciled, blended with his neighbour, but as one with him" (ibid., p. 4). Commentators from the fields of philosophy, classics, and literature regard the ecstatic quality of Nietzsche's Dionysian frenzy as comparable to Aristotle's cathartic purges (Pfeffer, 1972; Porter, 2016). In each the conditions for the spectator to undergo a subjective transformation rely upon an identification with the protagonist's struggle (through commiseration in Aristotle and through reconciliation and fusion in Nietzsche), after which the spectator is purged and/or renewed and thus enters into a higher moral state of being. In other words, the recuperated state is always within reach of the spectator but "triggered" by his/her ability to be moved, touched, engaged at the very level of his/her subjective core, and it is within the "moral" dimension that restoration takes effect, which in turn has psychological implications: namely that of restoring an essential "balance" to the psyche.

The notion of restoration of balance to the psyche is inherent in Sigmund Freud's notion of catharsis in psychoanalysis. Indeed, and not surprisingly, Bernays' study is also regarded as paving the way for Freud and Breuer's importation of the "cathartic method" into psychoanalytic therapy (Porter, 2015). In a neat little piece of serendipity, it was none other than Freud's uncle by marriage – the very same Jacob Bernays – who is credited as having advanced a specifically *pathological* reading of catharsis. Whether Freud would have come across Bernays' study of Aristotle had he not married his niece Martha is anyone's guess, but there can be little doubt that he was profoundly influenced by Bernays' thesis on catharsis as a fundamental psychical function of the spectacle of the Greek tragedy (Lacan, 1992, p. 247); no great wonder then that Freud would go on to focus on one Greek tragedy in particular in order to theorise an essential opportunity for catharsis at the core of human subjectivity: predicated upon the recognition and identification of the spectator with Oedipus, what is purged is nothing other than the ambivalent tensions experienced in our psychical relations with our parents.

> A single idea of general value dawned on me. I have found, in my own case too, [the phenomenon of] being in love with my mother and jealous of my father, and I now consider it a universal event in early childhood [...]. If this is so, we can understand the gripping power of *Oedipus Rex*, in spite of all the objections that reason raises against the presupposition of fate; and we can understand why the later "drama of fate" was bound to fail so miserably. Our feelings rise against any arbitrary individual compulsion, such as is supposed in *Die Ahnfrau* and the like; but the *Greek legend seizes upon a compulsion which everyone recognises because he senses its existence within himself.* Everyone in the audience was once a budding Oedipus in fantasy [...].
>
> (Freud, Letter to Fliess, 15 October 1897; *our emphasis*)

The first mention of Freud's "Oedipus Complex" is here presented in a letter to his close friend and theoretical ally at that time, Wilhelm Fliess (Masson, 1995). Freud's later treatment of the play in *The Interpretation of Dreams* again foregrounds the idea that the drama has a "profound and universal power to move" the spectator and moreover that if the play moves a modern audience no less than an ancient Greek one, this is because "there must be something which makes a voice within us ready to recognise the compelling force of destiny in the Oedipus" (Freud, 1900, pp. 261–262). What we can identify as Freud's *Aristotelian* claim is that Oedipus' destiny moves us only because it might have been ours; without this recognition and identification, we remain unmoved. Whereas, if we identify with Oedipus, it is because there but for the grace of (the) God(s) go I. For Freud there is even indication in Sophocles' text that the legend itself sprang from dream material which he takes as evidence for the trans-historicism of the "complex". Citing Jocasta's consolation of Oedipus by referring him to a typical dream that men have – that is, to lay (with) their mothers – Freud highlights the ambivalence men – then as now – experience in their relations with their mothers that has them dream of having sex with them one minute and speak of this with "indignation and astonishment" in the next (Freud, 1900, p. 264). Freud goes on to think about Shakespeare's Hamlet in a similar vein, regarding it as another "great creation of tragic poetry" (ibid.). Indeed, in his seminar on desire, the French psychoanalyst Jacques Lacan regards Hamlet as an Oedipal drama equivalent in functional terms to the tragic geneaology of the Oedipus complex (2019, p. 241–242). What is different in Hamlet for Freud is that between the two epochs of civilisation in which *Oedipus Rex* and *Hamlet* were conceived of, the advance of repression in the "emotional life of mankind" had laid claim to Hamlet. In the Oedipus drama, Freud sees the child's wishful fantasy brought out into the open and realised (as in a dream) whereas in Hamlet it remains repressed and as spectators we only discover the existence of Hamlet's fantasy from its inhibition. Hamlet can "do anything except take vengeance on the man who did away with his father and took that father's place with his mother" precisely because Freud argues the man shows him the repressed wishes of his childhood realised (Freud, 1900, p. 265). Where Freud moves from Sophocles to Shakespeare to examine the ambivalence of desire, Lacan takes Shakespeare's Hamlet as exemplar of the "tragedy of desire" in his sixth seminar (1958–1959), and Sophocles' Antigone as exemplar of the true tragic hero in his seventh (Lacan, 1992).

Freud's readings of Oedipus Rex and of Hamlet allow him to identify an unconscious ambivalence at the heart of the first human relationships: which for him constitutes a conflict and a tension in the psyche that he theorised as both trans-historical and universal. Critics of Freud's theory of the Oedipus complex come from every conceivable field including the one he invented himself: psychoanalysis. However, most critics appear to miss Freud's essential point that he attributes the Oedipus complex not to Oedipus but rather to the originally unknown creator of the legend *and* to the audience, and every variation of the legend subsequently. We could say, a bit like we said earlier regarding Henry VIII, that one of the reasons why accounts of Oedipal ambivalence continue to draw us in is because we are still riveted by the stagings of ambivalence which are otherwise repressed following Freud's very claim regarding Hamlet.

From a dream to a social theory

In Freud's invention of the myth that founds society, we find precisely this management of essentially conflictual material which Freud ultimately placed in relation to what Lacan would call the hateloving (*hainamoration*) of the father. In *Totem and Taboo* (1913), Freud elevates the mechanism that condenses Oedipal love and hate on one and the same person (i.e., the father) to the function of a theory that explains the very foundation of civilised society. The steps which led Freud from the theorizing of Oedipal to totemic psychical tensions can be seen to map his topology of an essential ambivalence at the core of human subjectivity and to ultimately propose it as predicated upon what he called the "father complex" (Freud, 1913, p. 157). The accent is first of all placed upon the affects of love/hate which are bi-located: love for the mother, hate for the father, which allows Freud initially to find Oedipus innocently guilty of the crime of loving his mother and killing his father, and Hamlet's neurotic inhibition supporting his incestuous wish, both tragic figures demonstrating what for Freud is already a core psychical tendency. Second: the affects are localised in different places in the subject's mind (Freud, 1913, p. 35). It is this second "take" on ambivalence that speaks to the very division of the subject itself (taken for granted and elaborated upon after Freud as the touchstone of the subject of psychoanalysis). Ambivalence in contemporary discourse is all too often banalised as the experience of "having mixed feelings", or even as "thinking or behaving one way but feeling another" (which legitimates the whole notion of "cognitive dissonance theory" as well as warranting aspects of the practice of CBT). However this essential Freudian innovation at the heart of his invented myth in *Totem and Taboo* situates ambivalence as the conflict between two equally strong currents – "localised *in the subject's mind* in a way that they cannot come up against each other" (Freud, 1913, p. 35, our emphasis) – since when one current or force is conscious, the other is unconscious. All accounts of the term ambivalence attribute its first use (and invention) to German psychologist Eugen Bleuler in 1909 (*ambivalenz*) and the introduction of the term into the English language for the first time only in 1910. Etymologically derived from the Latin *ambi* for both, *valentia* for strength/force, we argue that it was this fruitful term which allowed for Freud to theorise the bi-location of "lovehate" in the mind of the subject and retroactively found totemic law upon the tensions of the Oedipus complex.

In *Totem and Taboo*, Freud builds a conceptual bridge arising from his comparison of "taboo" in "savages" with his clinical observations of the obsessional neurotic tendency to substitute other objects and acts in place of prohibited ones, and his discussion of the presence of "ceremonials" in both to discharge the tensions inherent in the antagonism of desiring and yet feeling prohibited from acting in the direction of that desire (Freud, 1913, pp. 29–30). Freud found in both that the desire is unconscious and the prohibition conscious. Notably, the motives for prohibition have fallen under the sway of repression such that no more than the obsessional neurotic can tell you why s/he feels compelled to do (or undo) a certain act, neither can your average savage tell you the origin of his/her taboos (ibid, p. 31).

In his pre-staging of the "primal horde" myth, Freud remarks that as the most ancient and important taboo prohibitions are the two basic laws of Totemism: not to kill the totem animal and to avoid sexual intercourse with members of the totem clan of the opposite sex, he concludes that these must be the most ancient and powerful of human desires. These are in turn the very desires that Freud finds at the core of childhood wishes and as the "nucleus of neuroses" – aka the Oedipus complex.

Drawing on the case of Little Hans, Freud remarks that he had the typical Oedipal attitude of a male child towards his parents: the hatred of his father arising in him from rivalry for his mother had to contend against his old-established affection and admiration for his father (Freud, 1913, p. 129). Freud argues that Hans finds relief from the conflict arising from this "double-sided", "emotionally ambivalent" attitude towards his father by displacing his hostile and fearful feelings onto a substitute for his father (i.e., in Hans' case, the horse became a phobic substitute), although he concurs, the displacement does not bring the conflict to an end. In fact, Hans succeeds in transferring (displacing) his ambivalence onto the horse as well as identifying with it – jumping around excitedly and biting his father (Freud, ibid., p. 129)! As the essence of Totemism involves an identification of the subject with the totem animal as well as an ambivalent emotional attitude towards it, Freud feels justified in substituting the father for the totem animal in these preliminary remarks on the formula for Totemism (ibid, p. 131).

Splicing his research on Totemism together with his psychoanalytic observations Freud now advances via Darwinism with his own take on the hypothesis of the "primal horde" in order to theorise an organizing of the social bond with the "father-complex" at its very core. Commenting that in Darwin's version of the evolution of society there is no place for the functioning of Totemism, Freud instead supposes that once upon a time in Darwin's primal horde, the band of brothers came together, killed and (being cannibals) devoured the father of the horde, thereby bringing an end to the patriarchal horde. Together they managed something which was not possible for them to achieve as individuals. Now this act brought about a couple of consequences: on the one hand in devouring the father they accomplished their identification with him, even acquiring a portion of his strength through literal incorporation, on the other hand, being filled with the same kinds of contradictory, ambivalent feelings as children and neurotics with regard to the father they became filled with remorse and guilt (Freud, 1913, p. 143). This is the moment in the myth that seals the deal for Freud: the horde hated their father who had access to all the females and was able to prevent them from satisfying their craving for his power, and his sexual jouissance, yet they loved and admired him too. In killing him, they both satisfy their hatred and at the very same time complete identification with him. But afterwards, the old affectionate current returns the form of remorse and guilt. As Freud puts it, "the dead father became stronger than the living one had been" and adds, "events took the same course we so often see them follow in human affairs to this day" (ibid, p. 143). Why is the dead father stronger?

Because what he had prevented while he was alive is now actively prohibited by the sons themselves in the guilty constitution of two taboos: that of any act of killing of the totemic substitute for the father and that of any act of sex with the females of the clan. Freud's strong thesis in *Totem and Taboo* therefore foregrounds the idea that the social link is structurally underpinned by the unconscious hatred of the father (although this notion is at odds with the commonly accepted idea in our time of a weakening of paternal authority which we will say a whole lot more about in Chapters 4 and 5).

A secondary thesis but one which is most interesting is Freud's highlighting of the ambivalent aspect of the word "taboo" itself. Tracing the word to Wilhelm Wundt's use and explanation of its etymology Freud underscores the double meaning attached to it (Freud, 1913, p. 25). To begin with, Freud following Wundt calls attention to the single common characteristic that prevails in both of these states – "what may not be touched" – taboo, on the one hand referring to "something unclean" and on the other "something sacred" (ibid, p.25). It is only later in its usage according to Wundt that the term "taboo" becomes differentiated and eventually developed into its opposites – sacred/unclean (ibid, p.25). However, Freud argues that from the beginning of its usage "taboo" had a double meaning used to designate a particular kind of ambivalence and whatever arose from it (Freud, 1913, p. 67). He remarks that there were many words in early languages which expressed contrary ideas and that over time modifications in the pronunciation of the original word led to the expression of the ideas being separately achieved by two words. But this was not the case with "taboo". Here, the very ambivalence expressed by the word itself underwent diminution, and the term itself had fallen out of use to a large extent (ibid.). But what replaces the term for Freud is a new one: conscience, which he proposes may be experienced as a sense of guilt. If the prohibitions of taboo are themselves the consequences of an emotional ambivalence then the twist that Freud brings about in this thesis is to propose that the productions of "conscience" take over the importance psychical work of "taboo" via the dissimulation of an unconscious desire and its symptomatic counterpart: the guilt that is experienced when the prohibited unconscious desire is transgressed. According to this logic not even Oedipus could escape guilt even though he acted without awareness of his own crime (Lacan, 1992, p. 304).

Do this in memory of me ...

Tracing how Freud mythologises the origins of the social bond qua transform-ation of Oedipal ambivalence into Oedipal fraternal guilt, we catch an important glimpse of the functioning of the totemic meal, which allows for the staging of the tensions of ambivalence while at the same time serving to reinforce moral law. Freud's "Aristotelian" debt by way of Jacob Bernays has him support his references to his own primal horde myth via Sophocles' telling of the myth of Oedipus. If the resulting effect on civilised society of the social contract to agree to uphold the prohibitions on (maternal) incest and (paternal) murder is a fraternal guilt predicated upon an identification with each other (and our neigh-bour and our other semblables), then according to the thesis outlined by Freud back in 1913, there is a commensurate requirement for a totemic meal every now and then to identify (with) and work through our emotional ambivalence(s).

In Freud's advancement of his theory of the social bond at this time, he finds much of value in William Robertson Smith's research of 1889 put forward in his book *Religion of the Semites* (Robertson Smith, 2002). In particular he is struck by Robertson Smith's hypothesis that the ceremony of the "totem meal" had formed an integral part of the totemic system (ibid, p.132). What grabbed Freud was the function of the act of fellowship immanent in the sacrificial feast in which was stressed "confirmation of fellowship and mutual social obligations" (ibid, p. 142) together with the ceremonial aspect of the occasion involving the slaughter and devoration of the sacrificial (totem) animal. In other words, the totem meal celebrates identification of each member of the clan with each other through precisely a collective transgression, as well as ritualizing the identifica-tion of each member with the totem. What is forbidden to the individual member is justified only through the participation of the entire clan. Afterwards, the slaughtered animal is "lamented and bewailed" and this is followed by fes-tive rejoicing during which "every instinct is unfettered and there is license for every gratification" (ibid, p.140). This aspect of the totem meal suggests to Freud that this is how we can understand festivals in general: since it is an opportunity for permitted (nay, mandated) excess, it betokens the feeling that is produced when prohibition is lifted. But in addition we can see how the "lamenting and bewailing" is – as part of the ritual – akin to a staging of some-thing essential which should not be forgotten. Freud really underscores this aspect of the totemic formula since it is in the very "killing and mourning" of the totem animal (as a "substitute for the father") that he finds the "ambivalent emotional attitude" which characterises what he calls the "father-complex" in children and adults alike (1913, p. 141). First there is the tragedy, second there is the festival, or first a *slaughter* then laughter!

By contrast we argue that in our times our festivals do not adequately "stage" the tensions of ambivalence. Rather we see them functioning much more at the level of that which Lacan called the "*semblant*" (cf. Grigg, 2007): we are simultaneously seduced and deceived by the spectacle of the carnivalesque aspects of the festival while failing to identify entirely (with) the "action" or "drama" at the heart of it. In his speech at the Occupy Wall Street protest in 2012, philosopher Slavoj Žižek advised protestors not to fall for the *semblant* of the carnival – proclaiming that even though the "taboo" is broken it is still possible to be seduced into inactivity:

> Don't fall in love [with yourselves,] with the nice time we are having here. Carnivals come cheap – the true test of their worth is what remains the day after, how our normal daily life will be changed. Fall in love with hard and patient work – we are the beginning, not the end. Our basic message is: the taboo is broken, we do not live in the best possible world, we are allowed and obliged even to think about alternatives.
>
> (Žižek, 2011)

It is even the case that participants at festivals in our times suffer from the sense of obligation to enjoy without limits which puts into play a kind of anhedonic response, signalled in today's culture and psychoanalytic clinic as the "inability to enjoy". In times of compulsory enjoyment, today's subject is as likely to feel guilt and remorse not out of commemorating a moment of transgressive identification with his/her "tribe", but rather, out of his/her failure to enjoy the moment. The guilt associated with the inability to enjoy is an index of how what is transgressive in a culture changes epistemically (we will say more about guilt and its vicissitudes in Chapter 6).

Carnivals come cheaply in our times. Our time is one where Facebook and internet memes respond to events such as violent shootings or abuses of power. The taboo is broken as Žižek says: we can stage mass protests at the drop of a hat. Our discontents are "things" that can go "viral" at incalculable speeds. News is never "new". The hypermodern technologies of capitalism ensure a constantly "updated" news-feed and its counterpart in the form of endless threads, blogs, vlogs, tweets, snapchats, instagrams, and other digital bites. Is this the rather feeble twenty first century version of the Greek Attic chorus?

Greek scholar Francis Ferguson argues that for Aristotle the Sophoclean chorus is a character that takes on an important role in the action of the play, instead of merely making incidental music between the scenes as they do in the plays of Euripides (1949/1972, p. 29). The chorus may be described as a group personality – with its own traditions, habits of thought and feeling, and mode of being. It exists, it perceives, and it depends on the main protagonists to invent and try out the details of the drama. It is the function of the chorus to mark the stages of the action and to perform the suffering and perceiving part of the tragic rhythm (Ferguson, ibid, p. 30). In this way the function of the Greek chorus in relation to the staging of the tragedy can be seen to have mobilised essential representations of the tensions of ambivalence. For Lacan, the chorus is "the people who are moved", therefore, "your emotions are taken care of by the chorus" (Lacan, 1992, p. 252). Lucy Jackson argues that modern audiences faced with the spectacle of the Greek chorus experience it as a challenge: not Jackson emphasises because of an intellectual demand upon the audience but rather because the chorus prompts the audience to be become involved in the action of the drama (Jackson, 2016). This aspect of the chorus, its ability to both comment upon and operate as the locus of the signifying organization of conflictual material by "prompting" a response in the spectator is astutely observed in Woody Allen's 1995 film *Mighty Aphrodite*. Director Allen resurrects the chorus to its properly symbolic function in the film so that it is at once social commentator *and* repository of the tensions of ambivalence. (Allen of course works humour into the proceedings.) In one choral ode when the chorus prays to Zeus a voice is heard from the heavens saying "This is Zeus, I am not home right now. Leave a message and I'll get back to you." The chorus then responds at the beep saying "Call us when you get in, we need help!"

Is it not possible to see something of the same psychical business in the work of the Greek chorus and in the totemic ritual, as each offered opportunities for the catharsis of ambivalence? Ferguson claims that Sophocles' audience must have had as much appetite for the thrills and diversion as the crowds who – in our time – assemble for football games, music festivals, or Easter performances of Saint Mathew's Passion (Ferguson, 2007, p. 6). Perhaps this is true, but the proper symbolic resonance that struck Aristotle with the Greeks, and Freud with totemic tribal rituals is seldom at work in present day spectacles. Instead, we have a perpetual motion industry of homogenised totems: in lieu, then, of some totem we can love to death, today's subject is in danger of becoming her own kind of totemic pillar of narcissism.

In the absence of adequate practices to properly stage the (normal) tensions of ambivalence, we believe that there are outcomes at the level of individual psychopathology. One way to take the pulse of our psychical wellbeing is to examine our ways of story-telling, our own myths, which nowadays is more likely to be framed as a TV show or as a movie than its more traditional version as "fairy tale", folk tale, or puppet show.

That's (not) the way to do it!

Punch, the chief protagonist from the Punch and Judy puppet theatre show, celebrates some 356 years of existence. The show is characterised by a great deal of knock-about (and "slapstick" humour, so-called after the stick Punch uses to slap Judy and his other opponents with) and there is much fighting and killing. The story revolves around Punch who variously fights with the devil or a crocodile, beats his nagging wife and defenestrates his baby: on completion of his various murderous acts he cries out – "now that's the way to do it"! To celebrate his 350th birthday in 2012, Punch was the focus of a six-month-long exhibition at the Victoria & Albert Museum of Childhood (Rodriguez McRobbins, 2013). Punch however is not English in origin, as he derives from the "Italian puppet play" so-called by Samuel Pepys. Commentaries on the genre of puppet theatre agree that "Punch" arrived in England at a moment of great social upheaval. The country's recent brush with republicanism had gone spectacularly off the rails after its leader, the deeply puritanical Oliver Cromwell, turned England into a dead zone of no theatre, no dancing, no sports – no fun (Rodriguez McRobbins, 2013). With the abatement of Puritanism after Cromwell's death in 1658, artists and performing troupes from Europe began to arrive in England and the puppet "Pulcinella", the Italian clown character of the *commedia dell' arte* tradition, made his debut on the English stage. Through Anglicisation Pulcinella became "Punchinello" which eventually was shortened to "Punch."

Punch and Judy expert Martin Leech locates the puppet show as a theatrical form whose roots were firmly embedded in the cultural and political upheavals of the eighteenth century and explains the composition of the show as a response to the beginnings of the institutional repressions of a developing underclass (Leech, 1985). Leech has suggested that the emerging triumvirate of the law, religion, and marriage as forms of social control were manifest in the show as the Hangman, the Devil and Judy (cf. Reeve, 2005, p. 17). Spectators could therefore identify with Punch as he variously fought off and/or murdered the causes of his prohibited desires, which were also their prohibited desires. As such, there was the opportunity to witness the spectacle of their own ambivalent tensions vis-à-vis the Law, and the opportunity for a bit of cathartic action.

By the end of the eighteenth century, Punch had transformed from its original form as marionette into the glove puppet booth form and by the early nineteenth century new features were introduced into the show while retaining many of the features of the original one including his shrewish wife Judy, whom he regularly beat and killed, and his encounter with the Devil. Martin Reeve observes that several of the original puppet characters came to be associated with and transformed into actual figures of the time. "Scaramouch" became "Clown Joey" after Joey Grimaldi; the "Hangman" came to be named after "Jack Ketch", the most famous hangman of the early nineteenth century; and the servant "Nigger", or "Shallaballa" became "Jim Crow" after the very popular black-face music-hall character performed by T.D. Rice in the 1830s (Reeve, 2005, p. 50).

In Britain, Martin Reeve remarks that the show has not been subject to the same kinds of intervention by national or exterior agencies with agendas, which have shaped and transformed popular puppetry in some other countries (ibid, pp. 266–267). One of the reasons for this "resistance" to change according to Clifford and King (2006, p. 338) is due to its ambivalent position embodying the wild aspects of British popular culture as: "shifting, offensive, and anarchic". However, an article from British newspaper "The Telegraph" on the occasion of Punch's 350th birthday commented that the themes of domestic violence, assaulting police and general anarchic behaviour together with some of the more offensive characters (including the hangman) have been phased out. Journalist de Rosée (2009) argues that political correctness is Mr. Punch's archenemy, and that some British councils have attempted to ban the entire show. In 2004, one Women's Rape and Sexual Abuse Centre attempted to instigate a ban on the basis that children were encouraged to laugh at a family whose relationship was based on violence and in 2005, one of the local councils banned puppets of Saddam Hussein and Osama bin Laden, cast as the show's sausage-stealing villains (ibid.). Indeed individual "Punchmen" (the puppeteers of the Punch and Judy shows) remark that whereas they continue to use the Hangman in shows outside of Britain, they do not use that character in British performances.

As Kenneth Gross (2011, p. 7) has pointed out, puppet theatre has long enjoyed a certain edgy life as a marginalised art form able to take up a repertory of often forbidden works in certain historical contexts (he cites the example of players using puppets in Tudor England performing Medieval passion plays that were banned by the Protestant authorities). Indeed, there is a whole history and literature of commentary on the things that puppets can be made to do that human actors cannot (on stage, and increasingly on film: in recent years Charlie Kaufman's *Being John Malkovich* and *Animalisa* really stand out in this respect). Psychoanalyst Mark Rambert argues that it is precisely because puppets can do things that are normally "prohibited" that they are of great use in psychoanalytic work with children. He describes using Punch and Judy puppets with children up to the age of 13 or 14 years of age where the child invents the story and moves the puppets. According to Rambert this puts on stage for the analyst the child's conflicts and the cathartic action of the play/story is augmented by the gestures of the child and the emotion that accompanies them (Rambert, 1952, p. 150).

From his disruptive debut in sixteenth-century England welcomed and praised by Samuel Pepys, Punch has been hailed by great satirist Jonathan Swift in the eighteenth century ("observe the audience in pain when Punch is hid behind the scene but when they hear his rusty voice with what impatience they rejoice" Swift, 1728), and commended by Charles Dickens in 1849 for his cathartic effects which he cautioned would be spoiled by cleaning up his act and removing the violence from it.

What is clear is that the 350 year history of Pulcinella, Punchinello, or Punch, from Italy to England, and his counterparts, and European and further flung cousins – Kasperle in Germany and Austria, Polichinelle in France, Karakoz in Turkey, and Petrushka in Russia – has operated in order to represent and stage some of the tensions of the ambivalence experienced during these epochs. What is noted by diverse commentators in this field is the disruptive, anarchic, and cathartic effects produced in audiences. What is most interesting of course is that accounts from the early twenty-first century of attempts to remove aspects and characters of the puppet show because of the harm they may cause to children or the offence they may cause to spectators is both, as we observe, extremely recent and to a certain extent resisted (however what is foreclosed from the British show crops up in other places, and in other countries). What is most brilliantly illustrated for us is the literal removal from the stage of certain parts of the action (Judy is less often killed now and often returns unharmed at the end of the show) and certain characters (the hangman is removed altogether). According to most commentators of the art form, the Punch and Judy show offered ways for children and other spectators to identify with the hated aspect of key ambivalent figures (the mother, the law, the Devil, and death) and therefore helped to allow for the staging of Oedipal wishes and the resolution of Oedipal ambivalence. Taking the "punch" out of Punch removes all of the tension and the messiness of ambivalence. Perhaps, that's not the way to do it!

Once upon a time

In our time, with our notions of what is "good" for children (in turn predicated upon modernist humanist and developmentalist notions of "the child" and the pre- and proscriptions that emerge as associated practices), censoring boards' decision-making around what constitutes harm for children and young people lead to the production of a film, TV, and literature for today's young subjects, which features rather washed-out figures, emptied of jouissance and therefore of ambivalence. In his groundbreaking work *The Uses of Enchantment* Bettelheim argues that the child wishes to identify with the good guy or hero in a fairy tale. In contrast to "modern" children's stories, Fairy stories provided exemplars of "the good" and "the bad" as separate figures, a polarization that Bettelheim believed to also dominate the young child's mind (1976, p. 9). In this respect, he argued, the figures in fairy tales are not ambivalent, not good and bad at the same time "as we all are in reality": "A person is either good or bad, nothing in between" (ibid.). Ironically, in the ABC hit TV show (Kitsis & Horowitz, 2011–2018) *Once Upon a Time* set in the village of "Storybrook", characters continuously switch functions. The character who is the bad guy one season is "transformed" into the good guy in the next. *Once upon a time* we could say that the hero and the villain represented the polarised faces of our ambivalence and we were left with the task of psychically processing our identifications, guilt and remorse, whereas nowadays TV shows, and films, are geared up for audiences who apparently cannot tolerate the psychical gap that accompanies the working through of ambivalence (a gap that Bettelheim considered as constitutive in the psyche of the child). In this respect it is interesting how modern characters "written for children" are sometimes "rewritten" or indeed "overwritten". The cartoon character "Maya the Bee" which was the subject of a long-standing TV show and feature length movie in 2015 is praised for giving young children lessons in tolerance, responsibility and neighbourly kindness. Interestingly however the story first appeared in 1912 as the German novel *Die Biene Maja* and was written and read as a militaristic allegory warning against the imminent arrival of racially impure *Auslanders* (Clarke, 2015). Author Waldemar Bonsels was later a supporter of Hitler and contributed anti-Semitic tracts to the cause! Maya was not always a good little bee and crops up on Nazi youth websites in her more original version!

The well-rehearsed argument in favour of diluting violence and aggression in any of the media, which children and young people may get their hands on, is to prevent them from "learning" an anti-morality: in other words, the stories we read to children now are supposed to instruct them well in ways to love their neighbours. What is utterly repressed in such arguments are the historical representations of the cruelty and often sinister behaviour of the same cohort on film or in literature. We only have to think in this respect of such classics (in any of their formats) as *The Lord of the Flies*, and *The Children's Hour*.

Sometimes, however, in classic Freudian slip tradition, what is repressed slips out from under repression despite all attempts to prevent it. The whole business of keeping the horror, or "the bad", (the "alt right" poles of ambivalence) out of sight and therefore out of the minds of young children in order to preserve their psychological well being came to light recently in a darkly humorous way in cinemas this year. Irish times film critic and columnist Donal Clarke reported that while waiting for the film *Peppa Pig: Festival of Fun* to view, young children in Ipswich (U.K.) were inadvertently shown a trailer for the shocker movie *Ma* and became confused and tearful (Clarke, 2019, p. 3). In Montreal, meanwhile, "infants were propelled toward mental breakdown" when instead of *Detective Pikachu* appearing on screen, the opening scenes of horror film the *Curse of La Llorona* were projected! Clarke considers that the question we should be asking however is not, why this kind of outrage occurs so frequently these days, but rather, "Who are these weedy children collapsing into blubby puddles at the merest glimpse of a bloody stump?" (ibid.). Clarke points out that the Grimm brothers knew well that children's minds were primed by tales of horror (whether involving duplicitous talking wolves or carnivorous senior citizens) for the harsher realities of the world. Or at least, as we would argue, following Bettelheim, such tales prime them for managing the tensions of their ambivalence, and psychically processing some of the affects that are coordinated with such ambivalence.

References

Anderson, M. (1948). *Anne of the thousand days*. New York: Dramatists Play Service Inc.

Aristotle. (1941/2001). *The basic works of Aristotle*. Ed. R. McKeon. New York: Modern Library.

Bernays, J. (1857/2015). Outlines of Aristotle's lost work on the effects of tragedy (Grundzuge der Verlorenen Abhandlung des Aristoteles uber Wirkung der Tragodie. Sect. IV. 1857). Trans. J. I. Porter. In J. Billings & M. Leonard (Eds.). *Tragedy and the idea of modernity* (pp. 315–329). Oxford: Oxford University Press.

Bettelheim, B. (1976). *The uses of enchantment*. New York: Thames and Hudson.

Billings, J. & Leonard, M. (Eds.). (2015). *Tragedy and the idea of modernity.* Oxford: Oxford University Press.

Clarke, D. (2015). *Maya the Bee* review: Well-meaning, well-voiced and entirely devoid of character. *Irish Times*, 23 October. www.irishtimes.com/culture/film/maya-the-bee-review-well-meaning-well-voiced-and-entirely-devoid-of-character-1.2401515. Accessed 22 April 2019.

Clarke, D. (2019). These under-sevens really need to toughen up. *The Irish Times* print ed. May 25, 2019.

Clifford, S. & King, A. (2006). *England in particular: A celebration of the commonplace, the local, the vernacular and the distinctive.* London: Hodder and Stoughton.

de Rosée, S. (2009). Punch and Judy: That's the way to do it. *The Telegraph*, 4 September www.telegraph.co.uk/culture/theatre/theatre-features/6106556/Punch-and-Judy-that's-the-way-to-do-it.html. Accessed 12 June 2016.

Ferguson, F. (1949/1972). *The idea of a theatre and study of 10 plays, the art of drama in changing perspective.* N.J.: Princeton.

Ferguson, F. (2007). Oedipus: Ritual and play. In H. Bloom (Ed.). *Sophocles' Oedipus Rex* (pp. 5–16). New York: Chelsea House.

Freud, S. (1900). *The interpretation of dreams. The Standard Edition of the Complete Psychological Works of Sigmund Freud. S.E., IV and V., XIII*, pp. 1–164.

Freud, S. (1913). *Totem and taboo. The Standard Edition of the Complete Psychological Works of Sigmund Freud. S.E., XIII.*, pp. 1–164.

Gadamer, H.-G. (2004). *Truth and method.* New York & London: Continuum.

Gregory, P. (2015). *The taming of the queen.* London: Simon & Schuster Ltd.

Grigg, R. (2007). Semblant, phallus, and object in Lacan's teaching. *Umbr(A): a Journal of the Unconscious, 1*, pp. 131–138.

Gross, K. (2011). *Puppet. An essay on uncanny life.* Chicago & London: The University of Chicago Press.

Jackson, L. (2016). Greater than Logos? Kinaesthetic empathy and the chorus in Plato's laws. In M. Johncock & E. Sanders (Eds.). *Persuasion and emotion in classical antiquity* (pp. 147–161). UK: Steiner Verlag.

Kitsis, E., Creator & Horowitz, A. (Creator). (2011–2018). *Once upon a time* [Television series]. ABC.

Lacan, J. (1992). *The ethics of psychoanalysis, 1959–1960. The Seminar of Jacques Lacan. Book VII.* Ed. J.-A. Miller. Trans. D. Porter. New York: W.W. Norton & Co. (Original work published 1986).

Lacan, J. (2019). *Desire and its interpretation. The Seminar of Jacques Lacan. Book VI.* Ed. J.-A. Miller. Trans. B. Fink. Cambridge, UK & Medford, US: Polity Press.

Leech, R. (1985). *The Punch and Judy show: History, tradition, and meaning.* London: Batsford Academic and Educational.

Mantel, H. (2010). *Wolf hall.* London & New York: Picador Press.

Mantel, H. (2015). *Bring up the bodies.* London & New York: Picador Press.

Masson, J.M. (1995). *The complete letters of Sigmund Freud to Wilhelm Fliess 1887–1904.* Cambridge MA & London: Harvard University Press.

Nietzsche, F. (2003). *The birth of tragedy: Out of the spirit of music.* London: Penguin Books.

Pfeffer, R. (1972). *Nietzsche: Disciple of Dionysus.* Lewisburg, PA: Bucknell University Press.

Phillips, A. (2015). *Unforbidden pleasures.* London: Penguin Random House.

Porter, J. (2015). Jacob Bernays and the catharsis of modernity. In J. Billings & M. Leonard (Eds.). *Tragedy and the idea of modernity* (pp. 15–41). Oxford: Oxford University Press.

Porter., J. (2016). Nietzsche, tragedy, and the theory of catharsis. *Skenè, Journal of Theatre and Drama Studies*, *2*(1), p. 2016.

Rambert, M. (1952). Puppet shows in psychotherapy of children. *Pro Infirm*, *11*(5), pp. pp. 148–153.

Reeve, M.J. (2005). *Contemporary Punch and Judy in performance: An ethnography of traditional British glove puppet theatre*. PhD thesis. Royal Holloway College, University of London. Unpublished.

Robertson Smith, W. (2002). *Religion of the Semites*. New Brunswick & London: Transaction Publishers. (1889).

Rodriguez McRobbins, L. (2013). Are Punch and Judy shows finally outdated? *Smithsonian Newslettter*, 4 February www.smithsonianmag.com/arts-culture/are-punch-and-judy-shows-finally-outdated-10599519/ Accessed 12 June 2017.

Shakespeare, W. (1613/1997). Henry VIII. In *The complete works of William Shakespeare*. Hertfordshire: Wordsworth Editions Ltd.

Swift, J. (1728). A dialogue between Mad Mullinix and Timothy. In *The works of the Rev. Jonathan Swift*. Vol. 7. https://en.wikisource.org/wiki/The_Works_of_the_Rev._Jonathan_S wift Accessed 15 July 2017.

Wooding, L. (2015). *Henry VIII*. UK: Routledge.

Žižek, S. (2011). Carnivals come cheap—The true test of their worth is what remains the day after. *Afflictor.com,* 11 October https://afflictor.com/2011/10/11/carnivals-come-cheap%E2%80%94the-true-test-of-their-worth-is-what-remains-the-day-after/. Accessed 10 June, 2017.

Film references

Film versions of Henry VIII

1933 *The Private Life of Henry VIII*. Dir. Alexander Korda.

1953 *Young Bess*. Dir. George Sydney.

1966 *A Man for All Seasons*. Dir. Fred Zinnemann.

1969 *Anne of the Thousand Days*. Dir. Charles Jarrott.

1971 *Carry on Henry VIII*. Dir. Gerald Thomas.

1998 *Elizabeth*. Dir. Shekhar Kapur.

2008 *The Other Boleyn Girl*. Dir. Justin Chadwick.

Chapter 2

Why the zombies ate my neighbours

At present, one of the few locations where we can risk speaking outside of the terms of the politically correct in its neutering of difference, and about the tensions associated with this neutering, is the psychoanalyst's consulting room. We state the obvious here; psychoanalytic practice thanks to Freud has long attested to the symptom formation associated with the guilt – and anxiety – around wishing or dreaming that a horrid fate will befall a "loved one". Twenty-first century citizens are supposed to be free of hatred and hostility for loved ones, friends, and neighbours; they find no place for the working through of less favourable affects and ideas concerning the people in their lives, since increasingly, it is their "love" for his or her neighbour which is nurtured and in fact, demanded. So, to mess entirely with the classic lyric we ask: baby, baby, where did our hate go?

In the trailer for the pilot of the hit TV series *The Walking Dead* a very particular framing of the contemporary social bond is staged. Featuring a set of images and motifs, which will be repeated regularly throughout the series, the camera isolates what we can readily identify as the fantasmatic emblems of a "post-apocalyptic" scene: aimless wandering survivors torn from their homes; desolate, deserted, social, and urban spaces; streets strewn with corpses, stores and public buildings devastated and burnt out – and in this particular telling of the end of times – zombies, everywhere. Since the emergence of the sub-genre in the first part of the twentieth century through to the present day, the zombie figure on film and in TV shows, and more latterly, images of the zombie apocalypse, have been press-ganged into imaging and describing various tensions of the *human* condition. Commentators on the genre claim that it serves an ideological function (Dima, 2016); the zombie speaks to what is socially, politically, or even psychologically current during a given epoch, so that although the zombie *per se* does not speak, what the figure of the zombie speaks *to* is indeed worthy of our scrutiny (cf. Davis, 1988). As Lauro and Embry (2008, p. 86) remark:

> The zombie has become a scientific concept by which we define cognitive processes and states of being, subverted animation, and dormant consciousness. In neuroscience, there are "zombie agents"; in computer

science there are "zombie functions." We even find "zombie dogs," "zombie corporations," and "zombie raves" in the news. The ubiquity of the metaphor suggests the zombie's continued cultural currency.

And what emerges to be current or indeed to function as epistemic currency is for many zombie genre researchers entirely caught up with the fears, anxieties, and tensions of the time. The popular obsession with zombies and a zombie apocalypse may even reveal the potential reaction of a people to moments of real danger and national peril: in many ways a worrying reaction especially as indexed by a herd mentality, and culture of paranoia, accompanied by irrational thinking and scientific illiteracy (Davis, 1988, p. 5). Zombie frenzies, zombie merchandising, zombie runs (during which one has to complete a race while avoiding being infected by "zombies", cf. www.zombierun.com/zombiehow-it-works), and so on, occur only because the zombie touches something deep in contemporary subjectivity (Assef, 2013).

The question that mobilises much zombie film research is how an obscure monster rooted in Haitian mythology and depicted in black-and-white horror films stumbled its way into the mass consciousness of today's popular culture (Davis, 1988; Ozog, 2013). The figure of the monster in general can be seen to have emerged at a specific moment in history. The historian W. Scott Poole has argued that what comes to be constituted as an American "monster" emerges out of the central anxieties and obsessions that have been a part of the American psyche from colonial times to the present and from the structures and processes where those obsessions find historical expression (Poole, 2011). At one of its points of origin, and as Moon (2014) and others have observed, the zombie monster's emergence is bound up with representations of slavery and colonialism on Haiti. According to David Inglis,

> in Haiti's case, European and North American negative depictions of the country as a feverish inferno of Voodoo-induced depravity were very much stimulated by racist fears over what was in the nineteenth century a glaring socio-political anomaly, the world's first "Black republic".
>
> (2011, p. 45)

In his book, Mark Danner details the movement from slavery to republic on Haiti highlighting the point that this achievement was not unambiguously welcomed by the world's "first independent republic" – the United States, which despite its constitutional and revolutionary creed that all men are created equal, looked upon these self-freed men with "shock, contempt and fear" (Danner, 2009, 2010). In fact, Danner goes on to claim, to all the great Western trading powers of the day – much of whose wealth was built on the labour of enslaved Africans – Haiti stood for the representation of freedom taken too far, and fear rose around the idea that such revolt might spread across the sea to the states. According to Danner, this was why the United States refused for nearly six decades to recognize Haiti.

As such, and as David Inglis remarks, the literalisation of racist fears is captured in the history of Haiti's birth as a colonial entity populated by slaves displaced from their homes and the subsequent liberation of those slaves in the
Haitian revolution can be seen as having "fed" the North American obsession
with the threat of attack by swarms of liberated slaves. William Seabrook's
account of life on Haiti published as *The Magic Island* in 1929, with his stories of voodoo and zombies, was pivotal in the constitution of the characteristics of the zombie in the first feature-length film of the genre in 1932
(Seabrook, 1929). Victor Halperin's film *White Zombie* premiered at a time
when the U.S. occupation of Haiti was in its seventeenth year. The polysemous
constitution of the zombie monster is observable in the merging of the "working dead" Haitian slaves of Seabrook's accounts together with what was an
increasingly everyday sight for 1930's America: the out of work, destitute,
worker. For many researchers of the genre, the American horror boom of the
1930's is immediately tied to the economic crash of 1929 and the fiscal hang-
over along with its subsequent misery and destitution. The zombie monster of
the 1930s is also then, a carbon copy image of the out of work, destitute,
unemployed worker shuffling along the streets of America in soup-lines, representing what Russell has called "an economic zombification of terrifying proportions" (2005, p. 23).

Another important constitutive element in the formation of the genre as
well as in the characteristics of the figure of the zombie in early films is the
survivalist fantasy harking back to the American nation's birth on the frontier. Early settlers venturing into hostile environments; iconic frontier figures
forging territories against antagonistic foes devoid of morality and consciousness; nations regenerated through violence; all of which perpetuate powerful
survivalist ideologies of mythic proportions and extreme prejudice toward an
Other who is always portrayed without personality or psyche thereby allowing audiences to return to identifications of imperialist conquests without risk
of the guilt associated with colonisation (Stewart, 2013, p. iii; Moreman &
Rushton, 2011).

From the 1930's through to the present day the many mutations in the
trajectory and in the figure of the zombie invite academic scrutiny and comment – especially given the malleability of the zombie as signifier and as
allegory – and indeed as befitting a phenomenon that can be interpreted as
"saying something" about the human condition and the episteme of which it
belongs. In fact, there is no shortage of research in sociology, film theory,
cultural, and post-colonial studies, and there are many interesting political
and economical observations about the rise and rise of the zombie as a film
and TV figure. For example, the collection edited by Thompson and Thompson (2015) entitled "But if a zombie apocalypse did occur..." brings
together essays which consider the phenomenon's medical, military, governmental, ethical, economic, and other implications. From the point of view of
psychoanalysis there are fewer contributions. As psychoanalysts ourselves,

we are interested in foregrounding what of the psyche is represented by this figure and its changing characteristics; our questions are inflected therefore to interrogate the field of the unconscious, seeing as we do in the zombie and its particularity at given times, the materialised aspects of a figure who stands in for a specific "other", but where that other is a lot closer to home than is emphasised in other accounts and theories.

Love and zombies

When we began to watch *The Walking Dead*, we were immediately struck by the soundtrack used in the trailer – the *Walker Brothers* song "Without Love" from 1966 – which we remembered also featuring in the beautiful film *Truly, Madly, Deeply* from 1990. This idea of being "without love" operates as the very index for us of what we see functioning as an intolerance of ambivalence. We are going to think about this intolerance accompanying a kind of "final solution" to dealing with ambivalence in two versions: in the first moment here – in the zombie apocalypse, the foreclosure of hatred for our neighbour will return in the figure of the zombie in whom we isolate a jouissance we cannot recognise, and in the second – which we will get to in Chapter 3 when we look more closely at *Truly, Madly, Deeply* – the foreclosure of hatred for our loved ones returns in the figure of their ghosts. We could say then, that in the absence of being able to tolerate ambivalence, we love each other to pieces, *and* to death and back.

The lyrics to the song "Without Love" underscore something crucial for us about the form of ambivalence that inspired Jacques Lacan in 1972 to coin the neologism *hainamoration*, or hateloving (Lacan, 1999, pp. 90, 98). In his twentieth seminar, Lacan points out that it took Freud to remind us that we know nothing of love without hate (ibid., p. 91). Lacan prefers to use this term *hainamoration* in place of ambivalence to highlight the point where hatred reverses into love and vice versa, where the *semblable* is transformed into something unbearable (ibid., pp. 90–91, p. 100). There are just two verses in the Walker brothers' song, with just two lines each. The first verse is all about the loneliness of the ego, and its impoverishment when the love has gone. The second verse bemoans the emptiness and meaninglessness of life without love. The chorus is a series of laments: the sun doesn't shine anymore, the moon doesn't rise anymore, and tears are always clouding your eyes. These repetitive laments can be heard variously as the complaints of the neurotic that the big Other isn't holding up, is failing somehow. But the "without love" at the end of the chorus is what hits home hard. This is the lament of the bereaved, and what we also hear as the cry of what Lacan calls the one-all-alone (Lacan, 2018). This is the being who finds themselves outside the social bond, a horrific destiny which offers no refuge. In the post-apocalyptic scene from the trailer to the pilot episode of *The Walking Dead*, this state of existence is described using the *à-la-carte* identifiable emblems of loneliness. We see a lone rider coming into town on horseback (reminiscent of a scene from a Sergio Leone film) with enough ammunition to take down a whole town: in this case, "the bad guy" is not some Latino cigar-smoking hard-case in the back room of the local whorehouse, but rather, the flesh-eating zombie whose bite can infect you, kill you and return you to a state of existence where you will permanently be *without love*.

In his seminar of 1972–1973, published in English as *Encore – On Feminine Sexuality, The Limits of Love and Knowledge* – Lacan claims that love is what makes up for the non-relationship of speaking beings; this is where he elaborates upon the maxim of non-rapport in a sexual relationship (Lacan, 1999, p. 66). Love is also however the signified of the sexual relationship (ibid., p. 47); as such, it is both the sign of something not working out between the sexes, as well as the meaningful trace of sexed speaking beings attempting to make love. Love, Lacan argues, is impotent since it is not aware of its limits – those limits that he has identified: as that which accompanies the desire to be as One, an impossible fusion constituted out of the fantasy of mutual desire and an all-phallic jouissance (1999, p. 6) endlessly rehearsed in love songs and poems. This fantasmatic One (a union made up of two hearts, two souls, etc.) is revealed by Lacan as merely two Ones plus an *a*; this *a* being the object cause of desire with whom the One makes a jouissance partner. And Lacan says that this is all we can know about "making love", in the sense of *sexual* intercourse. The One all alone is correlated therefore, *with love*, as the very index of the failure of the sexual relation as relation.

It is in this sense that being *without love* is mobilised in a fairly radical Lacanian twist in *The Walking Dead*: what is laid bare are the Ones and their jouissance. In *Encore* (1999), Lacan also makes the claim that love marks the shift or movement from one discourse, one version of the social link or bond, to another. For us, the zombies – without love – represent the displaced and tattered remains of the social bond, what is left after the love has gone (so to speak). Unlike love, hatred does not depend upon a discourse – or a song – to support it, and perhaps it is no coincidence that zombies do not speak. The hatred Lacan speaks of in *Encore* is the hatred that springs forth from jealousy. Coining the term *jealouissance*, he glues this hatred to jouissance, a jouissance incarnated in the neighbour, the semblable (ibid.). We believe that what is represented in scenes of human end times is precisely this unbearable *jealouissance*, which finds expression in the most horrific, brutal and abundant zombie killings – scenes which indicate the extent to which the speaking being cannot bear his (former) neighbour's mode of jouissance. In this sense, the zombie is a fall guy, a stand-in, a stooge, for the semblable, and as such, a substitute for the ambivalent figure of the neighbour, the one who is there, just too close for comfort. And this "too close for comfort" ambivalent figure in American history has all too often been the African American. In his ground-breaking analysis of racism in American society, Lacanian scholar Sheldon George argues that racial fantasies which figure the (black African American) other's enjoyment as being alien and excessive when compared with the jouissance of white Americans spring from *jealouissance*; the "frustrated hatred" arising from the conviction that the other has access to a "bountiful bliss" that the subject lacks (George, 2016, p. 5). This *jealouissance* is precisely what in George's analysis drives the hatred and aggressivity at the core of much racial violence.

In a post-lecture discussion at MIT in 2014, Noam Chomsky was asked his opinion on the American cultural preoccupation with zombies and the notion of a zombie apocalypse. He opined that the US is a nation unusually populated with fear, a fear that he claims goes back to the colonies. In Chomsky's argument the narrative switch which takes place in popular American myths transforms the oppressed into oppressors: as such, defending Indians become "merciless Indian savages"; slaves who revolt are in fact planning on killing all the white men and raping all the white women; Hispanic narco-traffickers are going to come in and destroy society, and so on. In this way, zombies are the new Indians and slaves in white America's collective nightmare. The zombie functions as the representative of the realised colonial object, proxy for the marginalised unseen, unwanted denizen, offering American audiences an opportunity to variously sublimate and/or displace what they find intolerable in the Other (King, 1981; Saunders, 2012). As Thompson has usefully remarked: the zombie figure is a perfect sublimated symbol for what culture finds unassimilable – famine, holocaust, plague, toxic waste, genetic mutilation, borderless chaos, racial warfare, urban riots, mindless consumerism, et cetera (2015, p. 22. See also Spivak, 1988). In this way we can regard zombie post-apocalyptic representations of the human condition as the stagings of the tensions of ambivalence we cannot articulate or express, as well as the stagings of the unbearable experience of *hainamoration*.

Freud and zombies

The 2015 quirky Belgian film translated into English as *The Brand New Testament* depicts God as a surly middle-aged man living in a flat in Brussels with his wife and young daughter whom he bullies relentlessly. His divine Law has consisted of whimsying into being an ever-increasing set of impossibly cruel and sadistic rules applied to the human condition. His ten-year-old daughter decides to take matters into her own hands, and so she consults with her brother Jesus Christ who advises her to go amongst the mortals and recruit some new apostles who will write new gospel for the people. She effectively undermines God's unreasonable power over mortals by sending everyone in the world an email letting them know the date of their death, an act which radically affects human interactions. She then takes Jesus' advice and sets off to recruit her new apostles to write the brand new testament. In one scene, God – now furious with the effects of his daughter's intervention – follows her into the human world. Ill-equipped to feed himself there (no money, no idea how to obtain food) he soon finds himself along with the local down-and-outs in a soup-kitchen. His aggressive behaviour stealing food from other homeless people leads to him being counselled by a priest (pointing to Jesus on the crucifix) who urges him to "love thy neighbour" as God ordained. In a rewriting of what is taken as "Gospel" this Belgian God vehemently denies having so proclaimed. What is sharply observed in this film is that not even a God so cruel, so whimsical, so sadistic – as depicted here – would demand of human subjects that they love their neighbour.

In *Civilization and its Discontents*, Freud critically examines the Judeo-Christian dictate "Love thy neighbour as thyself" (Freud, 1930a). He asserted that although people would prefer to view themselves as "gentle creatures who want to be loved" the truth they disavow is that they are also aggressive beings, such that:

> Their neighbour is for them not only a potential helper or sexual object, but also someone who tempts them to satisfy their aggressiveness on him, to exploit his capacity for work without compensation, to use him sexually without his consent, to seize his possessions, to humiliate him, to cause him pain, to torture and to kill him.
>
> (1930a, p. 111)

In a Hobbesian moment, men, Freud claimed then, are wolves to each other. Nowadays, it would appear, that men, and women of course, are zombies to each other. Indeed, at the premiere of his 2006 *Land of the Dead*, Georgio Romero – director of the *Living Dead* trilogy and recognised virtuoso of the genre said: "Today the zombies are our neighbours". Here is Freud on zombies, or rather, neighbours:

> Not merely is this stranger in general unworthy of my love; I must confess that he has more claim to my hostility and even my hatred. He seems not to have the least trace of love for me and shows me not the slightest consideration. If it will do him any good he has no hesitation in injuring me, nor does he ask himself whether the amount of advantage he gains bears any proportion to the extent of the harm he does to me.
>
> (Freud, op.cit. 1930a, p. 110)

In an interesting echo of Freud's sentiments about the neighbour, Moon argues: "the zombie has become a general metaphor for the other, who threatens our peaceful lives, rapes our women, kills our fellow citizens, and threatens the freedom of our society" (2014, p. 204).

Slavoj Žižek has commented at length on the virtual enforcement of today's liberal discourse of tolerance involving a respect for, and openness towards others, making use of Freud and Lacan's insistence on the problematic nature of the basic Judeo-Christian injunction "love thy neighbour". Žižek fully brings out the attendant obsessive fear of harassment that accompanies liberal tolerance. In other words, and as he puts it: "the Other is just fine, but only insofar as his presence is not intrusive ..." (Žižek, 2008, p. 35). In place of the injunction: "Love thy neighbour as thyself", Žižek advocates a "Fear thy neighbour as thyself!" As he describes it:

> A neighbour is primarily a thing, a traumatic intruder, someone whose different way of life (or, rather, way of 'enjoyment' materialised in its social practices and rituals) disturbs us, throws the balance of our way of life off the rails, when it comes too close .
>
> (Žižek, 2016a, p. 74)

This also gives rise to an aggressive reaction, as noted by Freud and Lacan that aims at getting rid of this disturbing intruder.

The sociologist Anne-Marie Fortier, in an article entitled "Too Close for Comfort: Loving Thy Neighbour and the Management of Multicultural Intimacies", claims that under neoliberalism, new forms of multicultural intimacy are imagined in contemporary Britain. She examines how these new forms are invested with particular ideals of loving thy neighbour, and feelings for the nation. Fortier makes the point however that racial, ethnic, and cultural relations are not only negotiated and "managed" in literal spatial locations, but also imagined – we could say fantasised – through specific emotional and ethical injunctions, such as "embracing the other" and loving thy neighbour. Moreover, these injunctions are imagined in the ambivalent spatial terms of obligations to, and dangers of, proximity – an ambivalence that is inflected with articulations of "race", class, and gender. Exploring how the imperative of neighbourly love refers to the ambivalent desires for and anxieties about proximity to the neighbour, she argues that who gets close to whom, and under what circumstances, is not left to chance (Fortier, 2007). While for Nietzsche one's neighbour still had his uses, the neighbour of our times is a figure upon whom many of our fantasmatic fears and anxieties have become condensed.

Together with the imperative "Love thy neighbour!" there is a commensurate: "speak well of thy neighbour!" Not only does one's ambivalence about the neighbour not transform into pure and simple tolerance when the effort is made to avoid using the term "fag" and replace it with "LGB individual", but this strategy also fails to address the social, religious, and economic conditions which mark such a difference as meaningful and such a person as marginalized. While we can easily see how "politically correct" speech is in fact speech which has been corrected to serve the ideologies of various political hues, the blind-sidedness which accompanies much neoliberal slogan-mongering insists upon reference to figures of racial and other difference by different names, as if such re-naming does anything to alter the material conditions which give rise to these differences (we will say more about this issue in Chapter 8).

We argue that a consequence of the condensing of neoliberalist discourse onto the superegoic injunction "Love thy neighbour" creates the bizarre and often dangerous outcome of a redoubled imperative: in loving my neighbour as myself, there is absolutely no place for me to dispose of my inherent racism, and chauvinism, etc. We are reminded of an old Charlie Brown cartoon where he has been playing Cowboys and Indians using his right hand as a make-believe pistol. A speech bubble appears – containing his mother or father's command: "put the pistol away!" That's just it. There's no place to put the pistol away! The pistol is always already there. The same point is made in the second Mr. Bean movie; passing through the airport, Bean catches the eye of airport policemen and playfully places a hand under his jacket as if to finger a gun, a gesture immediately seized upon by the police officers who chase him and force him to lay his weapon on the ground. Bean's placing of his hand on the ground – pistol shaped – underscores once again our inherent act of weapon-ising in times of *perceived* adversarial necessity. The injunction "love thy neighbour!" is currently embedded in a discourse intended to support an ideology of liberty and equality for all, but the problem is that the notion of "fraternity" – that other term of the "social" contract – is basically unenforceable. Whilst it is possible to legislate against inequality and absence of liberty, it has thus far, at least, been impossible to make people "love their neighbours" without also hating them with passion.

This very tension can be seen at work in the everyday enforcement of kindness and tolerance (see Dean, 2009). The more we urge and are urged to extend the hand of loving neighbourly friendship toward our culturally or racially different semblable, the more, it seems, we want to eat or blow his or her head off. Disavowing this basic human tension – highlighted in racial violence nowadays – is at the same time a disavowal of the need for speaking beings to experience and in some way manage the tensions of ambivalence, and constitutive of a panic-producing frenzy of epic proportions around what may be articulated of fears of "difference". Ignoring this tension on the one hand fosters a fake tolerance at best, and on the other hand the nurturing of the narcissism of small differences building up into larger scale underbelly racism and hate crimes. Žižek's well-rehearsed point about the obscene underbelly of unpermitted enjoyment propping up the law of justice, fair treatment, and equality is also observable here: what is ignored is that ambivalent tensions run riot in the schools, in the workplace, and in organisations, increasingly so because today's citizen is exhorted to love his neighbour, his school friend, his workmate, more than ever before. What is repressed here is precisely what finds a way toward representation on film. It is obviously also what finds its way to the symptom as presented to a psychoanalyst. For example, one analysand persists in parking his car in such a way as to irritate his analyst's neighbour whose imagined potential wrath functions as both a source of anxiety during his session, but also, crucially, operates in such a way as to localise his desire to find a/the neighbour whose enjoyment is intolerable – here, there, and everywhere.

Taken to and beyond its limits, the injunction "love thy neighbour" is, as Lacan pointed out over half a century ago, to place egoism at the heart of love. If the ego is the seat of *meconnaissance* – and the site of the fundamental and paradoxical paranoid knowledge of the semblable, then to love your neighbour as yourself is, at the level of speech, to subject him to your hatred, your demand for his death.

Millenial anxiety and ambivalence

Most commentators agree that the figure of the zombie on film indexes a certain crisis of the age in which the narrative is conceived, indicating that the zombie sub-genre acts as an efficient barometer of cultural and social change and unrest. The zombie is regarded as an exemplary allegory of social discontents since as a "circulating symbol with contradictory range of meanings" (e.g., slaves, consumers, capitalists, communists, etc.), it can be used to make a point about contemporary political and economic issues in diverse contexts (Moon, 2014, p. 166). Practically every piece of research on the genre features an analysis of Georgio Romero's trilogy: *Night of the Living Dead* (1968), *Dawn of the Dead* (1978), and *Day of the Dead* (1985). And rightly so. Romero's series forms perhaps the sharpest commentary upon American cultural and political anxieties from the zombie genre. Regarded by most as game changers, the films are argued to have transformed the genre into a comprehensive allegory of social anxiety (Moon, 2014, pp. 175–196). What interests us is how astutely Romero observes and comments on the tensions of ambivalence at different moments of American economic and political history in each film. In *"Night"*, neighbours become monsters and attack other neighbours, soldiers and police shoot civilians, black men are mistakenly killed by white vigilante in scenes which Romero intended to be resonant with the images of the war in Vietnam and civil unrest which would have been familiar to American TV news audiences at the time. Later, in *"Dawn"*, which takes place in a shopping mall, what is staged is nothing other than a critique of consumer capitalism. In a violent and deadly parody: when the going gets tough, the tough go shopping. Under threat from the zombies, the shopping mall, itself a site of ambivalence, becomes at once a place of refuge as well as a place of jouissance: the desire for goods and the yearning for violence transform a shopping spree into a killing spree. In *"Day"*, the cold war with the Soviet Union and the rise of the American male heroic action figure once again capture the valence at work in prevailing notions of masculinity at this time but also, the condensing upon the communist Other of the fears of invasion and destruction of society associated with the cold war era under Reagan.

Romero effectively managed to take the pulse of American film audiences – at the different times of his trilogy – by representing on film the expression of paranoia, alienation, risk, and threat, allowing the zombie "to speak" for each cultural moment of the particular dangers seen as most threatening at each epoch (Badley, 2008; Glassner, 1999).

Commenting on the zombie film trail from the year 2000 onward Ozog (2013, p. i) argues that while the rise in popularity of zombie films is directly connected to "our fears and anxieties as a culture", the decade 2000–2010 was one of particularly heightened social fears and apocalyptic anxieties. This idea – unsurprisingly – finds full support among the zombie on film researchers. Everyone notes the exponential increase of films in production in that decade and the new one from 2010, and everyone connects that increase to the major fears emergent from the first decade of the twenty-first century: Y2K bugs, the attack on the World Trade Centre of 9/11, SARS and H1N1 viruses, pandemics, hurricanes, tsunamis, the war on terror in Iraq, collapses of financial and social orders, et cetera, et cetera, (Assef, 2013; Saunders, 2012; Stewart, 2013; Thompson, 2015). From the point of view of American audiences, Sewer (2009) remarks:

> Bookended by 9/11 at the start, and a financial wipe-out at the end, the first ten years of this century will likely go down as the most dispiriting and disillusioning decade Americans have lived through in the post – world war II era.
> (Sewer, 2009, p. 30)

What is increasingly referred to as "millenial dread" is according to Kirsten Thompson (2005) simply an extension of an American apocalyptic tradition which in cinema was first represented in the seventies in science fiction and demonic horror films as an expression of cold-war anxiety, then gathered momentum via a turn to social conservatism in the eighties, and gradually reached a hysterical peak in the nineties in a cycle of horror, disaster, and science-fiction films explicitly focused on the approaching millennium. After 9/11, this "dread" took new forms with anxieties about the rise of Islamic fundamentalism and terrorism from within (Thompson, 2015; Stewart, 2013, p. iii). As such then, and as Thompson argues, "social anxieties, fears and ambivalence" about global catastrophe under the label of "apocalyptic dread" took explicit narrative form in the cinema of the late nineties and early twenty-first century. In this way, the zombie, and zombie apocalypse films of the new century are seen to articulate something of the ambivalence of our times. Bishop (2010, p. 24) argues that "a post 9/11 audience cannot help but perceive the characteristics of zombie cinema through the filter of terrorist threats and apocalyptic reality".

In our research, we discerned a commensurate trend in film representations of the zombie, and of zombie invasions or intrusions into the human field. From its emergence in the film *White Zombie* of 1932 through to the 1980s the zombie appears most often as a supernatural conjuring, a monster from beyond the grave, or from beyond this world. This suggested to us that "the undead" as the roused dead neighbour, conjured into this state via some supernatural mechanism, is the zombie materialised of the real as a kind of payback for human's meddling with the laws of Nature or of God. As Žižek has remarked, the return of the dead is a sign of a disturbance in the symbolic (1992, p. 23).

We had a hypothesis however, that at a certain time in film making, something would have changed: the cause of the zombie invasion was not going to be the result of the evoking of the "undead" by black magic, voodoo ritual, or disturbing of graves. Rather, we thought, that after a specific and recent time in our human history, the zombie and zombie invasions would be caused by something pertaining to human warfare, to the conflict of speaking being with his living neighbour. We were right. After 9/11, by far the greater number of zombie films feature the idea that becoming a zombie, or being invaded by swarms of zombies is the result of mysterious viruses or plagues, of humans meddling with chemicals, sometimes in the development of chemical warfare toxins. The notion of being "infected" therefore features as a dominant theme, as well as the idea of not knowing if your neighbour is already infected. If you survive, you will not be alone; you will in fact be surrounded by all your (dead) hostile neighbours. In the words of Robert Neville from the film *I am Legend* – in which he is the lone immune survivor of the mysterious plague that has transformed everyone on the planet into zombie monsters – "God didn't do this. We did." God and/or the supernatural don't cut the mustard any more when it comes to explaining global collapse, or apocalyptic doom. Rather, in our contemporary forebodings, it is the abuse of science, power, and even capital that harken the arrival of zombie plagues and devastations (Rasmussen, 1998, p. 41). To quote Jones (2000) here: "[w]e do not know the cause of what is going wrong, for we are the cause of what is going wrong." In what Assef (2013) has referred to as an anthropomorphic plague, man becomes the pathogenic agent of his fellow man, a point we are emphasising here, as it is in the morbid twist which transforms one's next-door neighbour into one's next-door zombie, that we see the "hypermodern decline of Hobbes' thinking" such that man is in our times a zombie to man.

Film obviously allows for the optimum representation of ambivalence (Jones, 2000), and the genre of the horror film is exemplary in this respect. In his remarks on the gothic horror tales of Hoffman, Freud had observed that the acme of the uncanny is represented by anything to do with death, dead bodies, revenants, spirits, and ghosts (p. 48). We can agree with Moon (2014) and Assef (2013) that the zombie causes an uncanny effect in our times. However, we argue that in fact *it is the foreclosure of ambivalence in the symbolic that leads to the returning of this ambivalence – materialised in the figure of the zombie – in the real.*

In other words, the contemporary zombie is the result of interfering with the human world rather than the supernatural or spirit world. Whereas before 9/11 your worst enemy was a zombie from another dimension – underworld/grave/ even outer space – post 9/11 your worst enemy is a zombie created by your "fellow man", your very own neighbour.

The new figure of ambivalence – the suicide bomber who is your airline traveller neighbour, the gun-toting murderer who is your dancer neighbour at a nightclub – is the *semblable* who incarnates pure terror, whose act devastates entire human landscapes, and whose desire is caused by an object whose jouissance is incomprehensible to you, but not any less deadly to you for that. If pre 9/11, the <u>foreclosure of ambivalence</u> resulted in the return of the ambivalent figure as a "zombie" from another dimension, we could say, *the real*: post 9/11, the <u>disavowal of ambivalence</u> has produced its perverse counterpart – the "zombie" from next-door.

Hypermodern zombie/hypermodern ambivalence

The new century's zombies and the rise of the global zombie apocalypse are interpreted as the sign and symptom of fear and anxiety gone global. Most zombie on film researchers agree that the zombie narratives of the 2000's have undergone major shifts and that after Romero, these narratives have become forms of "thought experiment" (Moon, 2014, p. 196). The emphasis is upon the collapse of the current *global* world order, with the accompanying questions of who gets to survive the apocalypse, who dies first, what people rise up as leaders, and ultimately, what are the differences between zombies and humans (Moon, ibid). The cause of the zombie is most often currently the result of a viral infection, and the time between being bitten, dying, and reanimation of the dead is radically speeded up. Some researchers link this phenomenon to the millennial lust for, and expectation of, speed in the millennial generation.

Others see current representations of zombie epidemics as hypermodern versions of the apocalypse. In his Yale lecture of 1975, Lacan argued that what is called history is the history of epidemics (Lacan, 2013). As such, there exists a link between a frightened society and the fictions that circulate in it (Assef, 2013). For Lacan, a plague is nothing other than what is established as such in the social discourse of a time. As psychoanalysts Eric Laurent and Jacques-Alain Miller have argued, U.S. hysterias can be interpreted in the light of epidemics of fear such as those that circulated around "mad cow" disease, avian flu, swine flu, economic crises, global terrorism, and so on (2005, p. 43). In light of these interpretations, it is easier to imagine the end of the world than the end of capitalism (Assef, 2013).

Making the link between what constitutes the subjectivity of our times and our current global economies of consumption under capitalism, some zombie researchers highlight the image and function of the "excessive consumer" parodied in the figure of the zombie who ceaselessly and without desire, devours and destroys. As we move from economies which revolve around a capitalism of production to economies of consumption, where the market distributes everywhere at high speed, where the consumer is never satiated and endlessly wants more, where technology is ever more productive, the image of the excessive consumer is ridiculously isomorphic with that of the zombie. The zombie apocalypse on the screen can be seen to bear a strong resemblance to the typical media coverage of "Black Friday" shopping featuring images of mobs and mayhem as swarms of shoppers fight over merchandise following Thanksgiving in the U.S.

The pressure to consume generates a subject primed for devoration and addiction; it is a subject ill at ease with the deferring of satisfaction, unaccustomed to tolerating a gap between desire and enjoyment, incapable of bearing the ambivalence around his/her relationships with the semblable, the neighbour. In this figure of the contemporary zombie, we see in fact what is the mirror image of the speaking being who is all alone, unable to make social bonds, moving en masse with his fellow shoppers after the objects which he consumes, without speaking.

To quote Jorge Fernandez Gonzalo:

> The Cartesian "I think therefore I am" has become "I eat therefore I subsist". The zombie would be then, the perfect icon of our insistent cultural habit of considering not only reality but also our neighbour, our companion, our friend, our lover, or our relative, that is others, as mere fuel at the service of our jouissance.
>
> (2011, p. 53, quoted in Assef, 2013, p. 10)

Ambivalence and zombies

There is an outbreak of zombies on film. It is undeniable. However, this is no mere interesting statistical (fun) fact. We began this chapter by arguing that in times of apparently increased "tolerance" of difference, there is less "tolerance" for the articulation/expression of the experiences of the tensions of ambivalence in encounters with different *others*. We have been tracing the ways in which the zombie figure can be read as a representation of some of the tensions of ambivalence we experience in our relationships with our semblables – our fellow human being – but which are inarticulable or unmanageable by other means. We find support for this idea in our observation that in times of public expression of ambivalent tensions and conflict, zombie films are made in much lower numbers compared with times of intolerance of expression of difference and inter-subjective conflict (which we believe are only the outcomes of speech which is "politically corrected", and a barely concealed intolerance at that). In other words, ambivalence isn't erased, it simply goes underground; in this case the increase or surges in zombie film production are interpretable of this attempted repression.

The figures of zombie film production register a low but regular output of films between the 1930's and 1960's, and a substantial increase in the 1970's. There is a further doubling of this figure in the 1980s, which reduces almost by half in the 1990's. Zombie film researcher Moon (2014, p. 203) commenting on the decline of zombie film production in the 1990's argues that this was due to the good economic outcomes of an apparently advanced global world order together with the proliferation of neoliberal capitalism. The cold war was over! The Berlin wall had fallen! The Gulf war was won by global forces, and so on (ibid.). In the same vein, Bishop (2010) claims that when people see stability in their lives, zombies do not fit the mood any longer because zombies resonate more with times of widespread fear, anxiety, and the sense of being under threat. According to these (and other similar) analyses of zombie films in production over the decades, in times of peace, apparent stability, and global contentment, the zombie is not as functionally necessary as in times of instability, anxiety and threat. But what if, rather than simply seeing the times of fewer films in production as a consequence of stability we were instead to focus on the spikes, and on the general trend in increase. The first of these spikes takes place in the 1970's, the second leap in the 1980's: by a slight turn of the lens we can see such spikes as radically interpretable, as saying something via film which is otherwise unrepresentable at these times. This would point to something taking place during the preceding period of time in each case which has such a powerful effect upon film-makers and audiences so as to lead to a doubling of outputs from the previous decade. Following this line of argument, and taking into consideration that in the decade 2000–2010, some 400 zombie films were produced, and to date, we seem to be on track for the same figure since 2011, it does seem to be the case that aside from the 1990's when film output dropped compared to the 1980's, there is in fact a steeply inclining curve of zombie film production. We believe that in times of *apparently* well tolerated expression of social tension and conflict, the zombie figure on film is not at all charged with the same function and intensity as it is at times of intolerance of expression of difference and intersubjective conflict. Let us take the 1980's as a case in point. This was when zombie film production doubled from its output in the 1970's. During this decade some 25 million people died of the AIDs virus (https://ourworldin data.org/hiv-aids), and the so-called "gay plague" unleashed a moral panic of epic proportions involving a huge increase in paranoia, fear and prejudice around gay men in particular. But the expression of this fear and prejudice hardly found lip service in Hollywood movie production. One notable exception was Jonathan Demmes' 1994 film *Philadelphia* which, although portraying the human face of the AIDS virus only succeeded in fostering a reactionary tolerance and sympathy for gay men akin to the current reactionary trend towards refugees. Images of figures of abject difference – little dead refugees washed up on beaches, gay men infected with the AIDS virus, the homeless, the unemployed, et cetera, confuse the issue for many viewers, since they are circulated within a neoliberal discourse that supposedly supports an ideology of liberty and equality for all, while the conditions that give rise to such conditions of difference cannot be addressed by love, and therefore, are entirely at the mercy of ambivalence. This is an ambivalence which is increasingly silenced so that while it remains unspoken (much like the zombie), it is nevertheless menacingly effective. The stagings of the tensions of ambivalence, and opportunities for thinking about the experience of *hainamoration* are increasingly foreclosed under neoliberalism and take place alongside the injunction to love our neighbour. The effects of the return of what is foreclosed find some expression in the horrific portrayals of violent zombie massacres even as they condense on the figure of the zombie all our foreclosed ambivalence towards our neighbour. In times of foreclosure of ambivalence, eat your neighbour!

References

Assef, J. (2013). The Zombie epidemic: A hypermodern version of the apocalypse. *LC Express*, *2*(7), pp. 1–16. November, 2013.

Badley, L. (2008). Zombie splatter comedy from dawn to shaun: Cannibal carnivalesque in zombie culture. In S. McIntosh & M. Leverette (Eds.). *Zombie culture: Autopsies of the living dead* (pp. 35–53). Maryland: Scarecrow Press Inc.

Bishop, K.W. (2010). *American zombie gothic: The rise and fall (and rise) of the walking dead in popular culture*. Jefferson, N.C.: McFarland & Co.

Danner, M. (2009). *Stripping bare the body: Politics, violence, war*. New York: Nation Books.

Danner, M. (2010). To heal Haiti, look to history, not nature. *New York Times*, 21 January 2010. www.nytimes.com/2010/01/22/opinion/22danner.html

Davis, W. (1988). *Passage of darkness: The ethnobiology of the haitian zombie*. Chapel Hill & London: University of North Carolina Press.

Dean, J. (2009). *Democracy and other neo-liberal fantasies*. North Carolina: Duke University Press.

Dima, V. (2016). You only die thrice: Zombies revisited in the walking dead. *International Journal of Žižek Studies*, *8*(2), pp. 1–22.

Fernando Gonzalo, J. (2011). *Pensamiento zombi*. Barcelona: Anagrama.

Fortier, A.-M. (2007). Too close for comfort: Loving thy neighbour and the management of multicultural intimacies. *Environment and Planning D: Society and Space*, *25*(1), pp. 104–119.

Freud, S. (1930a). Civilization and its discontents. *The Standard Edition of the Complete Psychological Works of Sigmund Freud. S.E.*, *XXI*, pp. 59–148.

George, S. (2016). *Trauma and race: A Lacanian study of African American racial identity*. Waco, TX: Baylor University Press.

Glassner, B. (1999). *Culture of fear: Why Americans are afraid of the wrong things: Crime, drugs, minorities, teen mums, killer kids, mutant microbes, plane crashes, road rage, & so much more*. New York: Basic Books.

Inglis, D. (2011). Putting the undead to Work: Wade Davis, Haitian Vodou, and the social uses of the zombie. In C.M. Moreman & C.J. Rushton (Eds.). *Race, oppression, and the zombie: Essays on cross-cultural appropriations of the Caribbean tradition* (pp. 42–59). Jefferseon, NC: McFarland.

Jones, E.M. (2000). *Monsters from the id: The rise of horror in fiction and film*. Dallas, TX: Spence Publishing Company.

King, S. (1981). *Danse macabre*. New York: Everest House.

Lacan, J. (1999). *On feminine sexuality, The limits of love and knowledge, 1972–1973. Encore: The seminar of Jacques Lacan book XX*. J.-A. Miller (Ed.). Trans. B. Fink. New York & London: Norton.

Lacan, J. (2013). Yale university: Lecture on the body. In *Culture/Clinic*. 1 (May). Minneapolis, MN: University of Minnesota Press.

Lacan, J. (2017). *Formations of the unconscious 1957–1958. The seminar of Jacques Lacan book V*. J.-A. Miller (Ed). Trans. R. Grigg. London: Polity Press.

Lacan, J. (2018). *... or worse: The seminar of Jacques Lacan, Book XIX*. Ed. J.-A. Miller. Trans. A. Price. London: Polity Press.

Laurent, E. & Miller, J.-A. (2005). *El Otro que no Existe y sus Comité de Ética*. Buenos Aires: Paidos.

Lauro, S.J. & Embry, K. (2008). A zombie manifesto: The nonhuman condition in the era of advanced capitalism. *Boundary*, *2*(35), pp. 85–108.

Moon, H.-J. (2014). *The post-apocalyptic turn: A study of contemporary apocalyptic and post-apocalyptic narrative*. PhD thesis. University of Wisconsin-Milwaukee, December 2014. Unpublished.

Moreman, C.M. & Rushton, C.J. (Eds.). (2011). *Race, oppression, and the zombie: Essays on cross-cultural appropriations of the Caribbean tradition*. Jefferseon, NC: McFarland.

Ozog, C.A. (2013). *Fear rises from the dead: A sociological analysis of contemporary zombie films as mirrors of social fears*. MA thesis. University of Regina, Saskatchewan, January 2013. Unpublished.

Poole, W.S. (2011). *Monsters in America: Our historical obsession with the hideous and the haunting*. Waco, TX: Baylor University Press.

Rasmussen, R.L. (1998). *Children of the night: The six archetypal characters of classic horror films*. Jefferson, NC: McFarland and Company.

Russell, J. (2005). *Book of the dead: The complete history of zombie cinema*. Surrey: FAB Press.

Saunders, R.A. (2012). Undead spaces: Fear, globalisation, and the popular geopolitics of zombiism. *Geopolitics*, *17*, pp. 80–104.

Seabrook, W. (1929). *The magic island*. London: Harrap & Co.

Sewer, A. (2009). The decade from hell: And why the next one will be better. *TIME*, December 7, pp. 30–38.

Spivak, G.C. (1988). Can the subaltern speak? In P. Williams & L. Chrisman (Eds.). *Colonial discourse and post-colonial theory: A reader*. New York: Colombia University Press. 1994.

Stewart, G. (2013). *The zombie in American culture*. MA Eng. Lit. University of Waterloo, Ontario, Canada. Unpublished.

Thompson, A.L. & Thompson, A.S. (2015). (eds.). *But if a zombie apocalypse did occur: Essays on medical, military, governmental, ethical, economic, and other implications*. Jefferson, North Carolina: McFarland and Co.

Thompson, J.F. (2015). The rise of the zombie in popular culture. In A.L. Thompson & A.S. Thompson (Eds.). *But if a zombie apocalypse did occur: Essays on medical, military, governmental, ethical, economic, and other implications* (pp. 11–25). Jefferson, North Carolina: McFarland and Co.

Thompson, K.M. (2005). *Apocalyptic dread: American film at the turn of the millennium.* Albany, NY: State University of New York Press.

Žižek, S. (1992). *Looking awry: An introduction to Lacan through popular culture.* Harvard: M.I.T. Press.

Žižek, S. (2008). *Violence.* London: Profile Books.

Žižek, S. (2016a). *Against the double blackmail. Refugees, terror and other troubles with the neighbours.* London: Allen Lane.

Žižek, S. (2016b). Left forum 2016. Closing Plenary: *Rage, Rebellion, Organising New Power – A Hegelian Triad.* May 22, 2016. https://vimeo.com/173570587

Chapter 3

Raising the dead
Mourning and ambivalence

Anthony Minghella's 1990 film *Truly Madly Deeply* beautifully illustrates how ambivalence in love manifests in the process of mourning. The story revolves around Nina, listlessly going through the motions of life, the sun having stopped shining for her since her husband Jamie died unexpectedly of complications from a cold. Profound mourning, Freud tells us in his paper "Mourning and Melancholia," involves a "painful frame of mind", a "loss of interest in the outside world," a "loss of capacity to adopt any new object of love (which would mean replacing him)," and "turning away from any activity that is not connected with thoughts of him" (Freud, 1917e, p. 244). The protagonist of *Truly Madly Deeply* is stuck in this arrested process of mourning when, following the both/and logic of disavowal, something magical seems to happen: her husband, as a flesh-and-blood ghost, comes back to life. Nina, then, may have thought at some level, "I know very well that Jamie is dead and can never return, but all the same I prefer to believe that he is living once more." With her love "living" once again, she too returns to life. After they reunite, they gleefully sing the Walker brothers' song which we found in the TV show *The Walking Dead* and jumped up and down about in Chapter 2. (Check out this sweet rendering of the song from the film with Juliet Stevenson as Nina and Alan Rickman as Jamie here: www.youtube.com/watch?v=AZ52td1GMT0).

The words as they are sung here clearly resonate with Nina's state of mourning – defined by loneliness, emptiness (a lack of desire), and a lack of hope ("the sun ain't gonna shine anymore ..."). The twist is that Jamie has returned to her life as an embodied ghost, and they now paradoxically belt out the lyrics to the song as if it were a song about reunion or the bliss of union. We see disavowal at work in Nina's saying – or singing, rather – that she is mourning for her dead husband at the same time that she prefers to believe that he has returned to her and the song is an occasion for joy.

The protagonist, instead of symbolically remembering her love, symptomatically repeats it through having loved her husband to death and then back again. Whereas the successful process of mourning involves public mourning rituals (such as funeral rites and services) and private conversations and activities (such as looking through photo albums) in which the mourner is often progressively able to speak of both the good and the bad aspects of the deceased, Nina's whole life has been reduced to wishing an idealised version of Jamie would return. Before the bodily spectre of Jamie returns, Nina told her therapist that she has imaginary conversations with Jamie and that she could see no point in going to or getting out of bed because Jamie is not with her. She was angry at the couples she saw together since they had something that she had permanently lost. When Nina's sister asked if her son, Harry, could have Jamie's cello for his cello lessons, Nina responded angrily, saying, "It's practically all I've got left of him. It is him. It's like you're asking me to give you his body!"

We can only speculate as to what had caused her to cling to her object without letting him go. But clues arise that it had something to do with a denial of ambivalence when her blissful reunion with his ghost quickly sours. He annoys her by bringing a crowd of dead friends to stay with them, watching black and white movies on a loop, moving the furniture around, and turning the heating up full blast (because, of course, as a flesh-and-blood ghost he is perpetually cold). Instead of continuing to idealise him, she begins gradually to be able to remember him as he was – as someone she *deeply* loved but who also, at times, made her *madly* angry. For, in life, as in death, he could on occasion be most annoying. It is through this staging of her ambivalence that she becomes able to truly mourn so that she may again be with, instead of without, love. The resolution of her mourning consists not so much, as Freud suggests in "Mourning and Melancholia", in the mechanism of remembrance functioning to completely de-cathect Nina's libido from her deceased husband and forget him (1917e, p. 245); rather her mourning proceeds through commemorating him in the symbolic as someone special that she *both* loved *and* hated.

In the film *Bleu*, which is the first part of Krzysztof Kieślowski's *Three Colors* trilogy, the protagonist Julie (played by Juliette Binoche) attempts to achieve the fantasied final result of Freud's conception of mourning as depicted in "Mourning and Melancholia":

> Each single one of the memories and expectations in which the libido is bound to the object is brought up and hypercathected, and detachment of the libido is accomplished in respect of it … when the work of mourning is completed the ego becomes free and uninhibited again.
>
> (1917e, p. 245)

Julie, having lost both her husband, Patrice, and her daughter, Anna, in a car crash from which she emerged as the sole survivor, does everything she can to completely decathect her libido from her dead husband and daughter. Unlike in Freud's conception of mourning, however, she attempts to skip the process of mourning and remembering and cut straight to becoming "free and uninhibited" (p. 245). She tries to kill herself by swallowing pills from the hospital medicine cabinet, but when she finds herself unable to swallow them she opts instead for a kind of living death.

Although Julie tries her utmost to negate her loss(es), as with all negation there is a flaw. Blue, the colour of the French flag which represents liberty, in this film represents both personal liberty and its restrictions insofar as Julie is free to sell her things, cut herself off from all of her relationships, and to try to live a life of nothingness, but ultimately she is not "master in her own house" and cannot ignore the part of her that is blue, that loved and lost. Another part of Julie does want to remember, and that manifests for instance in her choice to keep her daughter's blue crystal chandelier as well as in the excess in her vehement attempts to forget. Instead of a denial of ambivalence regarding her opinions of Patrice and Anna, Julie denies her ambivalence about mourning itself. Believing she has already moved on, Julie consciously tries to have nothing to do with mourning; attempting to turn herself into nothing or into just-another-woman, but her repressed desire here is to remember, to whine, cry, be sad, and commemorate how special and irreplaceable Patrice and Anna were to her.

In Freud's "Mourning and Melancholia" (1917e), Freud explicates the pathological structure of melancholia by way of a comparison with the normal experience of mourning. According to Freud, although both mourning and melancholia are the result of the loss of the object, in mourning the loss is typically the death of a loved person – "or to the loss of some abstraction which has taken the place of one, such as one's country, liberty, an ideal, and so on" (p. 243) – while in melancholia the loss tends to be due to a disappointment in love. However, whereas the mourner is conscious of whom he has lost, the melancholic may be aware of the loss which precipitated his illness "but only in the sense that he knows *whom* he has lost but not *what* he has lost in him. This suggests that melancholia is in some way related to an object-loss which is withdrawn from consciousness" (p. 245). Freud tells us that the distinguishing mental features of melancholia are a profoundly painful dejection, cessation of interest in the outside world, loss of the capacity to love, inhibition of all activity, and a lowering of the self-regarding feelings to a degree that finds utterance in self-reproaches and self-revilings, and culminates in a delusional expectation of punishment (1917e, p. 244). He further points out that, with the notable exception of "self-reproaches and self-revilings," the same traits are manifested in mourning. The task of the mourner is to come to grips with the reality that her loved one is dead. The work of mourning is "carried out bit by bit, at great expense of time and cathectic energy, and in the meantime the existence of the lost object is psychically prolonged ... [and] when the work of mourning is completed the ego becomes free and uninhibited again" (p. 245).

Although the work of melancholia involves a similar mechanism of gradual de-cathexis, a crucial difference rests upon the melancholic's self-reproaches. Indeed, Freud says that "dissatisfaction with the ego on moral grounds is [melancholia's] most outstanding feature" (1917e, p. 248). For Freud, the key to understanding this difference between mourning and melancholia is that the melancholic's self-reproaches are in fact displaced reproaches against a loved one. At the time that the melancholic suffered the loss, instead of his libido being withdrawn from the lost loved one and directed toward a new love, his libido was withdrawn into his ego as part of his narcissistic identification with the abandoned object. In Freud's classic statement, "[t]hus the shadow of the object fell upon the ego, and the latter could henceforth be judged by a special agency, as though it were an object, the forsaken object" (p. 249). The melancholic works through his loss by berating his ego as if he were the once loved object.

Importantly for our argument, at the root of melancholia is ambivalence about the object. Freud notes that the ambivalence is either constitutional, that is, is an element of every love-relation formed by this particular ego, or else it proceeds precisely from those experiences that involved the threat of losing the object. In melancholia, accordingly, countless separate struggles are carried on over the object, in which hate and love contend with each other; the one seeks to detach the libido from the object, the other to maintain this position of the libido against the assault. According to Freud, the location of these separate struggles cannot be assigned to any system but the unconscious (1917e, p. 256). The pathological condition of melancholia, then, is formed on account of ambivalence about the object which resists conscious articulation. That being said, Freud points out that mourning can also become a pathological process if the mourner suffers from unprocessed ambivalence. Ambivalence, in other words, instigates symptomatic processes in both conditions; the difference between pathological mourning and melancholia, then, lies mainly in the function of the shadow of the object falling upon the ego – that is, the melancholic's identification with the loved and hated object. In fact, Freud remarks that the loss of a loved one serves as an "excellent opportunity" (p. 250) for the emergence of ambivalence. When ambivalence affects the mourning process of the obsessional neurotic, the mourner reproaches himself for the loss of the loved object, feeling guilt for having killed the object with his hateful thoughts. In both pathological mourning and melancholia, the superego wages its sadistic and punitive war upon the ego.

Lacanian psychoanalyst Russell Grigg has argued that in contrast to mourning, which is produced by the loss of the object, "it is the very presence of the object, rather than its loss, that is critical in ... melancholia" (2015, p. 152). Even though there may be loss at the level of an imaginary object, the melancholic individual, seen as suffering from one form of psychosis, is at the mercy of the invasive presence of the object in the real. In Grigg's words,

> What makes melancholia so different from mourning is that the melancholic subject turns out to be defenceless against the object. The object cannot be memorialised, as in mourning, and instead remains forever there in the Real. The collapse of semblants that otherwise veil the object persists, and the "grimace" of the object, like the grimace of a skull behind

a beautiful face, is exposed; for the melancholic, the veil of semblants, the i(a) over the object *a* falls altogether.

(ibid., p. 153)

Seen in this light, when the imaginary veil covering the object falls, melancholia results as a way to manage the overproximate real. Furthermore, it is our thesis that *the emergence of melancholia – beginning with the collapse of semblants that veil the object – is due to a foreclosure of ambivalence in the symbolic returning in the real.* In this sense, what we see in melancholia is not *repressed* ambivalence but rather, *foreclosed* ambivalence.

Although Freud's "Mourning and Melancholia" was written prior to his formulation of the death drive, we can read the death drive in the following remark about melancholia: "This picture of a delusion of (mainly moral) inferiority is completed by sleeplessness and refusal to take nourishment, and – what is psychologically very remarkable – by an overcoming of the instinct which compels every living thing to cling to life" (1917e, p. 246). Likewise, in "The Ego and the Id," published in 1923, Freud said that we see "a pure culture of the death instinct" (Freud, 1923b, p. 53) in melancholia. A Lacanian reading of the death drive reveals its repetitions manifesting within the symbolic realm as a breaking away from social norms and symbolic roles. This is beautifully portrayed by Kirsten Dunst's character, Justine, in Lars von Trier's film *Melancholia*.

We meet Justine on the eve of her wedding day. At the lavish reception hosted by her sister and brother-in-law at their mansion, we witness painfully inappropriate wedding toasts – Justine's mother says she does not believe in marriage and advises the couple to "enjoy it while it lasts" – and Justine's boss, the head of an advertising firm, introduces her to his nephew who is his newest employee while informing her that his nephew would be fired if he failed to convince her to give him a tagline for a new ad campaign on her wedding night. Justine's brother-in-law points out to her the huge sum of money he spent on her wedding reception and says he will only feel it is money well spent if she, as someone with a history of melancholia, agrees to "be happy." Justine smiles, agrees, thanks him, and as she walks away we see her practicing her smile before her expression returns to something much more like a scowl. In other words, as she later tells her sister, Justine "really tried" to play a role in the social fabric of her world despite her underlying disdain for the social order. For Justine, it is a world filled with narcissism, manipulation, greed, and the lack of love. After the night's events, even her sweet-natured new husband's request that they make love is something she cannot tolerate. She refuses his advances, goes outside to the golf course, and savagely fucks Tim, her boss's nephew (possibly in full view of her husband, who could have watched from the upstairs window). In this act we see the death drive at work. In this expression of her disdain for the social order she at the same time repeats a compulsion of her inability to function within it; we see her husband departing with his suitcase, because Justine had succeeded in destroying her marriage in less than a single day. Her actions lead to a kind of living death. Justine, then, is perfectly poised to become the heroine at the film's conclusion, when Earth's doppleganger planet, named "Melancholia", hurls its way from a distant solar system to collide directly with Earth. In a social world in which critiques of ideology – such as the superegoic command to "be happy" or to "become wealthy" (embodied by the boss and the brother-in-law) – are not tolerated, the planet Melancholia functions as a kind of return of ambivalence in the real.

Now we can also think of the figure of the zombie as exemplifying certain key aspects of melancholia. The zombie, who does not speak, has rejected or been ejected from the social bond. The Lacanian conception of the death drive reveals it as an endless repetition – precisely the kind of living death embodied in the zombie. What is more, the operation of the oral drive in the zombie, the drive to eat human flesh or human brains, reminds us of Karl Abraham's influence on Freud's depiction of melancholia. In the Editor's note to "Mourning and Melancholia," Strachey cites Ernest Jones' (1955, pp. 367–8) account that Freud submitted a first draft of the paper to Abraham who, in turn, made the "important suggestion that there was a connection between melancholia and the oral stage of libidinal development" (Strachey, 1957, p. 239; Freud, 1917e, p. 250).

We also see the oral drive at work in a case vignette Karl Abraham provides that highlights the connection between mourning and ambivalence. In his 1924 paper, Abraham discusses the case of a man whose wife and child died following a Caesarean section childbirth. After this tragic loss, the man had developed an uncharacteristic aversion to food that lasted for weeks. In Abraham's view, the man's disinclination for food "was reminiscent of the refusal to take nourishment met with in melancholics" (p. 79), although its disappearance on the night of an important dream made it clear that the man was not melancholic. Instead, Abraham remarked that the man in his dream "had reacted to his painful loss with an act of introjection of an oral-cannibalistic character" (ibid.).

The man dreamt that he was present at his wife's post-mortem. In one scene, in a twist reminiscent of Dr. Frankenstein's monster,

> the separate parts of the body grew together again, the dead woman began to show signs of life, and he embraced her with feelings of the liveliest joy. In the other scene the dissecting-room altered its appearance, and the dreamer was reminded of slaughtered animals in a butcher's shop.
>
> (1924, p. 80)

The man's associations to the dissected body in the latter scene included the meat he had eaten the night before for dinner. This meal had been the first he had eaten with a good appetite in weeks. And so his appetite for life was only able to return when his ambivalence could be staged; he saw himself in the first dream scene as wishing for his wife to become whole and alive and then in the second scene as desiring to consume her and reduce her to the dissected parts that remind us of the fragmented body of the mirror stage (cf. Lacan, 2006).

From our own clinic, an analysand – an obsessional neurotic – had a dream. *A cult was trying to raise the dead. If they succeeded in casting their spell, thousands of bodies would be reanimated and then controlled to wage a devastating war upon humanity. As the bodies were being levitated into the air, the analysand, an onlooker, decided he would try to stop them by singing Beethoven's "Ode to Joy." He became triumphantly happy when he realised his song was working, and that instead of the bodies coming back to life as warring human monsters, he was directing them to fly up to heaven.* A key association to the dreamer's singing "Ode to Joy" reminded him of its dual or ambivalent usage in the movie *A Clockwork Orange*; and in fact he himself identified with Alex, the protagonist of the movie.

In *A Clockwork Orange*, upon first experiencing the "Ode to Joy" Alex is overcome with jouissance when a woman at a bar sings an excerpt from it. Prior to that point in the film, the viewer had witnessed Alex and his gang of "droogs" beat up an old man, engage in a brutal fight with a rival gang, steal a convertible, and then pretend to be in distress so as to gain entrance into the Alexander family home; once inside, they promptly destroyed the house and then forced Mr. Alexander to watch as Alex raped Mrs. Alexander. The scene at the Korova Milkbar when Alex is bewitched by the sound of "Ode to Joy" follows this series of horrific acts and marks the birth of the viewer's ambivalence about Alex. Alex even reprimands one of his Droogs for being disrespectful to the beauty of the song. With Alex's rapturous admiration, the viewer is no longer able to purely hate Alex, but instead develops a kind of love for him as well.

In Žižek's (2012) film *A Pervert's Guide to Ideology*, he questions the function of Alex's identification with the music from Beethoven's Ninth Symphony. Žižek points out the seemingly paradoxical nature of Alex, the "ultimate cynical delinquent" being so fascinated by a piece of music which espouses an ideology of all humanity uniting in solidarity and joy. This ideological assertion of "all" humanity belies the truth that some are excluded, and Žižek locates Alex in that place of exclusion. In the second part of Beethoven's Ninth, the tone of the music changes into a "carnivalesque rhythm," and this shift occurs "precisely when Alex enters a shopping arcade" and is like a "fish in the water." Žižek comments that the first part of the Ninth, "which is falsely celebrated today" and can be heard in many official events, corresponds to the political ideology in Beethoven's time. Then, Žižek goes on to argue "the second part tells the true story, of that which disturbs the official ideology and of the failure of the official ideology to constrain it, to tame it." In this way, Beethoven carried out a musical critique of ideology.

According to Žižek's argument then, "Ode to Joy" is itself an expression of ambivalence – making use of the dominant cultural ideology while at the same time more profoundly rejecting it. In *A Clockwork Orange*, Alex subsequently plays an audio tape of Beethoven's Ninth which then functions as the sound-track to his perverse fantasied images: a drawing of a naked woman with a snake slithering its tongue near her vagina, beneath which four painted ceramic statues of the crucified Jesus appear to be dancing in synchrony as if in a chorus line; a woman in a wedding dress is hanged, which we see from a below "upskirt" viewpoint; Alex's face appears as a grinning vampire, revealing his fangs and blood dripping down his chin interspersed with shots of large explosions, presumably as he climaxes. Indeed, "Ode to Joy" and all classical music becomes associated with Alex's enjoyment of violence. Later on in the movie, of course, the imprisoned Alex is classically conditioned via "Ludovico's Technique" – which reminds us of "Ludwig," Beethoven's first name – to feel physically ill at the thought of either violence or classical music, which are paired.

In the analysand's dream of the would-be killer zombies, he stages an ambivalence as a way to manage his obsessional guilt over the jouissance he obtains from aggressive fantasies. In the dream, as the onlooker who subverts the zombies' potential for violence by sending them peacefully up to heaven, he derives jouissance from seeing himself as a do-gooder who saves the world. On the other hand, in singing "Ode to Joy" as it figures in *A Clockwork Orange*, the analysand also identifies with the cult who experience jouissance in their power to raise the dead and unleash murderous rage. The analysand's ambivalence is also manifested in his mourning of the dead; does he wish them to return to life or go to heaven? This analysand's ambivalence constitutes his obsessional doubt and difficulty making choices (e.g., double-checking, second-guessing, letting "fate" decide for him) that stem from, amongst other things, guilt over his death wishes for his father and younger brother.

Indeed, one of the functions of the dream as a formation of the unconscious in psychoanalysis is its framing–staging – of ambivalence and indicating where in the work of mourning an analysand may be. One analysand, a man in his mid-twenties at the time of coming for treatment, had lost his father to cancer at the age of fourteen. His relationship with his father from the onset of puberty had been difficult. The analysand had been repeatedly in trouble for smoking, stealing from his mother's purse to finance the purchase of cigarettes, hanging around corners with other young boys, and so on. His father would punish him severely, grounding him for weeks on end, hitting him on many occasions, and refusing to speak to him. On the night his father died, he had been at a friend's house when he was called to the hospital, but it was already too late to say goodbye. His idea for years had been that as he had often wished that his father would die, he had in fact successfully caused his father's death. The guilt that resulted and manifested in his symptoms was substantial. Working through his wish-come-horribly-true in his analysis led to the production of dreams about his father. To begin with, the dream would be darkly lit, with the father standing silently and menacingly in corners. As the treatment went on, the dreams were more brightly lit, and the father began to speak, saying very ordinary, banal things, for example giving advice to his son about which car to buy. Commensurate with the dreams, associations led to the articulation of conscious ambivalence around his father: no longer solely the punitive, intolerant, hard man, he went on in the analysand's dreams and waking associations to become a living "degradable" father, just like any other. We are reminded of the beloved Jamie who comes back to haunt Nina in *Truly, Madly, Deeply*. When speaking to her therapist about the idea she has that Jamie is sometimes "with her", she says that he does not tell her things about God, or the after-life, rather he tells her quite ordinary things: "make sure the back door is locked," "brush your teeth up and down not side to side!"

Zombies and vampires and ghosts, oh my!

An analysand whose father had died dreamt *that he was in a haunted house. There was something gurgling in the garbage disposal that was going to come up and attack him. He grabbed a spatula and a meat cleaver and was preparing to beat it back down when he encountered a zombie in the form of an old man who was trying to eat him.* He awoke in fright. In associating to the dream, the analysand noted that "old man" is a way of referring to one's father. Ghosts seeking vengeance, haunting the people who harmed them, can serve, as in this case, as depictions of neurotic fantasies of punishment. Following Grigg's thesis we could say that the fright and uncanny that zombies, ghosts, and other depictions of the dead can elicit is a function of the object *a* being unveiled. In this dream, the oral drive, via the zombie's attempt to eat the dreamer and the regurgitations of the garbage disposal (whose contents consist of bits of uneaten food) is the drive whose object is horrifyingly unveiled. Dreaming of being haunted by the zombie of a father is one way to work through ambivalence about the father, such that the zombie father wanting to harm the subject may represent both a punishment for the son's sins against the father (going against his wishes, not living up to his expectations, and so on) and its opposite, the son wanting to harm the father. Both the son's desire to go against his father's wishes and his desire to be the apple of his eye must be worked through in mourning.

Since the mark of the proximity of the object *a* is jouissance, it is appropriate to recall here that individuals seek out horror movies depicting ghosts, zombies, and vampires because they are in some way "enjoyable". As Freud had noted – "many people experience the feeling [of the uncanny] in the highest degree in relation to death and dead bodies, to the return of the dead, and to spirits and ghosts" (Freud,1919h, p. 241). What we see then is that the experience of the uncanny or *unheimlich* which is often elicited by zombies, vampires, and ghosts in dreams and on the screen, corresponds to the subject's encounter with the object *a* and an unsettling anxiety. And in our clinical work we have observed that individuals tend to have a penchant for a certain type of figure of horror on the screen which accords with their complaints in analysis. What fascinates and scares us the most is something intimately related to our object *a*.

Russell Grigg, in his article "Remembering and Forgetting" (2016), depicts the work of mourning as inscribing the "imaginary features of the object, which he describes using Lacan's matheme – i(a) -, into signifiers lodged in the Other." Grigg continues on to describe how the pain we experience in mourning can be attributed to,

> the fall of the semblants that love and desire attach us to, as Freud taught us; but – and this is what Freud did not capture – the work of mourning is the transformation of these semblants into signifiers registered in and endorsed by the Other.
>
> (Grigg, 2016, p. 3)

In other words, to mourn is to remember and to *privately and publicly commemorate* who and what we have lost. The link to the uncanny is revealed when we consider the role the object *a* plays in mourning. In mourning, the painful loss of one's semblants exposes the underlying object *a*, ordinarily hidden by the object's ideal features (Grigg, ibid.). The real of object *a* can manifest in nightmares concerning the lost loved one, nightmares such as the one in Abraham's case of the man who lost his wife and child and had a dream in which he "was reminded of slaughtered animals in a butcher's shop" (ibid.).

The figure of the zombie, whether in dreams or on the screen, thus provides the spectator with a possible opportunity to work through mourning and ambivalence. The subject may have difficulty commemorating in the symbolic the bad as well as the good aspects of his father and to put into words both the loving and hateful wishes he had about his father. The unconscious formation of the deceased father as a zombie makes it socially permissible to express aggression toward the zombie father, to wish him dead, and even to kill him.

In fact, the TV show *The Walking Dead* is full of stories of someone's parent, sibling, spouse, or child dying and being reincarnated as a zombie, bringing new meaning to the idea of "complicated mourning." In Season 1, Amy, who was 12 years younger than her sister Andrea, resented that prior to the zombie apocalypse Andrea did not return home to visit very often and was not a large part of her life. After Amy is bitten in the neck by a zombie, Andrea cradles her in her arms all night in devastation. When Amy awakens, having been reincarnated as a zombie, it happens to also be the occasion of her human birthday. Andrea apologises to Amy for never having "been there" for her, crying, before she kills Amy. Through her apology, it is as if Andrea feels somehow responsible for Amy's death before she then actually kills Amy. Presumably, Andrea feels guilty for having at one time treated Amy as though she did not exist, an action which may have existed side by side with a fond regard for Amy. It is through relating to Amy as a zombie that Andrea's ambivalence comes to the fore and can be worked through.

The apparently distant relative of the zombie in the TV and film horror genre has also returned flashing his/her incisors. In on-screen depictions of vampires, the uncanny manifests when someone who seems familiar, like us, flashes her or his fangs and tears into the neck of an unsuspecting victim. The delights of the oral drive, of feasting on one's neighbour or lover, elicit both a scare and a pleasurable excitement in the viewer insofar as the viewer may identify with both the victim and the vampire. The immense popularity of vampire films and television shows since the 1990s (*Interview with a Vampire*, *Buffy the Vampire Slayer*, the *Twilight* series, *TrueBlood* among others) is undeniable, and we will speculate about what the figure of the vampire condenses and represents on the cultural and psychical stage in Chapter 5. In terms of mourning, the vampire, who is often a main character in contemporary films, functions as a fantasy of eradicating loss and mourning. Since a vampire is immortal, unless ultimately killed off by being exposed to the sun or by a wooden stake to the heart (such ferocious breaking of the heart in this manner of killing also peculiarly indicative of loss of love), vampire couples on film do not have to deal with losing one another through death, and sometimes vampires, unlike zombies, have chosen to become vampires in order, precisely, to have eternal life. Indeed, in many screen depictions of vampires, a vampire falls in love with a human, and in some cases turns the human into a vampire on account of his love for her. (Typically, it is a male vampire who "turns" or creates a female vampire out of a human woman, thus making her both his child and his lover – a combination which is rarely made explicit.) For instance, in *Interview with a Vampire*, the male vampire protagonists take pity on a young girl whose family has been killed in the plague, and since they are unable to tolerate that this innocent young creature should die, they turn her into a vampire. As another example, in the *Twilight* series, the female human protagonist consents to be turned into a vampire by her love so that they will be together for eternity and she will not have to be mourned. Accordingly, in her now extended lifetime she will have to witness the deaths of her human friends and family and thus perhaps mourn more and not less. So there is a sense in which the character cannot escape mourning, even if she can escape death. We could argue therefore that the popularity of the vampire on the screen in recent decades has something to do with its depiction of the fantasy of not having to go through loss – whether it be a loved one or one's own beauty and youth. Certainly, vampires on the screen tend to be young beautiful, handsome, strong, and sexually voracious. This fantasy of "eternal youth" reflects our contemporary obsessions, in which consumer goods and products

("Eternity", "Forever Young", etc.) are invested with the function of the fetish. The fetish serves to deny lack. As addictions are increasingly normalised, the relentless search for enjoyment in the forms of *having*, or attempting *to have*, can be seen as fetishistic and thus perverse denials of lack and of loss.

This leads us to suppose that nowadays we all too often approach the process of mourning as satisfaction-seeking consumers. Perhaps the modern or hypermodern condition of depression is a response to loss which cannot be staged or worked through. For example, when someone's dog dies, people often advise that person to "get over it" by getting a new puppy in short order; sometimes they will even present the mourner with a puppy as a present. This mentality makes objects equivalent and replaceable. When a woman suffers a breakup, her girlfriends supply her with ice cream that night and the next night take her out on the town to find a new man to fill her lack. A little girl who is the daughter of a friend was playing a game with a toy she had received for her birthday from her father some months before, when her friend accidentally broke it. The girl cried and was not consoled by her father's promise to get her a new, physically identical toy. The father realised that there was an aspect of the toy that had been broken, as something special she had been given by him for her birthday, which was forever lost and needed to be mourned. And so it may be that even objects that are, from a certain angle, replaceable, can and should still be related to as uniquely valuable. In the face of loss, the message from the Other of our times is "pick yourself up and move on! Find someone new and you will be whole again." The push to jouissance promoted by our culture is completely antithetical to the proper process of mourning. We need time and space to mourn both the loved and hated aspects of the object. Meanwhile, we argue, any attempts to fill the void without considerations of ambivalence are symptomatic.

References

Abraham, K. (1924). A short study of the development of the libido, viewed in the light of mental disorders. In R.V. Frankiel (Ed.). (1994). *Essential papers on object loss* (pp. 72–93).New York and London: New York University Press.

Freud, S. (1917e). Mourning and melancholia. In *The Standard Edition of the Complete Psychological Works of Sigmund Freud. S.E., XIV*, pp. 237–258.

Freud, S. (1919h). The uncanny. In *The Standard Edition of the Complete Psychological Works of Sigmund Freud. S.E., XVII*, pp. 217–252.

Freud, S. (1923b). The ego and the id. In *The Standard Edition of the Complete Psychological Works of Sigmund Freud. S.E., XIX*, pp. 1–66.

Grigg, R. (2015). Melancholia and the unabandoned object. In *Lacan on Madness* (pp. 151–170). London: Routledge.

Grigg, R. (2016) . Remembering and forgetting. *Lacanian Compass Express, 3*(2), pp. 1–8.

Jones, E. (1955). *Sigmund Freud life and work*. Vol. 2. London and New York: Basic Books.

Lacan, J. (2006). The mirror stage as formative of the I function as revealed in psycho-analytic experience. In *Écrits: The first complete edition in English* (pp. 75–81). Trans. B.Fink. New York: W.W. Norton & Co.

Strachey, J. (1957). Editor's note in Mourning and melancholia. In *The Standard Edition of the Complete Psychological Works of Sigmund Freud. S.E., XIV*, pp. 367–368.

Zizek, S. (2012). *The Pervert's Guide to Ideology* [Motion picture on DVD]. Director S. Fiennes. United Kingdom: Zeitgeist Films.

Chapter 4

On letting the right one in
Heisenberg and vampires

The father serves different functions in Freud's Oedipal myth and in his myth of the primal horde in *Totem and Taboo* (1913). The Oedipus complex is supposed to explain how desire and jouissance are regulated by the law. The law is present from the outset, and the father himself is beholden to this law. As the one who transmits the law to the child, the father is seen as preventing access to jouissance. Jouissance is symbolised as occurring when a subject transgresses the law, and so the law shapes and conditions desire. In *Totem and Taboo,* this relationship between the law and jouissance is inverted; jouissance is present at the outset and the law follows. The one who ostensibly has jouissance at the outset, however, is restricted to the father of the primal horde, who somehow enjoys all the women and through his position of power restricts his sons' access to the women. Unlike the Oedipal father, the primal horde father acts as an exception to the law. His sons murder him in protest, imagining that after his death they will gain access to jouissance. Although both the Oedipus myth and the myth of the primal horde involve the murder of the father, the consequences of this murder are the opposite in each case. In *Totem and Taboo*, patricide is not our unconscious wish but instead, according to Freud, a prehistoric event that actually had to occur to allow humans to pass into culture from the animal world. In other words, whereas in the Oedipus complex the perpetual postponement of enacting the unconscious wish is what is responsible for sustaining the symbolic law (as committing incest would abolish the symbolic prohibition that defines the cultural world), in the myth of the primal horde the murder of the father is a precondition for being within the symbolic. Crucially, in *Totem and Taboo* the result of murdering the father is not the fantasied access to jouissance via incest but instead the rise of the dead father returning as the name of the father who in his death has become more powerful by embodying the symbolic law and serving as barrier to jouissance. Underpinning this seemingly paradoxical result of the transposition of the primal father to the symbolic father is the *guilt* experienced by the sons. It is on account of their guilt that their hatred for their father becomes unconscious; the conscious side of the ambivalence is their love and respect for the father, in whose honour they agree to uphold a symbolic law, establishing the two fundamental taboos of prohibiting killing the father and having sex with the mother. The Oedipal complex and the myth of the primal horde, then, function in tandem. The former prohibits jouissance and the latter regulates desire. Both myths function to cover over a necessary structure that allows the subject to cope with the drives and the body's jouissance. In reality, there are limits to how much jouissance the subject can tolerate. *In the father complexes, the impossibility of jouissance is symbolised as a prohibition, and the result is the birth of the subject's ceaseless desiring and symptom formation.* The mother or woman stands both for the possibility of and the prohibition on jouissance once the father figure translates the impossibility of jouissance into a prohibition.

Return of the primal father

Although faulty Oedipal fathers in some cases still manage to sufficiently transmit the symbolic law, such that we see Oedipal guilt playing a role in the symptoms of some analysands (as we argue further in Chapter 5), increasingly we are seeing a rather different type of father figure functioning. The Freudian Oedipus complex functions as such if there is a father who *properly* lays down the law regarding access to jouissance by threatening castration. But Freud knew from his clinical practice that Oedipal fathers do not manage to lay down the law all by themselves and they do not manage to castrate, still less threaten it. In short, Oedipal fathers are not always, or even not at all scary. It only takes a brief review of the fathers in Freud's clinical cases to see that Oedipal fathers are far from perfect vessels for the transmission of symbolic law. Dora's father suffers a chronic illness, is impotent, has an affair with Frau K., and tries to use Dora as an object of exchange with Herr K. (Freud, 1905e). Little Hans' father does little to come between Hans and his mother, only protesting feebly at Hans cuddling in the marital bed with his mother (Freud, 1909b). The Rat Man's father married for money instead of love, living off his wife's fortune and functioning weakly in the social realm as a noncommissioned officer (Freud, 1909d). Indeed, psychoanalysis is full of such accounts of patients complaining about the weaknesses and shortcomings of their fathers. One of our patients repeatedly included his father in the count of his brothers; he had only one brother but would say over and over "my brothers". Over time he recognised that he could not allocate his father a status above that of his brother because of his ineptitude and what he regarded as his generally pathetic position in the family. In "Family Complexes in the Formation of the Individual" (1938), an article written early in Lacan's career, he considered the degradation of the figure of the father to be the main cause for psychological illness, even going so far as to suggest that the inception of psychoanalysis was a response to the shortcomings of the father and an attempt to mend the corresponding crises. It is in this Oedipal series of what Lacan dubs "faulty fathers" that the sickly and financially impotent Walter White of *Breaking Bad* initially belongs (see Lacan, 2016, for his discussion of James Joyce "symptom" as a substitution for the faulty, and foreclosed, Name-of-the-Father).

As such, these faulty fathers or Oedipal dads need to be "bigged up" in order to function in the kind of way Freud imagined. Freud therefore needed a kind of conceptual upgrade for the Oedipal father: and this is what is achieved in his take on Darwin's myth of the primal horde "father". This second father is the father of jouissance, for whom everything is allowed and whose murder in turn brings about the operation that Lacan identifies as that of the transformation of jouissance into desire. Let us take another look at *Breaking Bad*. At the beginning of the series, Walter White is a version of the faulty Oedipal dad, playing the role of the symbolic name of the father. White goes to work and teaches chemistry to uninterested students. After that, at his job at the car-wash, we see White on his hands and knees cleaning the hubcap of a flashy car owned by a disrespectful student who laughs at him. His son, "Walter Junior", later refuses to respond to that name and instead goes by "Flynn." But then White breaks out of his humiliated and degraded status as Oedipal dad by breaking bad. White transforms into "Heisenberg" – the name he chooses for himself as methamphetamine cooker – and as Heisenberg, is the cruel superegoic primal father, a master of jouissance.

There is more than one Name-of-the-Father. More than one, and at-least-two. As we have indicated, the combination of the two myths mobilises the following Freudian father formula: the murdered primordial father of jouissance finds a return in the guise of symbolic authority incarnated by the father in the Oedipus complex. However, in *Breaking Bad*, in what we want to call the "Heisenberg Myth", the order of succession described by Freud in *Totem and Taboo* is apparently reversed: the deposed symbolic authority returns as the obscene real tyrant. This twist – in which the primordial father makes a reappearance – is recognised by a number of Lacanian commentators.

Žižek remarks, for instance, that "in all emblematic revolutions, from the French to the Russian, the overthrow of the impotent old regime of the symbolic master (French King, Tsar) ends in the rule of a far more 'repressive' figure of the anal, father-Leader (Napoleon, Stalin)" (Žižek, 2005, p. 206). Psychoanalyst Paul Verhaeghe argues:

> Normally, it's the real primal father who is done away with, with the result that the symbolic paternal function can be established […]. In the reversed version, instead of the real primal father, it's the symbolic function which is destroyed, thereby setting loose […] a figure who is only on the lookout for his own jouissance.
>
> (Verhaeghe, 2016, p. 3)

Indeed, in most of the anti-Trump discourses that circulate, this is the most frequent outcry: that a certain symbolic function immanent in Obama's regime appears to have been replaced by the jouissance-led and ultimately repressive actions of Donald Trump.

One of the guiding principles that Lacanian psychoanalysis works with today is that whereas at one point in history the singular Name-of-the-Father may have allowed for the naming and describing of the double function of prohibiting jouissance and mobilising desire, now it is necessary to speak of a pluralisation of names, a plurality of fathers, with a multiplicity of different functions. The different versions of the father complex all function to explain the subject's relation to her/his desire and how s/he experiences being barred from a certain quantity of jouissance. But, in our time this also means that the subject sees the primal father, rather than the Oedipal father, as once again standing in the way of her or his enjoyment. The Names-of-the-Father as mobilised in *Breaking Bad* can be regarded as such as a kind of handbook for understanding the Names-of-the-Father in contemporary society. In a time of an inexistent singular Name-of-the-Father, the subject is deprived of a universal one-size-fits-all possibility of symbolising authority, which regulates jouissance. This deprivation leads to structural consequences as noted by Verhaeghe:

> The emergence of a social reality characterised by the breakdown of civility, rising belligerence, paranoid delusions, social fragmentation, widespread anomie and outbreaks of irrational violence.
>
> (2009, p. 138)

And the psychoanalytic point not to be missed here is that there are symptomatic consequences to this deprivation. As Verhaeghe goes on to argue, the subject can engage in a number of supplementary alternatives, for example looking for symbolic authority in other places such as in identification with a charismatic leader, or in forms of fundamentalism, as well as in imaginary and rivalrous identifications with others who are also disenfranchised and who come up with solutions to the lack of symbolic guarantee in drug dependency and other addictions (ibid.).

We see this range of practices most vividly sketched in *Breaking Bad*, in the assemblages of subjects around the figures of the various drug kingpins, and in Heisenberg's ultimate fundamentalist passage into "the one who knocks". In our time, when the lack of symbolic coordinates give rise to the increasing impetus to get our symbolic bearings, our recourse to the imaginary in search of a solution may in turn lead to the constitution of the tyrant, who shadows our every move, who lurks behind the door waiting to knock. We should be careful then, to *let the right one in*.

The jouissance (and bloody ambivalence) of vampires

The vampire, it is said, needs to be invited in. Rather like the zombie, the figure of the vampire on the screen has also been put to work in representing some of the tensions of human ambivalence. Whereas the zombie may be seen to represent something of our foreclosure of ambivalence about the neighbour, we see the vampire portraying repressed ambivalence about sexual jouissance. The vampire, as such, is a figure of modernity insofar as Western modernity has been characterised by the regulation of and restrictions upon sexuality. This was the case at least until the 1990's.

Many commentators have remarked upon the allegoric power of the vampire to portray the repressed sexuality of modern times. In his essay, "The Monster in the Bedroom: Sexual Symbolism in Bram Stoker's Dracula", Christopher Bentley argues that Count Dracula embodies the Freudian id (1972). Christopher Craft (1984) comments upon Dracula's homosexual undertones and sees Stoker's Dracula as a "characteristic, if hyperbolic instance of Victorian anxiety over the potential fluidity of gender roles" (p. 112). Speaking of Bela Lugosi's 1931 film version of Dracula, Jeffrey Andrew Weinstock points out that the "film's real energy is the contest between Dracula and the men who pursue him, which includes the memorable scene of Dracula's failed 'seduction' of Van Helsing" (2012, p. 53). The male and female vampire as potentially or actually homosexual has been a theme in vampire films since their inception. The figure of the vampire, as a creature of the night, has depicted transgressive sexuality in a number of key ways: by being excessive, gender-bending, female (i.e., fantasies of women's sexuality as being castrating or subversive simply by virtue of depicting a female as having sexual jouissance), extra-marital, homosexual, and even verging on cannibalism via the oral drive to suck the blood of a human.

The type of vampire film most common until the 1990's is one that relies upon a traditional Oedipal structure to stage ambivalence about sexual jouissance. The vampire in these films is depicted as the neurotic subject's fantasy of a pervert: the subject who is not subjected to Oedipal law, not subjected even to the limits of death, who is not inhibited by guilt and relentlessly pursues jouissance at the expense of others. The lusted-after victim of the vampire, however, operates within the symbolic law. Before the victim realises the true nature of the vampire, s/he is often portrayed as falling under the spell of the attractions of the vampire, and it is in this state of not being aware of her or his sin that the victim experiences Oedipal guilt. The victim is sometimes punished for her unconscious desire, for example when the victim becomes a vampire herself and is no longer able to hide the guilty secret of her sexual jouissance.

In Werner Herzog's 1979 remake of *Nosferatu* – a late entry in this classic scenario – the male protagonist is portrayed as guilty of the sin of greed, and it is because of this that his homeland is punished with the vampiric plague. He brings the vampire to his homeland because he ignores sign after sign that his journey to Transylvania will be an encounter with evil (his wife's foreboding and pleas that he forego the journey, the terror-stricken warnings of the townspeople near Count Dracula's abode, etc.) on account of wanting to earn the hefty sum of money promised to him for his services (as a lawyer who can ratify the Count's purchase of land in Germany). The vampire in this type of film that is common before the end of the twentieth century represents a sexual jouissance that, once discovered, must be eliminated by those acting in the name of the father. Faulty Oedipal dads and other characters are able to triumph against unholy sexual jouissance in the name of God the father whose power is symbolised in using communion wafers and crucifixes as weapons against vampires.

A faulty Oedipal dad saves the day in a very early iteration of the vampire story that predates and even partly inspired Bram Stoker's *Dracula* (1897): Joseph Sheridan Le Fanu's 1871 *Carmilla*, about a female vampire who preys on the unsuspecting 18-year-old Laura who is eager for a friend. As it happens, Carmilla is a distant relative of Laura, and so Carmilla's sexualised affections for Laura – not to mention Carmilla's enjoyment of drinking Laura's blood while she sleeps in her bed – are not only crossing the taboo against homosexuality that was prominent in that day but also the incest taboo. Le Fanu portrays Carmilla's sexuality with Victorian-era circumspection:

> Sometimes after an hour of apathy, my strange and beautiful companion [Carmilla] would take my hand and hold it with a fond pressure, renewed again and again; blushing softly, gazing in my face with languid and burning eyes, and breathing so fast that her dress rose and fell with the tumultuous respiration. It was like the ardour of a lover; it embarrassed me; it was hateful and yet overpowering; and with gloating eyes she drew me to her, and her hot lips travelled along my cheek in kisses; and she would whisper, almost in sobs, "You are mine, you shall be mine, and you and I are one for ever".
>
> (Le Fanu, 1871/2003, Chapter 4)

In addition to her love object, Carmilla's victims were exclusively female. Laura's father and another father figure are depicted as overcoming their original positions as dupes in time to protect the virginal Laura. They find Carmilla's coffin and drive a stake through her heart. Although Laura's father takes her on a year-long holiday tour of Italy, she never fully recovers, and she is thus punished for her unconscious desire for Carmilla. The tale of Carmilla is thus a Gothic horror story, since her victims are portrayed as being guilty of yielding to a perverse, sinful temptation that has lasting consequences on them. The Oedipal father in this story is depicted as weak, but once his eyes are opened to the sinful activities of Laura under the sway of Carmilla, he is able to act on behalf of God the father and prohibit further sin. Carmilla served as the prototype for the figure of the lesbian vampire (Keesey, 1998). Most iconically, the story of Carmilla was filmed in Roger Vadim's 1960 *Et Mourir de Plaisir* (translated as "To Die of Pleasure", but released in the U.S. and the U.K. as *Blood and Roses*), in which the lesbian eroticism was cut significantly for its release in the U.S.

As a fun fact we observe that the 1913 film *The Vampire*, directed by Robert G. Vignola, was the first film to depict a vampire which did not portray an undead vampire as we know it today, but instead showed a vamp, or a female femme fatale. Inspired by Rudyard Kipling's 1897 poem of the same name, the vampire is a seductress who will be the undoing of any man who falls for her charms. Correspondingly, Kipling's poem includes the lines, "(We called her the woman who did not care)/But the fool he called her his lady fair." Just two years later, Theda Bara's starring role as the "Vampire woman" in *A Fool There Was* (1915) – which was also based on Kipling's poem – popularised the term "vamp". Bara's character almost magically seduces several men, including a U.S. government official serving as special representative to England who quickly abandons his post and his family for the vamp. Right from the start of the vampire genre on film, then, we see one of the key ways in which the vampire functions allegorically. In a time when the women's suffrage movement was hotly contested, the female vampire on film depicted the horror of what might happen if women were given more freedom. Characters such as Bara's Vampire woman simultaneously stage a male fascination with a hypersexualised female ideal and a *jealouissance*: hatred, and fear of feminine jouissance that fuels misogyny.

In more general terms, the vampire in its various iterations functions to represent sexual desire and jouissance. The vampire on the screen is often depicted by an alluring sex symbol of his or her day: the dashing line-up including Christopher Lee, Lauren Hutton, Tom Cruise, Brad Pitt, and Delphine Seyrig, to name but a few. In other instances, such as the original 1922 *Nosferatu* and Herzog's 1979 *Nosferatu*, the vampire, although himself unattractive or grotesque, fixates and feeds on a beautiful love object/victim, his lust being the cause of his eventual demise. In these retellings of the story of Dracula, Count Dracula, as a member of the aristocracy, has the financial means to transport himself – in a coffin, of course – and some soil from his native Transylvania to another country (England, in the original Bram Stoker tale and Germany in the 1922 F.W. Murnau and 1979 Herzog renditions). The foreign Count Dracula brings the plague on the local commoners, feeding on them, making this version of the vampire story about class and ethnicity distinctions as well as the prohibition of sexual jouissance. The blood-lust of the vampire either kills, or that lust becomes contagious, begetting a new vampire out of a previously upright citizen. Vampires, unlike zombies who are driven by pure drive to bite and consume humans, are depicted as deriving great jouissance from sucking human blood – especially the blood of the prototypical beautiful woman. As the living dead, their sexual jouissance brings to life Lacan's comment that all drives are sexual drives and every drive is a death drive (1997, p. 199).

What happens in the re-tellings of the vampire story as the twentieth century progresses is of great interest to our question about the status of ambivalence and Oedipal guilt today.

Vampire vegetarianism or, loving (instead of sucking the blood of) thy neighbour

The hugely popular *Twilight* films and the *True Blood* television series, both based on books written after the turn of the twenty-first century, feature a new kind of vampire: we will call it the "vegetarian" vampire. Fighting against his supernaturally lustful nature, this vampire abstains from drinking human blood and killing humans. In the *Twilight* films, the Cullen family survives by drinking animal blood. They are an attractive white vampire family complete with heterosexual parents and children who appear to be teenagers (although they are actually centuries old). The Cullens try their best to fit into daily human life, adhering to the human symbolic law and themselves feeling guilty about their previous sins against humans. Year after year the unfortunate vampire children are subjected to the trials and tribulations of high school. Edward Cullen, one of the "teenage" vampires, falls in love with Bella Swan, a beautiful human high schooler. Bella soon becomes the target of a coven of evil vampires – Laurent, Victoria, and James – who are manifestly not vegetarians. The Cullens, as the realization of the hysteric's fantasy of the infallible Oedipal father, rescue Bella again and again from the evil vampires. Meanwhile, Bella has a faulty human Oedipal dad whom she loves but rebels against and complains about. In the *Twilight* films, Eros is entirely domesticated through the Oedipalised vampire family but also through the moralistic tale of Bella's love for Edward in which the two of them abstain from sex and from her transformation into a vampire or a vamp – the latter being necessary so they can "safely" have sex and love each other for eternity – until she has had time to consider her choice carefully and truly consent. The *Twilight* story is therefore revealed for its repressive and neo-conservative promotion of regulated sexual jouissance. Unsurprisingly, there is seemingly no unconscious sinning going on in this twenty-first century series. Correspondingly, we may assume that the invention of vegetarian vampires is an index of our all-too-conscious contemporary guilt. The *Twilight* movie viewer identifies with the privileged, white, middle-class, and vegetarian vampires – those who themselves are subject to Oedipal guilt and do not wish to hurt their neighbour humans despite being clearly superior to them (enjoying privileges such as eternal life, beauty, wealth, enhanced senses, supernatural powers, and incredible strength), paternalistically exercising great restraint of their powerful sexual drives in order to refrain from hurting their racially and culturally different human neighbours. In the twenty-first century version of the vampire tale, the co-occurring presence of the good and evil vampire covens gives us a clue into its continued staging of ambivalence about sexual jouissance but also to what has changed in our culture and in our contemporary subjectivities.

In Lacan's essay "The Neurotic's Individual Myth," (1979) the neurotic constructs a myth in which the paternal figure is redoubled, and the two sides of the father, the Name-of-the-Father and his obscene, cruel, superegoic dark side, are incarnated in two different people. In the *Twilight* series, the vegetarian vampires can be seen as in the position of the symbolic fathers who are at war with the perverse superegoic carnivore vampires. These at-least-two names of the father are functioning in contemporary times where the singular Name-of-the-Father no longer reigns.

Again, in the 1994 film version of Anne Rice's *Interview with the Vampire* two vampire protagonists are figured. Tom Cruise plays Lestat, who is the traditional perverse carnivore vampire existing outside of the symbolic law. He becomes the vampire father of Louis, a human who has lost the will to live following the death of his wife and child. Louis, played by Brad Pitt, having transformed into a vampire feels guilty about his hunger for human blood and soon turns to feeding on animals. Louis becomes a vampire Oedipal dad when he is no longer able to fight off his hunger for human blood and feeds off of a ten-year-old girl whose mother has just died from an outbreak of the plague. Louis is horrified at what he has done, and so when Lestat turns the girl, Claudia, into a vampire it is to entice Louis to stay with him by simultaneously playing off of and assuaging his guilt. Both vampires are fathers, in their own way, to Claudia. The supergeoic father of obscene jouissance commands that Claudia enjoys. Although she has her fun for a time, when she discovers her lack in the form of not being able to mature into womanhood, she is furious at Lestat. Louis and Claudia try to murder primal father Lestat on two occasions on account of his monstrous nature. After the second attempt, they discover other vampires – much to the delight of Louis who had thought his dysfunctional family constituted the only remaining vampires. However, with this connection to vampire society they discover the existence of the symbolic law of vampires: never kill another vampire – which is at the same time a prohibition on killing the father owing to the capacity that each vampire, whether male or female, has to father a vampire. Having unknowingly committed this sin, they are nevertheless accountable for their Oedipal guilt; Claudia, who was primarily responsible for the murder attempt, is punished by being burnt to death (via exposure to the sun). We could see her murder attempt as staging what results from efforts to kill the obscene superego: an even greater punishment is delivered to the subject. As such, the primal father resists being killed, and he persists as a threat to the Oedipal law (which in these stories is oddly contemporaneous with the primal father); this twist indicates further the diminution in our times of the Name-of-the-Father.

These vampire stories clearly stage the ambivalences about sexual jouissance that corresponds to a more traditional version of the Oedipal complex and Oedipal guilt. However, the second cycle of vampire stories, becoming commonplace in the 1990's, portray the two faces of the father in two different figures. Moreover, the previously faulty human Oedipal dad is raised to super-human status, gaining the same powers as the perverse vampire – immortality, strength, mind control, speed, the ability to turn into a bat, and so on – but retaining his characteristic guilt and sense of morality. This shouts out to the contemporaneous proliferation of superhero – and supervillain – movies. The new Oedipal father is now propped up, almost not lacking, in a gesture toward the fantasmatic hysterical solution. Adding further support for the hysteric's fantasy, the male symbolic father vampire tends to fall in everlasting love with a human female – his one lack being the lack that she tries to fill via desire and love. (*TrueBlood* and *Buffy the Vampire Slayer* are other contemporary versions of the hysteric's vampire myth.) In Žižek's words, "beneath the hysteric's rebellion and challenge to paternal authority there is thus a hidden call for a renewed paternal authority, for a father who would really be a 'true father' and adequately embody his symbolic mandate" (1999, p. 404). Whereas in the first cycle of vampire films the faulty Oedipal father sufficed to do the job of eradicating the evil vampire and bringing guilt to the subject, this new superhuman – or supervampiric – version of the vampire Oedipal dad attests to the decline of the belief in the symbolic function of the father, which, according to Žižek,

> is losing its performative efficiency; for that reason, a father is no longer perceived as one's *Ego Ideal*, the (more or less failed, inadequate) bearer of symbolic authority, but as one's *ideal ego*, imaginary competitor – with the result that subjects never really 'grow up', that we are dealing today with individuals in their thirties and forties who remain, in terms of their psychic economy, 'immature' adolescents competing with their fathers.
>
> (1999, p. 404)

Indeed, the vegetarian vampire or superhero as one's ideal ego lends itself to super-powered pissing contests on the screen, with fighting being omnipresent in the newer versions of the vampire story. The vampire story no longer functioning primarily to stage ambivalence about sexual jouissance; this newer version of the vampire myth re-stages ambivalence about the function of the father. Consciously, these stories are about how the law always triumphs over lawless jouissance even if only via segregation rather than elimination, but the unconscious desire belied by the Oedipal father as ideal ego vampire is for the Other's completion.

The remains of oedipal guilt: Make way – yet again – for the primal father

We have been arguing that in our times the subject imagines that the primal father, rather than the Oedipal father, is standing in the way of her or his enjoyment. Whereas in pre-modern societies the cultural totality was unified by the reigning master signifier and subjects shared a single ego-ideal, by contrast our *post-modern* societies lack any such unifying symbol or point of identification. This postmodern "lack" is itself the result of the democratising of societies and attempts to generate rational societies by getting rid of the arbitrary power of the ruler. However, ditching the ego-ideal as the point of symbolic unifying identification results not in the appointment of a new master emptied of superego, but its obverse, rather a superego without a master.

In the absence of a strong symbolic authority, the vampire as superego without a master is an emblem of our times. In the 2008 Swedish vampire film *Let the Right One In* (based on the 2004 novel by John Ajvide Lindqvist), the relentlessly bullied 12-year-old Oskar lives with his mother and occasionally visits his uninvolved alcoholic father. Oskar tries and fails at avoiding the bullies who take pleasure in physically and psychologically torturing him. Oskar does not fight back, but we see signs of his fantasy of the primal father in his habit of keeping newspaper clippings of murders and other violent crimes. Oskar meets and befriends his neighbor Eli, who appears to be a girl about his age. The two begin a kind of romance, although Oskar learns that "she" is really a 200-year-old vampire and, moreover, a castrated boy. Paradoxically, Eli's castration serves to bolster "her" status as a primal father as "she" exists outside of the order of symbolic law and sexuation. At the school swimming pool, Oskar's bullies threaten to pluck out his eye – in an apparent reference to Oedipus – if he does not manage to hold his breath for three minutes. Eli rescues him by brutally killing the bullies. The moral of this contemporary vampire fantasy is marked by the failure of the symbolic authority to intervene to stop the bullies. Teachers and parents are impotent. There is no guilty other to which to appeal. In this postmodern narrative, the only way to prohibit jouissance, to stop bullying, is through the brutal force of the superegoic figure without a master. If you align yourself with the primal vampire father, he will kill all your enemies. In the absence of Oedipal guilt there is nothing but the fantasy of being the primal father, and in the face of the weakness of the Oedipal law there is only anxiety.

The Oedipus Complex nowadays is judged to be of dubious clinical value but on the other hand Oedipal dads – or faulty fathers if you prefer – are in abundance. We know from our clinics that modern sons (and daughters) do not straightforwardly identify their fathers as representatives of patriarchal authority. As the security and protection associated with that authority has disappeared, the result is ever-increasing levels of anxiety and aggression in young people who are condemned as such to the level of the juvenile, forever the kid, the perpetual adolescent (cf. Verhaeghe, 2009, p. 38). Lacan himself claimed that perhaps the Oedipal show has run its course, but we are not convinced. What we see Oedipally speaking rather is how the father is *still* the symptom of the son. We will not be surprised then to find that postmodern experiences of ambivalence, and its correlates of enjoyment, transgression, and guilt, will be affected accordingly.

References

Bentley, C.F. (1972). The monster in the bedroom: Sexual symbolism in Bram Stoker's *Dracula*. *Literature and Psychology*, *22*(1), pp. 27–34.

Craft, C. (1984). Kiss me with those red lips: Gender and inversion in Bram Stoker's *Dracula*. *Representations*, *8*, pp. 107–133.

Freud, S. (1905e). Fragment of an analysis of a case of hysteria. In *The Standard Edition of the Complete Psychological Works of Sigmund Freud. S.E.*, *VII*, pp. 1–122.

Freud, S. (1909b). Analysis of a phobia in a five-year-old boy. In *The Standard Edition of the Complete Psychological Works of Sigmund Freud. S.E.*, *X*, pp. 1–148.

Freud, S. (1909d). Notes upon a case of obsessional neurosis. In *The Standard Edition of the Complete Psychological Works of Sigmund Freud. S.E.*, *X*, pp. 151–318.

Freud, S. (1913). Totem and taboo. In *The Standard Edition of the Complete Psychological Works of Sigmund Freud. S.E.*, *XIII*, pp. 1–164.

Keesey, P. (Ed.). (1998). *Daughters of darkness: Lesbian vampire stories*. San Fransisco: Cleis Press.

Lacan, J. (1938). *Family complexes in the formation of the individual*. Trans. C. Gallagher. Retrieved from www.lacaninireland.com.

Lacan, J. (1979). The neurotic's individual myth. *The Psychoanalytic Quarterly*, *48*(3), pp. 405–425.

Lacan, J. (1997). *The four fundamental concepts of psychoanalysis the seminar of Jacques Lacan book XI*. London: W.W. Norton & Company.

Lacan, J. (2016). *The sinthome: The seminar of Jacques Lacan Book XXIII*. London & Harvard, MA: Polity Press.

Le Fanu, J.S. (1871/2003). *Carmilla*. Google Books. Retrieved from www.gutenberg.org/files/10007/10007-h/10007-h.htm

Lindqvist, J.A. (2007). *Let the right one in*. Trans. *Ebba Segerberg. London: Quercus. (Original work published 2004)*.

Stoker, B. (1897). *Dracula*. U.S.: Doubleday and Co.

Verhaeghe, P. (2009). *New studies of old villains. A radical reconsideration of the Oedipus complex*. New York: Other Press.

Verhaeghe, P. (2016). *The tactics of the master: Paranoia versus hysteria*. Retrieved from Jcfar.org.uk/wp-content/uploads/2016/03/The-Tactics-of-the-Master-Paul-Verhaeghe.pdf.

Weinstock, J. (2012). *The vampire film: Undead cinema*. London and New York: Columbia University Press.

Žižek, S. (1999). *The ticklish subject: The absent centre of political ontology*. London and New York: Verso.

Žižek, S. (2005). *Metastases of enjoyment: Six essays on women and causality*. New York and London: Verso.

Film reference

1915 *Was, A Fool There*. Dir. Frank L. Powell.

Chapter 5

Guilty secrets (Walter White, Walter Mitty, and the Manosphere)

Psychoanalytically speaking, our guilty secrets can be understood as indexing our forbidden (unconscious) desires and the phantasy of their satisfaction. Freud went as far as arguing that there are parallels between the criminal and the neurotic, since both keep a guilty secret hidden, but whereas the criminal keeps it hidden from the Other (variously manifested), the neurotic keeps that secret hidden even from her or himself (Freud, 1906c, p. 108). The neurotic *hides* his/her secrets in such a way that s/he suffers from symptoms which are constituted on the basis of her/his repression. They are therefore plagued by these symptoms in the same way that a criminal may be disturbed by a guilty conscience. This type of – neurotic – guilt is correlated with an Other which installs the incest prohibition in the subject: a law which later in his teachings Freud would nominate as being enforced by the superego. In this logic, it is the superego set up at the time of the dissolution of the Oedipus complex which forbids a particular enjoyment. In this way, the neurotic's guilt is what we can call Oedipal guilt, since what is hidden from the neurotic subject is the unconscious desire to get rid of the father – fantasmatically figured – as the obstacle barring his access to keeping the mother all to him/herself. But more broadly, the guilt which follows our more banal transgressions (cheating on our expenses, keeping the extra change at the checkout, and so on) may also be described as Oedipal since it belies a displacement of a more radical desire – the unconscious desire – to live without, or perhaps better described, *outside*, the Law, whereas typically that Law is the one we do not dare except in humour (or, perhaps porn fantasies) to question.

Years of stand-up comedy routines testify to thinly veiled murderous impulses around male authority figures (belying the Oedipal parricide desire) as well as the wink-nod currency attached to the idea that men end up with women who in some ways resemble their mothers (belying the Oedipal incest desire). Notwithstanding the fact that most of these jokes are orientated around men (and heterosexual men at that), according to Pornhub, millennials (compared with any other age group) disproportionately look for porn featuring family members with the most popular search terms including mom, "milf" (*aka* mother/mom/mama I'd like to fuck), and stepsister. Once a secret neurotic fantasy, taboo incestuous sex now termed *fauxcest* is big business for the porn industry. But, in certain essential ways, what we are calling Oedipal guilt is the symptom that is glued to, and, that is a necessary tendency of, civilised subjects. The lament "Ohhhh, I feel so guilty" following any declaration of excessive consumption, or transgressive enjoyment, betokens a common experience which in some ways (and perhaps in the absence of "other" ways) binds people to groups and communities (even if according to Freud, those "communities" might be considered to be pathological, cf. Freud, 1930a). The guilty pleasures we experience go some way towards mitigating all those forbidden pleasures we have craved unconsciously. At the same time, the guilt which roams free of its original sin – so to speak – is, rather like a smart phone insofar as it can be plugged into many ports and made to function in many ways. Indeed the fully mobile telephone device in its manifold modalities (hybrid mini-computer, Wifi hotspot, all around monitor of its user's habits even providing GPS coordinates of its user's whereabouts) can provide both the means to engage in all sorts of forbidden pleasures as well as the means whereby one's guilty footprints can be tracked. Guilt, originally the index of what is hidden from the neurotic's consciousness, testimony to the fact that the subject has been Oedipalised, and therefore, civilised as a subject of society, bound by its laws (against incest with the mother, and murder of the father), can (rather like the mobile telephone device then) "fit" many purposes as it can register as resonant with all sorts of acts. The subject's original ambivalence – hateloving the father, lovehating the mother, and vice versa – and repression of one or other of these poles of tension, finds expression in all sorts of ideas ... and symptoms.

A young woman analysand recounted waking recurrently during her eighth year with the thought "I am bad". And the guilt accompanying feeling so "bad" hounded her throughout this time and well into adolescence. The crime for which she felt morally reprehensible took some time to discover, embedded as it was in the convoluted dynamics of growing up with an emotionally detached father and alcoholic mother whose accidental pregnancy when the girl was seven-years old led to the frequent "worry" that something bad would befall her parents and this latecomer sibling. Through the analytic work, gradually this "worry" was realised – subjectivised – as a "wish" that in fact something "bad" *would* happen to them, and the feeling that she was a "bad girl" and the guilt that ensued found its due psychical location. The woman's long dedication to being the perfect daughter and perfect sister and her accompanying sense of self-loathing and inferiority could eventually shift gears and find a new direction.

A man who had a panic attack at work worried despite evidence to the contrary that he would be unable to complete a project assigned to him. His fear belied a wish that he would not be able to complete it, in protest to his boss who had unfairly assigned him an overload in order to give his favoured female employee a lighter workload. If the man was unable to complete it, he would be punished by a negative employee evaluation. His anxiety, manifestly tied to worries about inadequacy, was guilt transformed and disconnected from his repressed desire to let his temper loose on his boss. The situation was metonymically related to his ambivalence and aggressive desires toward his father by way of a shared trait between the boss and the father. His guilt, as an index of his forbidden desire, became transformed and displaced.

Another young man wished that his father would just "fuck off" and leave him alone after his sense of being persecuted and criticised by him in the years leading into adolescence. The father died soon after. The boy unconsciously took the psychical rap for that death as he had *wished* for it to happen. Coming into the work of analysis, this man was plagued with guilt for all sorts of things. What he found most difficult to understand was why he would leave things lying around so that his partner was bound to trip over them; then he would feel compelled to move them to a safer place so that his partner would no longer trip over them but then would set to worrying that this "safer place" could turn out to be a risky place after all and would feel compelled all over again to move things back to their original place. This free-floating guilt, displaced from its original location tormented him daily in the form of new worries, which were debilitating and time-consuming. Only when he was able to suture his guilt to his wish that his father would go away and "leave him alone" and recognise the function of that in the context of his "love-hate" relationship with him, was he at last able to consider how "worrying" that something would happen to a loved one was also an expression of his ambivalence toward that person – a realization that allowed him to work through his ambivalence with his partner.

The original "worrier" in the Freud case-book is Ernst Lanzer, *aka* the "Rat[s] Man" (Freud, 1909d). If ever there was a man who suffered from ambivalence it was Ernst. Coming to Freud as a "youngish man of university education" Ernst Lanzer introduced himself with the statement that he had suffered from obsessions ever since his childhood, but with particular intensity for the last four years. The chief features of his disorder were fears that something might happen to two people of whom he was very fond – his father and a lady whom he admired. Besides this he was aware of compulsive impulses – such as an impulse to cut his throat with a razor and he also produced prohibitions – sometimes in connection with unimportant things. From an early age, he had a strong wish to see girls naked but in wishing this he had an uncanny feeling that something would happen if he thought such things and the idea that he must do all sorts of things to prevent it. What might happen? His father might die. Thoughts about his father's death occupied his mind from an early age and for a long period of time and greatly depressed him. At this point, Freud discovered to his astonishment that this fear was still present even though Ernst's father was already dead. According to Freud, the obsessive wish to see naked girls, and the obsessive fear that something bad would happen if his thinking went in that direction, constituted the inventory of an obsessional neurosis. The thing that brought Lanzer to Freud was his obsession … with rats. During a halt, Lanzer – a young officer in the Austrian army finds himself sitting next to a figure whom he names as the "cruel captain". This captain tells of a "specially horrible punishment used in the East" (ibid., 1909d, p.166). The torture consisted of rats being trapped under the seated rear of a man and forcing their panicked escape up through his anus. At the moment that Lanzer heard about this torture the idea flashed through his mind that this was happening to his lady friend and to his father. This idea seemed nonsensical to him as his father had died some years previously. Lanzer then told Freud the details of his father's illness and death. The father had been suffering from emphysema and one evening Lanzer asked the doctor when he thought his father's condition might be considered as out of danger. The evening of the day after tomorrow had been the reply. It had never entered his head that his father might not survive. That night he had lain down for an hour's rest and when he woke up he was told that his father had died. He then reproached himself for not being present at his death.

For a long time, it was as if Lanzer had not "realised" the fact of his father's death. When he would hear a good joke he would say to himself "I must tell father that". 18 months later the recollection of his neglect had recurred to him and tormented him as guilt. Freud explained to Lanzer (and to successive generations of readers of the case) that when there is a misalliance (a false connection) between an affect and its ideational content it is because the affect "belongs" elsewhere. The sense of guilt is not in itself open to criticism but belongs to some other content which is unknown (unconscious). Lanzer wondered, how could the information that the self-reproach, *the sense of guilt*, was justified have a therapeutic effect? Freud explained that it was not the information that had this effect, but the discovery of the unknown content to which the self-reproach was really attached. Lanzer then remembered another childhood memory. When he was 12-years old he had been in love with a girl, the sister of a friend of his. She had not shown him much affection and he immediately had the idea that she would be kind to him if he suffered from some sort of misfortune, an instance of which might be his father's death. This idea also occurred to him six months before his father's death in relation to another woman. Financial obstacles made it impossible to think of an alliance with her and the idea came to him that his father's death might make him rich enough to marry her. In defence against this idea, he had come up with the wish that his father might leave him nothing at all so that he would have no compensation for his loss. The day before his father died he had the idea that "now I may be going to lose what I love most" (Freud, 1909d, p.179) and then came the contradiction "no there is someone else whose loss would be even more painful" (Freud, 1909d, p.179). Freud interprets: every fear corresponds to a former wish which was now repressed, and furthermore the unconscious must be the precise contrary of the conscious. So Lanzer's incredulity that he might wish his father to die given how much he loved him so was actually the precondition of the repressed hatred for him, betokening his ambivalence. On the one hand, some connection keeps his hatred for his father alive, on the other hand, his intense love prevented it from becoming conscious. Nothing remained therefore but for it to exist unconsciously since the idea of getting rid of his father as an interference, originally emerged when he had not loved his father more than the person he had desired sensually. This classical style of ambivalence in an obsessional neurosis is, psychoanalytically speaking, "text-book"; according to Jacques Lacan's later expression, the neurosis highlights the "architecture of contrasts" between contradictory, ambivalent desires at the heart of the structure of obsessional neurosis (Lacan, 1958, p. 630).

If the neurotic in general, and the obsessional neurotic in particular, is guilty of persistent unconscious (and contradictory) forbidden desires, and of finding symbolic coordinates in order to render such guilt meaningful – a way that is, from its original cause, how are we to make sense of the so-called "pale crim-inal", the one whose forbidden desire and sense of guilt that attends it leads to the very carrying out of a criminal act?

Pale criminals

In the third of three essays under the heading "Some character-types met with in psychoanalytical work" from 1916, entitled "Criminals from a sense of Guilt" Freud observed that a certain type of criminal carries out forbidden actions pre-cisely because they are forbidden and in doing so obtains a certain "mental relief". The guilt *precedes* rather than *succeeds* the act. As Freud put it:

> I must maintain that the sense of guilt was present before the misdeed, that it did not arise from it, but conversely – the misdeed arose from the sense of guilt. These people might justly be described as criminals from a sense of guilt.
>
> (1916d, p. 332)

Remarking that a friend called his attention to the fact that Nietzsche had also written about the "criminal from a sense of guilt" in Zarathustra's sayings "On the Pale Criminal", Freud speculated that future research would decide how many criminals are to be reckoned among these "pale" ones.

From his clinical experience, Freud believed that this obscure sense of guilt derived from the Oedipus complex and was a reaction to what he called the two great criminal intentions of *killing the father* and *having sexual relations with the mother*. Compared with these two archaic horrific intentions, other crimes were committed in order to locate the sense of guilt in relation to some-thing else, and indeed something concrete, which in turn provided relief to the sufferers. Freud considered that this was akin to the way a child misbehaves in order to be punished for a previous deed which causes a guilty suffering. Restating his strong argument for the universality of the two great human crimes – parricide, and incest with the mother – Freud claimed that human conscience itself is acquired in connection with the Oedipus complex.

A man is caught with his hand down the front of his pants in a busy shopping area in a big town. When the police officer asks him what he is up to, the man stares down at himself in disbelief. He is detained for questioning, but not charged, on condition that he speaks to a "psychologist". When he speaks, he explains that he had no idea that he was touching himself and only remembered "zoning out". He spoke of feeling surprised that he felt relieved when being questioned by the police, and equally relieved when invited by the analyst to speak. And then he began to speak about his guilt. He had been having an affair with the wife of his best friend for several years, and all four of them socialised together, went on vacation together, and had raised their kids alongside each other, and the guilt and the corresponding fear that he would be caught was becoming intolerable. Guilty of transgressing the written and unwritten laws of his relationships – his marriage, his friendship, even his relationship with his children – which are all simulacra for the arrangements of our social relationships under Oedipal law, he found a way to be caught in another sexually transgressive act. To be "caught in the act" was the tormenting signifier which acted as lynchpin between the archaic desire to possess the mother (behind the father's back), and the fear of being destroyed by the father should he find out. This version of Oedipal guilt and the accompanying jouissance mobilised in the rehearsal over years of the unconscious fantasy, is the very precondition – just like Freud's criminal from a sense of guilt – for his acting-out.

The TV show *Breaking Bad* (2008–2013) opens onto a shot of khaki trousers flying in the air and falling to the desert ground of New Mexico as they are trampled by an RV. The RV is being driven madly by the protagonist Walter White – in his "tighty-whities" underwear – ostensibly the owner of the abandoned trousers. We see that White and the man in the passenger seat are wearing gas masks, and that the passenger as well as two men we see sliding on the floor in the back of the RV, appear to be passed out or dead. White crashes the RV into some brush off the side of the desert road, and he gets out upon hearing sirens in the distance. Assuming the police are coming for him, he takes the gun from the hand of one of the men on the floor, grabs his wallet and video camera, puts on a shirt, and begins recording a video. He states his name, his address, and declares: "to all law enforcement entities, this is not an admission of guilt. I am speaking to my family now." He pauses, placing the palm of his hand over the camera lens to hide his tears. Removing his hand, he continues speaking:

> Skyler [his wife], you are the love of my life. I hope you know that. Walter Jr. [his son], you're my big man. There are ... there are going to be some things, things that you'll come to learn about me in the next few days. I just want you to know that no matter how it may look I only had you in my heart. Goodbye.

White is referring to the fact that, having been recently diagnosed with terminal lung cancer, he started "breaking bad" – a slang term in the southern U.S. states which indicates turning off the path of standard moral conventions – and began cooking crystal meth with a former high school chemistry student of his in order to provide financially for his son, pregnant wife, and his soon-to-be born daughter.

Although White tells his hypothetical law enforcement audience that his video is *not* an admission of guilt, we read the situation and surmise his sense of guilt; we take our cues both from his negation and from his characteristically neurotic assumption that the sirens indicate that the police were coming to arrest him. This Althusserian moment of interpellation is where the "*hey you there!*" of a police officer on the street calls on the neurotic's sense of guilt such that he believes the shout concerns him in particular. In a twist which is a trademark of the series – each episode begins with its own ending prompting the audience to ask, "How did he get here?" – the scene follows White to a morning three weeks earlier when he is sitting down to a home-cooked breakfast with his family in a lackluster celebration of his 50th birthday. Above all, this is a question about White's guilt. Early in the show, as he begins to steal, sell drugs, and even murder, White displays full-on neurotic Oedipal guilt for transgressing the symbolic law, the guilt which we have been arguing is the marker of the normative relation to the law and the social bond. White's Oedipal guilt in the pilot episode belies his ambivalence; his conscious desire on the one hand to be a loving father and husband, providing for them financially when he is gone, and on the other hand his repressed desires for power and vengeance (against his billionaire and Nobel-Prize-winning former business partners who refused to give him a piece of the pie) and the recognition, money, and jouissance that go with it. As White transforms and becomes more and more identified with "Heisenberg" (associated with Heisenberg's uncertainty principle), the pseudonym he provides for himself to drug lord Tuco Salamanca in Season 1, the audience wonders what has happened to his guilt, and, by extension, to him. "Heisenberg" as a signifier belies White's ideal ego: an unpredictable force provoking the Other to be fascinated by futile attempts to catch and pin him down.

Oedipal law and ambivalence

Freud constructed three versions of what might be called a father complex. These father complexes all serve to prohibit jouissance and regulate desire and have to do with the installations of the superego and the ego ideal. In the first version, the Oedipus complex, the law is present from the outset, and then it is transgressed alongside a production of jouissance and guilt. The Oedipal father functions to prohibit jouissance by laying down the law and threatening castration if the subject does not comply. The law of the Oedipal complex is inescapable, as it demands punishment even when the infraction has been committed unknowingly or unconsciously, existing for the individual as an unconscious sense of guilt. To have an unconscious desire metonymically related to killing the father (e.g., usurping the father's place in the symbolic world or in the mother's eyes) or having sex with the mother (e.g., to desire a woman who shares a key trait with one's mother, such as being married for example) is sufficient cause to feel guilty. And when a desire is repressed, the affect associated with it is displaced and/or transformed.

At the centre of the father complexes are processes of identification. In Freud's chapter on identification in *Group Psychology and the Analysis of the Ego* (1921c) the first of the three forms of identification he speaks of is primordial identification, which is the earliest libidinal tie with an object. This libidinal tie retroactively emerges in the Oedipus complex as a fundamentally ambivalent one in the sense of *hainamoration*.

A man began treatment for depression after he had begun to have suicidal thoughts. His suicidality emerged after his girlfriend of one year broke up with him without explanation by moving away and ceasing to speak with him. He complained of feeling a perpetual guilt – a guilt he explained by pointing to his failures to achieve more symbolic success. He also suffered from a series of nightmares in which *a man had been killed and he was trying to bury and hide the body so the police would not hold him responsible for the murder*. In a Lynchian moment, a severed hand was found in one version of the dream. Key in alleviating his depression was uncovering his ambivalent relationship to and identification with his father, who had divorced the patient's mother at age five, and after a few false promises of visiting with the patient, abandoned the patient entirely although he had only moved to an adjacent town. In the patient's adult life, fearing he was like his father, he had a string of romantic relationships which he ended prematurely (and later regretted so doing) the moment he doubted his commitment to the woman. He had reasoned at the time that by ending things quickly he was avoiding being like his father, who was at fault for marrying, having children, and then deciding he did not want anything to do with them. Of course, in another sense his habit of leaving women for insufficient reasons made him similar to this father. It was not until the girlfriend in question left the patient and moved away, in an act that metonymically linked her to his father, that he once again was in the position of being abandoned by a loved one. Interpreting his recurrent dreams uncovered that the dead body was that of his father, for whom he had murderous wishes. Consciously, he had thought he had forgiven his father and was indifferent towards him. The guilt that manifested in his depression and suicidality, however, belied unconscious aggressive desires which he turned around on himself – all the more so for his identification with his father. In his essay on the discontents of civilization, Freud argued that when an instinctual trend undergoes repression, its "libidinal elements are turned into symptoms, and its aggressive components into a sense of guilt" (1930a, p. 139). In other words, when aggressive thoughts are repressed, they are handed over to the superego and turned against the individual to create guilt.

The severed hand brought to the patient's mind several associations, including "to give someone a hand," which he had in fact done as a little boy in his father's garage workshop – his job having been restricted to handing his father tools. Recalling this memory brought him to tears, and he remarked that he was surprised to have remembered a time in which he both loved and was loved by his father. He had repressed his loving thoughts for his father because they were associated with the pain of being abandoned and feeling as though he was not loved by or special to a father who could leave him. The violence of the severed hand called to mind the phrase "I would give my right hand to ...". He finished this phrase with "be lovable enough that my father would not have left us," and subsequently also noted his desire to cut off his right hand in protest, as if to say he was never again going to help his father. In his case, the conscious current of the patient's ambivalence were thoughts that his father did not matter to him since he had been absent for the majority of his life. This apathy was a tell-tale sign of repressed hatred, but also in his case repressed love, as his love for his father was not only a betrayal of his mother but also brought about the painful self-judgment that he, as abandoned by someone who mattered to him, was unlovable.

Michael Haneke's 2005 film *Caché* is a most interesting *mise-en-scène* of Oedipal guilt and ambivalence operating on personal and political levels. The film follows Georges (played by Daniel Auteuil) and his wife Anne (played by Juliette Binoche), an upper-class couple, as they receive a series of mysterious video tapes, each wrapped in a child-like drawing involving blood. The first few tapes include hours of footage of their home and the passersby on the street. They are deeply disturbed by the simple fact that someone is watching them. The status of this gaze will become more precise as the film progresses. The next few tapes depict the vantage point of a car travelling on the road leading to Georges' childhood home. Various clues, including a drawing of chicken with a bleeding neck on the paper that enveloped one video tape, lead Georges to suspect Malik, a boy who had briefly been adopted by Georges' parents when he was young. Georges visits Malik who denies responsibility for the tapes. We learn that when Georges was a child he was jealous of the affections his parents were showering on Malik since Malik's parents, both servants of Georges' parents, had been killed by the police in the 1961 Seine River massacre during the Algerian War. (Malik's parents were Algerian and had been demonstrating on behalf of the pro-National Liberation Front.) Young Georges had ordered Malik to behead a chicken, handing him an axe, and then he told his parents that Malik had killed the chicken in order to scare him. This succeeded in convincing his parents that Malik was violent and could not continue to live with them. Malik was sent to an orphanage while Georges continued to live a life of privilege. Malik, at 40, rebukes Georges for his crime against him, which led to Malik's life of poverty and suffering, for which Georges refuses to accept responsibility. Georges returns to visit Malik a second time at Malik's request, and, in an act metonymically related to that of cutting off the throat of the chicken, Malik then cuts his own throat, committing suicide in front of Georges, with the implication that Georges was guilty of both crimes.

The film had opened with a sustained steady camera shot of the street view of what we later learned was the Paris flat of Georges and his wife Anne. After the viewer sees the videotapes, the opening scene retroactively takes on the function of the gaze directed at Georges and Anne, inviting the viewer to wonder how her or his gaze might be similar to that of the unknown videotaper. This gaze transitions from innocuous or naïve, perhaps even bored (viewers of the film have complained about these moments that "nothing" seems to be happening), to one that is experienced by Georges and Anne as predatory, and finally to one which regards George as guilty. Not only is Georges implicated but so too is France, which denied its involvement in the Seine River massacre for 37 years. In *Caché*, the function of the gaze is deployed to bring out the guilt in the Other (France) and the guilt in the subject (Georges). *Caché* may be translated as "mask," in its noun form, or, better, as "hidden," in its adjectival form, but we also speak of its function in computing, in which a cache is something that stores data. In other words, the film *Caché* speaks to the hidden guilt that is remembered and has symptomatic disruptive effects on Georges' otherwise happy life. In *Caché*, the foreclosed ambivalence about the Algerian neighbour returns as if from the outside when a stranger intrudes videotaped message and code phenomena on George's life.

Oedipal guilt can also "hide" in one of the symptoms of contemporary depression: anhedonia. In today's pleasure-seeking society, anhedonia, or the state of being without pleasure, can itself seem like a betrayal worthy of guilt. One patient became depressed shortly after his father was diagnosed with a terminal illness. He was curious about his anhedonia, which he experienced as blunting all of the emotions he would typically expect to feel. He remarked that he was noticeably lacking in concern or sadness related to his father just as he no longer took pleasure in playing golf with friends. The only intense feeling he had was when he would blame himself for being a failure – as a father, husband, friend, son, employee – and no amount of reassurance from his family to the contrary would convince him that he was being too hard on himself. Whereas popular therapeutic treatments such as cognitive-behavioral therapy or psychotropic drug therapy would see his guilt as "irrational" and his anhedonia as a meaningless but common symptom of depression, trying to cure him through medication or by getting him to argue against his irrational beliefs and cognitive distortions and force himself to engage in activities he used to find pleasurable, a psychoanalytic investigation reveals that he has very good reasons for his guilt.

The patient had a dream in which *his father was beheaded in a roller coaster accident, after which the dreamer was very sad and was being consoled by loved ones at the viewing*. The dream revealed a wish that the patient would on the one hand feel intense grief at losing his father and on the other hand would be able to display his grief for others and be seen as the properly grieving son. This wish functioned to hide still another wish – his desire to "behead" and kill his father. The patient remarked that beheading was an archaic punishment for treason, and then realised he found his father to be guilty of treason toward his own law; when the patient was young, the father had strongly emphasised to his son the importance of chivalrous behaviour towards women and had even commented that hitting a woman was "unforgivable," but when the patient was a teenager his father had lost his head, so to speak, and punched his mother in the face upon discovering she had slept with another man. The roller coaster was both one of his father's favourite leisure activities and a description of the father's temperament, and for these the patient disliked the father. At the same time, the patient felt he had inherited his father's temperament, and he took great pains to subdue it. The patient's anhedonia and self-loathing, then, functioned to punish him and disguise the repressed side of his ambivalence – his desire to kill his father, perhaps replacing the lacking Oedipal dad with himself as tyrant. In this sense we can read versions of contemporary depression – with its corresponding self-loathing – not as melancholia, but as directly related to Oedipal guilt, being a compromise formation related to the superego punishing the subject for his repressed desires. This patient, as a contemporary obsessional neurotic, shows that the hallmark of obsession is still Oedipal ambivalence.

Walter mitty – guilty thoughts (and other fake news)

"The Secret Life of Walter Mitty" begins life as a charming short story written by James Thurber, published in *The New Yorker* in 1939 and adapted for film in two versions, the first in 1947 featuring the inimitable Danny Kaye as Mitty, the second in 2013, directed by, and starring Ben Stiller in the title role. What is Mitty guilty of?

> Something struck his shoulder. "I've been looking all over this hotel for you," said Mrs. Mitty. "Why do you have to hide in this old chair? How did you expect me to find you?". "Things close in," said Walter Mitty vaguely. "What?" Mrs. Mitty said. "Did you get the what's-its-name? The puppy biscuit? What's in that box?". "Overshoes," said Mitty. "Couldn't you have put them on in the store?" "I was thinking," said Walter Mitty. "Does it ever occur to you that I am sometimes thinking?".
>
> (Thurber, 1939)

While Mitty is busy *thinking* – he is in fact slipping from one phantasy to another, at first glance triggered by the sometimes rather banal elements in his waking life. He is apparently enjoying himself. What makes Mitty charming is his innocence and his harmless day-dreaming; his escapism touches us because we recognise ourselves in those moments where we manage to escape for a minute from the tedium of the everyday. A closer reading however reveals the deft intelligence in the writing of Thurber's eponymous hero. What Mitty suffers from is not the guilt of a secret or forbidden enjoyment, but rather, its effects; in fact, he seems to suffer much more from the irritated response of his wife to his ability to escape from the here and now. But he is guilty nonetheless of escapism; of retreating rapidly into his rich inner life where he takes on one after another version of his ideal ego. And it is at very precise moments – namely, following the points in which he encounters the critical gaze of the Other – where he dons a better version of himself, an unconscious upgrade, so to speak. In a series of reversals, Mitty moves from hen-pecked husband driving too fast to the Commander of a huge Navy hydroplane saving the day (and the lives) of his crew in the "worst storm in 20 years"; from the scolding judgement by Mrs. Mitty that he is "no longer young" and needs to wear overshoes and gloves he becomes a master surgeon who has to operate on "a millionaire banker and close friend of Roosevelt's" suffering with a bad case of obstreosis, and whilst in the operating theatre also fixes the anaesthetiser machine which "no one else in the East" happens to be able to fix; and from being undermined by a young parking attendant he becomes "Captain Mitty" facing the German bombers as the "greatest pistol shot in the world" (ibid.). Mitty's "secret life" is what keeps him going; his unconscious phantasies belying his attachment to the ideals of being a man in all of his scenarios who is the exception to the rule, the one who saves the day, fixes everything and who even enjoys (brandy) like no other man. He has managed to find a solution to his experience of his wife's ambivalence about him (and by extension, his own ambivalence about himself) by retreating to fantasy. Whereas Walter White turns to a life of crime and transitions to a version of himself which is radically and nominally different (i.e., "Heisenberg", "the One who knocks", "the danger"), Walter Mitty turns inward and lives life as a series of fantasies where he is "the Commander", "the master", "the greatest pistol shot", and so on. They are both guilty in the terms of Oedipal law and suffer in different ways. White suffers from the guilt and fear of his transgressions, Mitty suffers from the consequences of his fantasmatic thoughts, following which he is castigated further for his "thinking". In a perfect moment of (almost certainly unwitting) parody, in a scene in *Breaking Bad* from its fourth season, Skyler White adopts the same tone as Mrs. Mitty warning Walter about the dangers that lie outside the door, pointing out that he is not safe. Next, in the magnificent reversal, which must surely have roused every hen-pecked emasculated viewer into applause, White rounds on Skyler in the classic response: "You don't know who you are talking to …", "I am the one who knocks …", "I am the danger". What Mitty also suffers from is his own fake news, highlighted by Thurber in the final moments of the story where Mitty stands by a wall smoking and finds himself facing a firing squad. Perhaps picking up on this moment, Ben Stiller's movie adaptation references the whole business of escapism, fantasy, and illusion as the various (but dubious) means to disavow what is real, actual, and true. Stiller as Mitty arrives in Greenland, and when he picks up his rental car he is asked if he wants the blue or the red car. This choice is a direct reference to Neo's choice given to him by Morpheus in *The Matrix*:

> This is your last chance. After this there is no turning back. You take the blue pill: the story ends, you wake up in your bed and believe whatever you want to believe. You take the red pill: you stay in Wonderland and I show you how deep the rabbit hole goes.

Since *The Matrix*, Neo's choice "Red versus Blue Pill" has taken on its own currency in cyberculture signifying the desire to see things for how they "really" are and an awakening from a life of disavowal and ignorance. Red "pillers" prefer the truth, no matter how gritty and painful it may be. In our analysis of Walter Mitty, he clearly prefers to take the blue pill, whereas Walter White goes for the red pill. Signifying the (at-least-two) poles of the legacy of our Oedipal ambivalence, the "red-pill" option has been taken up in a curious, and interesting way on the online community "RedPill" hosted on Reddit. Some 141,966 white, early 1930's, conservative, men (and counting) have adopted the Red Pill premise and its "rabbit-hole" theory, which is that women run the world without taking responsibility for it and there is no forum for their male victims to complain (Marche, 2016). Hence, Redpill. Women have become brainwashed by feminism into thinking that they want equality and respect when what they *really really want* (sic) is a return to traditional gender roles and to be dominated by men (ibid.) A related site, marriedmansex life.com, is compiled by "Redpill women" who not only agree and support the Redpill men's "rabbit hole" theory but are all about how to make men's lives better by swapping tips about being the kind of woman that man needs in order to make his life better.

We are living in a time when people are speaking about "Man Deserts", a reference to the relative disappearance from certain communities, and discourses, of men, and of the "roles" traditionally associated with them. The apparent downgrading or even degrading of "man" and/or "masculinity", and by extension "the father" in such man deserts, recalls Lacan's premeditations on the effects upon psychopathology and psychic structure of the degradation of the Oedipus complex in his very early work from 1938 to his comments on criminology in 1950 where he wrote about changes in family structures and the effects those changes have upon symptoms (Lacan, 1938, 1950). As such, the question for many psychoanalysts is whether the Oedipus complex is even a thing anymore, and in the case that it isn't, then what has become of "the father", or even the "Name-of-the-Father" (cf. Weatherill, 2017 in particular). In Lacan's teachings he arrives at a point in his conceptualization about psychic structure and the effects upon the subject of the Oedipus complex where he advances the idea that the importance of the father lies not in the actual person of the father but instead in his – or her – ability to transmit the Name-of-the-Father, which is a function. Because of this, the Name-of-the-Father can even take the form of the signifier for an absent or dead father. This is why Lacan refers so often to the paternal *function* rather than the Oedipal myth. In other words, in order to have Oedipal guilt and its resultant symptoms, there is simply the requirement for someone or something to stand in for what had been considered the traditional role for the father – someone who can separate us from the mOther's demand, signify her desire, and prohibit certain infantile modes of jouissance. The good-enough embodiment of the Name-of-the-Father stands in for the law, transmitting social norms such as the importance of sharing for instance, and this facilitates the child's attainment of a neurotic structure. If a subject is neurotic, s/he has internalised the symbolic law and is subject to Oedipal guilt for her or his transgressions. As long as there are neurotic subjects there will be ambivalence and "Oedipal" guilt. For us, it follows thus that as long as there is ambivalence – and this would be our strong argument – there exists neurosis as psychical structure which betokens a limited unconscious enjoyment and suffering.

For us, guilt is a quintessential index of a transgressive, ambivalent, desire, and we are interested to see how it is represented in our cultural products and in our social spaces and places – places from which "man" has apparently gone missing. We believe that in a time when – no doubt about it – masculinity faces all sorts of identity crises, the psychical operation involving an encounter with one's essential unconscious transgressive desire, an operation which Freud named the Oedipus complex, has itself undergone a displacement of sorts. We could say, for example, that Oedipus (and his ambivalent, paradoxical desires) has gone online.

Oedipus in the Manosphere

Journalist Stephen Marche writing about The RedPill forum in 2016 (ibid.) interviewed the principal moderator of the forum who goes by the pseudonym Morpheus Manfred. Manfred claims that the Manosphere (a network of websites dedicated to men's rights movements and guides for how to pick up women) "fundamentally became a surrogate father for the life lessons" he never got. Manfred argues in this interview that although Redpill men are accused of misogyny, there is no other place for them to express these views. According to Manfred, "there's nowhere else for a man to blow off steam". But, he emphasises, the endgame of their advice is not to encourage men to hate women, rather it is to help them how to understand them so that they do not have to be so frustrated by them (op.cit.).

Marche reflecting on the Redpill men asks if the forum is just another toxic technoculture product and then considers the all-important question "how shitty are men really?" (ibid.) In other words, how does the online behavior and opinion of such men translate into their non-digital lives. We are, of course, a long way from Walter Mitty's secret life. Marche continues: "are we our real selves on the internet or are we not?" (ibid.) He decides that the forum is "mostly feral boys wandering the digital ruins of exploded masculinity, howling their misery, concocting vast nonsense about women and craving the tiniest crumb of self-confidence and fellow feeling." (ibid.) But as Irish film and media scholar Debbie Ging points out,

> the issue is not whether there is a direct or meaningful correlation between the manosphere's articulations of antifeminism and the actual people who produce them. Rather it is in understanding the manosphere as a discursive system or network of systems and in seeking to determine the extent of the ideological, psychological, and material power it exerts.
>
> (Ging, 2017, p. 11)

For Marche, what is evident is that the truth of man's experience is contradictory and that "if you have a working dick and a working soul, you'd better get used to living with contradictions" (ibid.). The "contradictions" for which Red Pill "boys" lack the capacity are indexed by two dominant themes (incorporated into, and explained in the forum's glossary). On the one hand, the idea that men fall in love with women in the same way that boys love their mothers (obsessing about her even though she does not reciprocate), and on the other, the idea that "the girl of your dreams doesn't fucking exist" (ibid.) Among other things, Marche advocates that the boys on Red Pill need to read Freud, whom he quotes as saying that "every man wants to murder his father and sleep with his mother and [that] the only way to be civilised is to recognise that everyone is barbaric way down deep inside" (ibid.).

Or, as far as we are concerned, ambivalent. Red Pill boys and men voice their hatred of female independence and at the same time their passion for their mothers and their search for the one who is just like "the gal who married dear old Dad" (Von Tilzer & Dillon, 1911). But they do so anonymously. For all intents and purposes they live their lives like Walter Mitty; just as Mitty lives with his hen-pecking wife/mother and escapes to his phantasy world where he is "the Man" and gets the girl of his dreams, Red Pill boys escape into the Manosphere to complain that women are not like their mothers, and they escape to Pornhub to have sex with their mothers.

But then there are the "Blackpill" boys. Seemingly going where no self-respecting Red Pill man has gone before, the Blackpill movement has emerged from what is called the "incel community" – an internet tribe of involuntary celibates (almost exclusively heterosexual men under 30) – seeing themselves as victims of female cruelty and thriving on the circulation of incitements to kill women and praising killing sprees perpetrated on young women by other incels (Beauchamp, 2019). In September 2014, self-identified incel Elliott Rodger stabbed two male roommates and a friend, then drove to the nearby

Santa Barbara UC campus opening fire and killing three other young people and wounding 14 others before turning the gun on himself. Rodger's posted videos on YouTube lay out his grievances against women: "All I had ever wanted was to love women, but their behaviour has only earned my hatred" (quoted in Beauchamp, ibid.). Since his attack, Rodgers has become – according to Zack Beauchamp – the primary incel "saint"; his face photo-shopped onto paintings of Christian images and widely circulated. In April 2018, ten young women were killed in Toronto when a van driver pulled off the road and slammed into a group of pedestrians; the van driver was also a self-described incel. A dedicated fan of Elliot Rodger, in a Facebook post written just before his attack, Alek Minassian described himself as a "footsoldier in the broader incel war on society" and hailed the "Supreme Gentleman Elliot Rodger" (ibid.). "Going ER" is regarded by these incel members as all out activism against the wrongs perpetrated on them and their (sexless, relationship-less lives) by women, but also, by other men. As such, they rail against what they regard as a sexual class system. Men described as "Chads" (if white), "Tyrones" (if black) – with the right jawline, physique and other biological characteristics – are able to have sex with any woman since they are at the top of the male hierarchy. Hate and revenge are the principal driving satisfactions for Blackpillers targeted at women (especially fat women and Indian and Asian women because they only want to have sex with "Chads"); at men who have access to, and enjoyment of, and with, women; at homosexual men and women; and at people of any race or ethnicity other than white (Jaki et al., 2019).

The growing number of online hate communities where men espouse rage and violence towards women because they cannot get out of their involuntary celibacy existence indicates – unlike in the case of the Redpiller men – an entrenched extremist position situated at the absolute far-right potential of their hatred. What binds this community together is the gluey bond of hatred; they are not, as Waltman and Haas (2011, p. 34) point out, united by a common goal but rather by a deficit, or what we might call a minus, of jouissance, in that they cannot engage in sexual interaction. This is *jealouissance* writ large – as the jealous purview of the Other's fantasised enjoyment – but it is also vengefully Oedipal. Here, all men who are regarded as having the phallus, or as occupying the position of the primal father of Freud's mythological horde, or any version of the Oedipal father (as transmitters of social and civil law; as paternal function) are targets for the circulation of hate speech and/or violent fatal acts. But in a twist worthy of Tarantino working alongside Freud, women are also *both* the target of hate, violence, and revenge, *as well as* the longed-for, but forbidden object, out of reach, and out of bounds. (Waltman & Haas, 2011, p. 34). Freud long ago observed how an object of desire could undergo debasement indicating that "man" suffered from what he called, "psychical impotence" (Freud, 1912d, p. 183). This impotence, was conditioned upon an insurmounted "incestuous fixation" on the mother; In his thesis, the full-on libidinal attachment to the mother endured after puberty and new object-choices bearing the hallmark of the mother put up an obstacle to finding sexual (and loving) satisfactory encounters with such an object (ibid. pp. 170–181). Freud's classic axiom "where they love they do not desire and where they desire they cannot love" (ibid. p. 183) meant that for such a man, in order for him to experience sexual desire and enjoyment, he must debase the woman. Psychically, said Freud. In other words, what was unavailable to them (due to Oedipal law) had to undergo a psychical debasement in women who resembled the figure of their childhood passion and who was forbidden to them. What we see now however with these Blackpill men is real, violent, actual and potential eradication of the "object", since what is unavailable to them must be destroyed. This is a ferocious version of Freud's axiom. Commenting on the potential and real sinister aspect of the Manosphere Stephen Marche asks the six-million dollar question whether we are "our real selves online or off". On the one hand, the screen operates as the place where we do stuff that we would never dare to do offline. On the other, perhaps the screen offers the possibility for some to perform what Marche describes as "the truth of our being that the world of faces and consequences does not permit" (ibid.).

He concludes:

> Among men today, there is violence hidden under the virtue, and virtue hidden under the violence. The only constant is the hiding.
>
> (ibid.)

What is hidden, is forbidden, same as it ever was. But, of course, not all men subscribe to the mentalities expressed either covertly or overtly by the Redpillers or the Blackpillers; we give you "#notallmen". Tracing the alleged disappearance of men, and Oedipus, in the so-called "man deserts" up to this point has led us to the Manosphere where men's complaints of Oedipal dissatisfaction range from ugly misogynism to terrifying and fatal acts of *jealouissance*; the full gamut of conscious and unconscious ambivalence in other words. The #Metoo movement originated with activist Tarana Burke's campaign against sexual assault in 2006 but gathered massive momentum in response to actress Alyssa Milano's tweet in October 2017 "Me Too" where she suggested "If all the women who have been sexually harassed or assaulted wrote 'Me too' as a status, we might give people a sense of the magnitude of the problem." The rest, as they say, is history (or perhaps, herstory). The phrase "not all men" started life as the phrase "not all men are like that" as a counter to feminist critiques of male behaviour, and became an internet meme after Shafiquh Hudson's tweet in February 2013:

> Me: men and boys are socially instructed to not listen to us. They are taught to interrupt us when we_ Random Man: Excuse me. Not ALL men.
>
> (Hudson, 2013)

However after the Isla Vista killings – as Elliott Rodger's shootings have come to be known, the hashtag #Notallmen (are like Elliott Rodger) together with its counterpart #YesALLWomen (are affected by sexism and misogyny) have trended on Twitter and in the intervening years up to the present moment have spurred a rake of newspaper, internet blog, and scholarly journal articles.

We began this chapter by reflecting on Freud's claims about the similarity in disposition of the criminal and the neurotic. They both hide a guilty secret. Understanding that what is kept secret for neurotic subjects (who either act in criminal ways or not) is the very defining moment of their psychical structure, that is, the act of repression of their Oedipal desire is what makes them neurotic. Oedipal desire is shot through with ambivalence, and the tensions of that ambivalence are revealed in various ways as we have indicated in case vignettes, movies, short stories and on the Manosphere. Ambivalence – foreclosed, repressed, and disavowed – in other words variously negated, is at times troublesome in terms of psychical suffering and psychopathology, at other times in terms of criminal acts, and at others in the kinds of hostile discourse and promulgation of ideologies on the so-called Manosphere where a culture of hatred thrives alongside the big business of the porn industry which in turn piggy backs on the real news of our Oedipal forbidden desires. Red pill or blue pill? the choice is always already predicated on an essential ambivalence. True selves or fake news? This is a false question in light of each option serving as disavowal of the tension at the core of human subjectivity. We are strangers to ourselves in our desires.

References

Beauchamp, Z. (2019). Our incel problem: How a support group for the dateless became one of the internet's most dangerous subcultures. www.vox.com/the-highlight/2019/4/16/18287446/incel-definition-reddit

Freud, S. (1906c). Psycho-analysis and the establishment of the facts in legal proceedings. In *The Standard Edition of the Complete Psychological Works of Sigmund Freud. S.E., IX*, pp. 103–114.

Freud, S. (1909d). Notes upon a case of obsessional neurosis. In *The Standard Edition of the Complete Psychological Works of Sigmund Freud. S.E., X*, pp. 151–318.

Freud, S. (1912d). On the universal tendency to debasement in the sphere of love (contributions to the psychology of love II). In *The Standard Edition of the Complete Psychological Works of Sigmund Freud. S.E., XI*, pp. 177–190.

Freud, S. (1916d). Some character-types met with in psycho-analytic work: (III) Criminals from a sense of guilt. In *The Standard Edition of the Complete Psychological Works of Sigmund Freud. S.E., XIV*, pp. 332–333.

Freud, S. (1921c). Group psychology and the analysis of the ego. In *The Standard Edition of the Complete Psychological Works of Sigmund Freud. S.E., XVIII*, pp. 65–144.

Freud, S. (1930a). Civilization and its discontents. In *The Standard Edition of the Complete Psychological Works of Sigmund Freud. S.E., XXI*, pp. 59–148.

Ging, D. (2017). Alphas, betas, and incels: Theorizing the masculinities of the manosphere. *Men and Masculinities, XX(X)*, pp. 1–20.

Hudson, S., (2013). Shafiquah Hudson [@sassycrass] (20 February 2013). "ME: Men and boys are socially instructed to not listen to us. They are taught to interrupt us when we- RANDOM MAN: Excuse me. Not ALL men"

Jaki, S., De Smelt, T., Gwozdz, M., Panchal, R., Rossa, A., & De Pauw, G. (2019). *Online hatred of women in the incels.me forum: Linguistic analysis and automatic detection.* University of Hildesheim. Unpublished.

Lacan, J. (1938). *Family complexes in the formation of the individual.* Trans. C. Gallagher. www.lacaninireland.com.

Lacan, J. (1950). A theoretical introduction to the functions of psychoanalysis in criminology. In Ed. J.-A. Miller, *Écrits: The first complete edition in English* (pp. 102–122. translated by B. Fink). New York: W.W. Norton & Co. 2006.

Lacan, J. (1958). The direction of the treatment and the principles of its power. In Ed. J.-A. Miller, *Écrits: The first complete edition in English* (pp. 489–542). Trans, B. Fink. New York: W.W. Norton & Co., 2006.

Marche, S. (2016). *Swallowing the red pill: A journey to the heart of modern misogyny.* www/theguardian.com/technology/2016/apr/14/the-red-pill-reddit-modern-misogyny-manosphere-men.

Thurber, J. (1939). The secret life of Walter Mitty. *New Yorker.* March 18, 1939 issue. www.newyorker.com/magazine/1939/03/18/the-secret-life-of-walter-james-thurber.

Von Tilzer, H. (Music) & Dillon, W. (Lyrics). (1911). I want a girl (Just like the girl that married dear old dad).

Waltman, M. & Haas, J. (2011). *The communication of hate.* New York: Peter Lang.

Weatherill, R. (2017). *The anti-oedipus complex. Lacan, critical theory and postmodernism.* London: Routledge.

Film reference

2005 *Caché.* Dir. Haneke, Michael.

Chapter 6

Guilt, shame, and jouissance (and by the way, why your superego is not really your amigo ...)

A woman dreams that *she went to the supermarket to buy the ingredients for a dinner which her Italian mother-in-law was to attend. She pauses in front of the butcher's counter and sees a wall of hams. She decides to buy some. But upon arriving home, she finds to her horror that she already has hams, rows upon rows of them, squeezed into her refrigerator.* Through her associations to the dream she speaks of how she is often criticised by her mother-in-law; one criticism is usually around how she never finishes what is on her plate, nor even finishes an entire cup of coffee. Oh, the waste! The mother-in-law shames her for wasting what is precious, recounting hard times during and after war scarcities. The woman then goes on to speak about how in her work she feels great pressure to perform well. She feels she must cover up both her anxiety that she will not do the work properly as well as her worry about being found out for being what she feels is a sham. "Hams ... sham ... shame", the analyst restates. The woman realises how the signifier "hams" condenses the affect she feels before her mother-in-law's gaze – so many hams, so much waste – what she identifies as her shame, and the judgement of the workplace that will discover her as a sham. The unconscious production of the affect in the dream, is only gently distorted – by means of the displaced "s" and the elided "e" – in order to carry out the twin functions of calling attention to the sham of her being which is to say, her lack in being, as well as her shame under the gaze of the Other, where again we could say, something essential is exposed or revealed.

In his seventeenth seminar of the year 1969–1970 Lacan proposed that psychoanalysis should try to make the analysand ashamed (2007, pp. 181–183). Perhaps we can see this function at work in our little clinical vignette about the hams, since the dream of hams/sham/shame is addressed to a psychoanalyst. We observe in this instance that the analysand does not speak of feeling guilty or being made to feel guilty. Rather, she is (made) ashamed by being seen for squandering or pretending; both acts touching on the perverse conditioning of jouissance which Lacan in his late teachings identified as a kind of law that states that while you may enjoy your means, you must not waste them (Lacan, 1999).

In *Seminar XVII*, Lacan argues that Oedipal guilt has undergone radical transformation in light of what he saw as the decline in paternal authority (Lacan, 2007). Reworking the Oedipus complex and *Civilization and Its Discontents* (Freud, 1930a) in the first part of the seminar – which traced the works of Freud that deal primarily with guilt – he chose to draw out and elaborate upon the operation of shame. Lacan argues that Freud's assessment of the concerns of the world in the 1930's at the time of publishing *Civilization and Its Discontents* had become outdated. The source of our discontents was no longer exclusively to be found in the renunciations we are required to make on account of living in the social world, including prohibiting aggression against our neighbour and regulating our sexual jouissance – both manifest forms of our essential ambivalence. As we have argued, the psychical responses to the prohibition of aggression and the regulation of our sexual jouissance are the very things that zombies and vampires currently work very hard in our culture to address on our behalf. Instead, Lacan claimed that the new discontents of society have to do with permissiveness, such that the prohibition on prohibiting, so to speak, can create the conditions for great suffering for the subject. We catch sight of some of the effects of this "permissive" tendency in twenty-first century mainstream psychology discourse shouting out the ills of permissive parenting styles (as opposed to authoritative parenting, considered to be the hallmark of healthy parenting) potentially leading to impulse control and conduct disorders in children.

Modifying his previously formulated master's discourse in order to create the "capitalist discourse" – Lacan went on to speculate that it is the latter discourse, which structures the late modern subject (Lacan, 1970–1971, 1972). Inverting the two terms and writing the barred S above the line and the S1 (master signifier) below the line results in a split subject, who no longer has the master signifier, *aka* the ego ideal, or one of its avatars – "Oedipal dad", as a referent (Lacan, 1970–1971) Instead, the master signifier operating in the place of truth in the capitalist discourse is indicative of the false promises of consumerism under capitalism – that if only you purchase this S1, this sought-after product, you will be complete, undivided, without lack. "There is no longer any shame" Lacan declares (2007, p. 182). The absence of shame indicates, and indeed perpetuates, an ideologically functioning fantasy; guiltless jouissance, commodifiable, and marketable. Why? because you're worth it, of course. Returning shame to the gaze or eliciting shame for our jouissance is an effort then to reinstate the agency of the master signifier.

However, the master discourses of the first couple of decades of the twenty-first century interpellate us directly at the level of our guilt, attempting to alleviate or treat it through the (immensely profitable) mechanism of "forgiveness". Paradoxically, this involves the assumption that the subject is always already guilty while at the same time endlessly forgivable (this very element leading no doubt to the notion that Catholics are difficult to psychoanalyse properly since they can be so easily forgiven for their sins!). For example, the subject may be guilty of indulging in unhealthy foods, laziness, poor spending habits, environmentally unfriendly consumer choices, cluttering up their living spaces, not recycling adequately, and so on, but the subject is either encouraged to rebrand these activities as morally deserved, or, is addressed by religious, economic, psychotherapeutic, or spiritualistic discourses of forgiveness, not to mention Japanese house-tidying techniques, and the ubiquitous industry of "self-care". Above all, under neoliberalism, greed is recast as a good at worst, and as a moral imperative at best. Within the discourse of capitalism, forgiveness is commodified into various forms – chicken soup for the soul, mindfulness and yoga retreats, loan forgiveness, et cetera. Forgiveness can be seen therefore as an S1 operating as the truth of the capitalist discourse, a truth which is the false promise of overcoming subjective division. Against this, Lacan's solution of making the subject ashamed was supposed to function to dissociate the subject from the master signifier – a move which reveals the jouissance the subject experiences in relation to the master signifier. Making ashamed, then, would be opposed to trends in capitalist discourse that attempt to fix the subject's identity in a certain mode of consumeristic jouissance ("because they're worth it" for example).

The postmodern subject who enjoys without shame is without doubt the product of capitalist discourse. The neoliberal injunctions to "be happy" and "just do you" correspond to a subject whose guilt is revealed not by an Oedipal figure but instead by the primal father, the obscene superegoic jouisseur who punishes those who fail to "be themselves." Ultimately, this subject is essentially ambivalent about the function of the father. In a way, we could say that the pursuit of jouissance at the expense of desire relegates the Oedipal father to the repressed term of the ambivalence. However, it may also be the case that the subject's manifest desire to "be her- or himself" belies a repressed desire for a superegoic master, as figure, or as discourse; one which incarnates an impossible moral economy: spend, consume, enjoy, be unashamed, start over …

The super-duper-ego

In J.K. Rowling's (1999) *Harry Potter and the Prisoner of Azkaban* the children are gathered around Professor Lupin as he proceeds to take them through a new spell – Riddikulus! The children are encouraged to think about a feared object/figure in their lives – in most cases one that would destroy them, either physically, mentally or both – and then to imagine this feared object or figure made ridiculous. The spell is performed on a shapeless hidden form – a "Boggart" – which when released from its place of containment takes on the form and shape of the child's feared object/figure (Rowling, 1999, pp. 102–106). Once it is released, the child has to wave his/her wand in the direction of the Boggart which by now has assumed – what we can usefully think of as – the superego incarnate, in the first child's case beautifully exemplified in the form of a cruel and sadistic professor, and whilst conjuring up an additional feature to attach to the original ferocious form, one that in being judged "riddikulus" by let us say the child's ego (in this case his granny's handbag and hat), the child chants "riddikulus" and the entire class erupts in laughter. All at once the superego relents its inhibiting grip on the child.

This version of the superego reminds us of Simon Critchley's idea that at times your superego can be your *amigo* (Critchley, 2002). But, it is not at all straightforward to see how (or even if) this comes about in Freud's conceptual development of the superego. For while it is the case that Freud comes up with a fairly benign version of the superego in his paper "Humour" of 1927, in every other mention of the superego in his writings up to 1927 and beyond, it is superego in its various prohibiting, censoring, critical self-observing, conscience-upholding, and maintaining of the ego-ideal functions that we encounter (Freud, 1927d). Furthermore, and contrary to the example from Harry Potter's schooldays, it is not guaranteed that finding the ego's concerns ridiculous and petty is not at the same time experienced as cruel and sadistic. After all, in Freud's account and as Simon Critchley has observed, humour has the same internal logic as depression. In other words, whereas narcissism in humour leads to finding one's concerns silly, or funny, in melancholia it leads to a laceration of the ego. We bear in mind that finding one's self and one's concerns "ridiculous" when coordinated with melancholia may well provide grounds for abject despair, if not suicide (Owens, 2016).

Many Lacanian psychoanalysts take the view that desire opposes superego in so far as superego orders jouissance and is generally speaking responsible for creating situations and acts which appear not very much in keeping with the subject's desire, all things considered. What is usually thought of as the paradox of the superego consists of the giant leap from the Freudian strictly censoring/prohibiting of (incestuous) pleasure to the late Lacan conceptualisation of superego as agency of jouissance in its imperative conjugation. Strictly speaking, however, there is no paradox if we take into account that the superego does not effectively prohibit jouissance: rather it is the superego that pushes the subject into situations of transgressive enjoyment, which cause suffering rather than pleasure, and as Lacanian scholar Adrian Johnston has pointed out, the jouissance obtained is never what was expected (Johnston, 2002). When the obscene superego is in charge it commands the subject to enjoy at the expense of desire, and since the superego is fundamentally an injunction to jouissance nothing is more effective at blocking jouissance than the obligation to enjoy.

From the point of view of Lacan's great seminar on the ethics of psychoanalysis (1959–1960), the only thing the subject could be regarded as guilty of was having given up on her or his desire (Lacan, 1992, p. 319). Against this, our permissive twenty-first century societies authorise and even command jouissance, such that betraying, or giving up on your jouissance – not your desire – is the new "sin" of our times. Generally speaking, we no longer need feel particularly *guilty* or *ashamed* about our jouissance. Indeed in our times, jouissance is promoted and redefined under the guise of "authenticity" – as "you doing you" or "being true to yourself"; we are encouraged to take our mode of jouissance seriously and earnestly these days. You should only act in a certain way if you are "doing you"; if you do not feel like going to visit your grandmother then you should not go; if you do not want to practice piano then you should sit on the couch and watch Netflix on your iPad; if your heart is not really in the world of work, and if study is too onerous, stay at home and become an Instagram star! This modality of expressing ourselves authentically via our drives even produces a new form of "depressed" patient who should interpret the cause of her malady as not having found the right activity in life to express herself. What is most symptomatic in and of our culture today, however, is not merely to be found in a paucity of jouissance or not finding "authentic" jouissance but also in our having denounced the very operation of desire. Let us return to the "hams" woman; she felt shame(d) by the gaze of the (m)Other(-in-law) for "wasting" her enjoyment (jouissance), that is, for not finishing off the contents from her plate or from her cup (she failed, we could say, to enjoy everything). But in fact, it was the patient's very desire that was at stake, as she preferred to leave something, or rather, have a portion of nothing. In other words, her unconscious desire was to preserve a space for the *objet a* ("the nothing"); as such, betraying this desire should be the condition for her guilt, which according to Lacan has an ethical status. But in our time, the spaces for experiencing the ambivalence of our desire, are increasingly threatened by the new rules of enjoyment. Lacan famously cautioned that the anorexic, whose desire is to eat "the nothing," was the model for how one's desire can kill if the jouissance at work in the desire is unrecognised (Lacan, 1958, p. 502). Perversely, one of the consequences of the foreclosure of ambivalent tensions, including those about our own desire, is that, today's overeater may be the new model for how one's jouissance can kill if desire is not installed. Orchestrated by the superego and the shaming gaze of the Other which incarnates the new rules of enjoyment ("you must enjoy", "you must not waste the means of your enjoyment"), desire, and its ambivalent characteristics including guilt (both Oedipal and ethical) risks remaining uninstalled and/or unrecognised.

A young analysand practicing bulimia to the brink of organ failure brings two dreams to her analysis. In the first dream she sees herself handing a book of poems to the analyst by the poet Patrick Kavanagh. In the dream she visualises the first verse of his poem – *Advent*.

We have tested and tasted too much, lover –
Through a chink too wide there comes in no wonder.
But here in this Advent-darkened room
Where the dry black bread and the sugarless tea
Of penance will charm back the luxury
Of a child's soul, we'll return to Doom
The knowledge we stole but could not use. (Kavanagh, 2005)

Associating around the dream she discovers a conundrum; she recalls seeing the book in the analyst's hands but noticing that the book bore the name of another poet – Yeats.

In the second dream she is walking along and finds that she is "allowed to enjoy" the walking. Suddenly she notices a single crow, who doesn't scare her. But all at once there are many and they are screaming to her: EAT, EAT, EAT. And then she concludes that she must have eaten because then she felt just as bad and as "fat as normal" and started to drain away into a hole in the ground.

This young analysand believes herself to be a wicked person, not allowed or entitled to "have" the things that she considers the dues of a good person. There's a tight logic which she has rehearsed for a good many years where she believes herself to be a "wicked monster" who takes and takes, a "selfish whore" who eating everything up, using something of value, something good for bad intention reduces her to an eating, vomiting, cutting, wasting, and moralising machine. As such, she is not allowed, doesn't deserve, to eat. If she eats, she has to vomit, since only good people are allowed to eat. And in between all this eating and vomiting, she is not allowed to "test or taste" in the words of Patrick Kavanagh from her dream, any of life's other pleasures: walking, reading, listening to music, watching a movie or doing anything which is not in some way about "getting better" which of course contains the moral imperative to transform herself into a "better" self.

In her associations to the first dream, she recalled studying the poem in her last year in secondary school, a time of great turmoil and distress as she had in her own moral reckoning failed to become a better person and this was when she began what would be a year-long anorexic fast. Advent is the four-week period in the Christian calendar leading up to Christmas and at the time of the poem's writing it was a period of fasting and penance. She connected the testing and tasting in the first line with her overeating and bulimic feasting, and the fasting of the dry black bread and sugarless tea to her anorexic three hundred calories a day solution. But she also noted that there is the reference to the stolen fruit, which for her conjures up so much of her monstrous and wicked whoring as she describes her bulimia. And then we come to this enigmatic reference to Yeats. She sees it as "Yeats" – another great Irish poet – whose name printed on this poetry book mystifies her in its inaccuracy. It is only when the analyst enunciates the "Y" separately from "EATS" that she hears her own question – Why eat?

The second dream emerges later in the analysis and functions as a response to her question – why eat? The one crow is not threatening, but the many compel her to eat and die. She recalls – to her surprise – that the collective noun for crows is "a murder" (of crows) and indeed the prevailing theme emerges in this dream as murder, albeit a self-murder that leads her to the hole in the ground which is of course both a grave and a toilet wherein she and all the contents of her body are drained away.

These dreams allow us to catch a glimpse of the superego functioning as it is variously coordinated with Law, pleasure, shame, and jouissance. The delimiting of a time to eat in the first dream; a time to fast and a time to feast is encapsulated in the Law of Advent (God's Law so to speak). It is a beautiful law for this girl since it allows for a pleasure that is entitled, not shamefully stolen. The poet's nostalgia attests to this domain of regulated pleasure and its importance for moral well-being broadly understood. We see this appetite for a regulated oral pleasure in the diet trend from a few years ago, which proposes weight loss, good health, and longevity by following a fast/feast regime. Essentially, the dieter eats "normally" for five days a week and "fasts" for two days. Subscribers to this diet proclaim that what is wonderful about this method is that one can "enjoy" eating unrestrictedly for those five days because of having to restrict eating for the two day fast. For us the reason this diet fails (and many others of course) is because it ignores the strictly Lacanian truth: in times when everything is permitted ... nothing is permitted. In times when one must enjoy, one radically fails to do so, even if it is for a "permitted" two days a week. Insofar, as a question emerges in this young woman's dream, it testifies to the fact that the beautiful Law – God's law of fast and feast – although beautiful doesn't explain everything. Another way to say this is that the ego ideal, though rational and in keeping with the pleasure principle fails as a moral guide. Why eat? Here we see most clearly the obscene underside of the ego ideal, in this case heard as the super-egoic command: eat-eat-eat! Unto death! Why eat? Because we say so! You don't feel that you are allowed to but you must! In her encounters with various members of the helping and/or psychiatric/medical professions, the response to her question of why she should eat is met with ... "*because you must*".

Slovenian philosopher Alenka Zupančič has astutely observed that for the subject who does not know whether what she wants to do is right or wrong, whether it is pathological or not, such a subject finds in the superego a sort of practical guide that at least gives her the clue that the best of all possible actions is always the one that makes her suffer the most (2000, p. 163).

In the psychoanalytic clinic we hear increasingly of a new type of guilt related to the failure to attain the happiness which we are supposed to achieve touted by prominent neoliberal and capitalist ideologies of our times. We are encouraged to earn and to spend, consume, acquire, and otherwise endlessly pursue an enjoyment which we labour after, and either never obtain, or (perhaps) worse ... catch hold of and never manage to regulate. These two interconnected new forms of guilt are conditioned on the subject having what is needed and wanted but feeling guilty for remaining unhappy, and/or, feeling guilty for the inability to regulate jouissance (which we are ironically indicating as the "new rules of enjoyment"). Contemporary suffering is described in overeating, overspending, "overthinking", and all of the other symptoms which betoken the inability to establish a limit to jouissance. It is interesting that in the latest revision of the DSM-V there are a plethora of diagnoses reflective of excess enjoyment in the sections on "Feeding and Eating Disorders" and

"Substance-Related and Addictive Disorders" in particular. Clearly tied to the capitalist and consumerist ethos of our day are the newly minted "Gambling Use Disorder" and "Binge Eating Disorder", which did not appear in the previous iteration of the DSM (2013).

However, these sufferings exist alongside of, and sometimes in symbiosis with anxiety, anhedonia, and other depressions. "Too much", yet, "not enough", doesn't fully capture this "twisty-turny" kind of business whereby guilt insinuates itself around *shame* in new psychopathologies. Whereas guilt was (and still is in some instances) one of the indexes of the fantasy of transgression of Oedipal desire, and as such, conditioned by unconscious ambivalence, under the requirements of a push to enjoyment guilt becomes welded to shame in an operation that belies not ambivalence but rather, onanistic devotion to jouissance. Where once you felt guilty because of your excessive forbidden (enjoyment) jouissance, now you are encouraged to be shameless in the pursuit of jouissance since it is your duty to enjoy yourself. But wait ... you can't enjoy yourself! Or maybe you can't stop enjoying.

Now there is no excuse for your lack of jouissance, and no need for shame anyway since if your jouissance is guilt-free the only thing you can be guilty of is not enjoying enough. This apparent "re/vision" follows a similar logic to the Žižekian-imagined enjoyment without jouissance; coffee without caffeine, beer without alcohol etc., a list to which we believe we can now add sex without kink, and ultimately, causing poor Jacques Lacan to turn over in his grave, the sexual relationship without impossibility (the only thing that is impossible is impossibility it appears). The subject of our times thus escapes into the fantasy of an enjoyment without limits or consequences, where to be "guilt-free" is not only fantasmatically mobilising of all sorts of practices, but also the new hallmark of the object under late capitalism. Take for example the so-called "Snackwell Effect" resulting from the record breaking sales of the "fat free" Snackwell cookies marketed in the 1990s as "guilt-free" cookies. The Snackwell Effect specifically referred to the observation that individuals tend to consume greater quantities of an item advertised as guilt free or somehow healthy, which can ironically lead to gaining excess weight. Lacan back in 1973 warned us that our jouissance was going off the track because it took its bearings from the ideal of an "overcoming" [*plus-de-jouir*] (Lacan, 1974/1990, p. 32). This *plus-de-jouir*, "coming" too much, or excess of jouissance is authorised by our times since the master signifier has lost its value and given way to a permissive society which denounces desire. And we can see then why the speaking being is caught there, in a kind of perpetual state of liminality vis-à-vis her jouissance, her desire, her guilt, and her shame.

"Sex addiction": a problem with (ahem ...) coming too much

By his twentieth seminar, Lacan had radically recast jouissance according to what he called the field of the "right-to-jouissance", *you may enjoy*, and, the law of the superego, which compels the subject to enjoy, *you must enjoy* (Lacan, 1999, p. 3). Jouissance makes no sense *and yet* it is everywhere. There's no getting away from the superegoic imperative (ibid.). Whereas once, guilt was the price you paid for giving up on your desire, now guilt can be just another name for jouissance. We can see this reframing of jouissance in the (so-called) new symptom of "sex addiction" as represented on film.

Between 2011 and 2013 a number of interesting films emerged dealing with the theme of sex addiction in various framings. Žižek has famously claimed that cinema teaches us how to desire (1992). We could say that insofar as on the big screen the sex act can be mobilised as perverse, dangerous, addictive and harmful, cinema is trying to teach us to desire from the place of the addict in recovery. Here, it is *sex addiction* (or we could say the way each subject experiences the excessive dimension of their jouissance), and not in fact an essential and structural impossibility at the very level of masculine and feminine jouissance, that acts (any longer) as an obstacle to the successful sexual relationship. By invoking sex addiction as a symptom, cinema makes use of epistemic concerns press-ganged into service as an apparatus of jouissance-regulation. In other words, even as we are learning how to desire – within the context of a "good healthy relationship" where there is the right kind of sex taking place and so on – we see that sex from the position of the pervert (to make the well-rehearsed Žižekian point) or voyeur. In other words, the cinematic trick is to show us how to desire by showing us how not to desire and therefore colliding or collapsing the gaze of the cinema-goer with the gaze of the addict. In itself this is a curious moment to pause and think. According to Lacan the operation of shame relies upon our being aware of the gaze of the Other in our *plus de jouir*, but in these films the gaze of the (cinematic) Other is sutured to the gaze of the "sex addict" (we see, whatever it is they are riveted to, through their eyes), and as the jouissance is subsequently framed within discourses of disease and illness (as an addiction), responsibility for jouissance is eradicated, since the subject cannot be held responsible for his illness. Nonetheless, it is clear that from its emergence as a "symptom" in the mid 1970's, sex addiction has to be regarded as a specific and distinctive category of addiction (Carnes, 1983); one that is to say that has been tied to a specifically right-wing moral agenda from the beginning. Sex addiction groups modelled upon the 12-stepping programmes of AA were set up during the 1970's and built therapeutic collateral in the form of Patrick Carnes' bestselling *Out of the Shadows: Understanding Sexual Addiction* (Carnes, 1983). In the preface to the 2001 reprint of his book, Carnes for example, tracks the emergence of the AIDS epidemic as *itself* the result of compulsive engagement in unprotected sex acts and proof therefore of the phenomenon of sex addiction, even arguing that Bill Clinton and Monica Lewinsky's affair is essential testimony and example of how men and women go astray because of sex addiction (ibid.).

Despite its foreclosure from the DSM-V, and serious attempts to have it included under the special category Hypersexual Disorder (Kafka, 2010), and despite there being no current medical or psychiatric grounds for the classification of some human sexual behaviour as "addiction", sex addiction – for so long the apparition of a radical right moralising discourse – reappears on film in the second decade of the twenty first century. Of course, the constitution of any moral panic is predicated upon epistemic rather than paradigmatic conditions. In other words, it is precisely epistemic knowledge about sex which allows for it to be posited and understood as an object of addiction, and for a whole business and film industry to grow up around this object with a set of practices and legitimated warrants and treatments to emerge and be sustained.

"Sex addiction" is then an instance of how cinema demonstrates that it is able to capitalise on the essentially undetermined inscrutability of the excessive nature of the sexed speaking being. And at moments like these we see how the subject's excess (*plus de jouir*) may be interpreted as *either* the missing piece that will unite the social field *or* as the obstacle to its coherence, which means that the social field – here in its cinematic variation – becomes productive at the points when fantasies about the other's desirability or danger mobilise defences to ward off the effects of excess (Rothenberg, 2010, p. 43). Secondly, "sex addiction" becomes a particular name for the subject's *plus de jouir* (or coming too much) understood strictly as a fantasmatic obstacle to the successful sexual relationship. Within sex addiction ideology, it is not all sex that is forbidden, just the "empty, meaningless" kind that is out of bounds. And this takes on the same crazy logic as saying to the alcoholic: give up all your dirty boozing, licking the dregs of the week old beer cans, turpentine bottles, and whatnot, and take instead a glass of this exceedingly fine wine which you may legitimately savour with your supper. In other words not only does cinema attempt to teach us *how to desire* but in addition, *how to enjoy* in order precisely to avoid an enjoyment of the kind that is regarded as beyond the beyonds, sick, etc. – or in other words, how to enjoy without shame, or guilt. Freud's "salmon mayonnaise" joke comes to mind here (Freud, 1905e, pp. 49–50). An impoverished man borrows money from an acquaintance, later that day the acquaintance sees him in a restaurant with a plate of salmon mayonnaise in front of him and he reproaches him. "What? You borrow money from me and then order yourself salmon mayonnaise?", "I don't understand you" the borrower replies, "if I haven't any money I *can't* eat salmon mayonnaise, and if I have some money I *mustn't* eat salmon mayonnaise" (ibid., p.50, emphasis in the original). Notwithstanding Freud's analysis of the joke, what he also notices is something of the logic of enjoyment. The "can't" and "mustn't" (which he italicises) denoting what is possible and what is permissible in the realm of enjoyment is also marshalled in the whole business of what sexual enjoyment is possible, and what sexual enjoyment is permissible; conditioning a logic of shameless, guilt-free enjoyment.

In this new sub-genre of film there is always a scene which depicts the disposal of the object, and the signifiers of sick jouissance. In *Thanks for Sharing* (2012) one sex addict helps another to empty his flat of everything and anything that he has used in his masturbatory practices. Together they set fire to all of these objects. In *Shame* (2011), Brandon tears through his apartment dumping magazines, videos and finally his laptop into black refuse bags into which he also throws left-over food slops parodying the practices of eating disordered subjects who conceive of ways in which to make previously desirable objects unpalatable by throwing other forms of rubbish onto food objects. In *Nymphomaniac* (2013), Joe under the instructions of the leader in her sex addiction group removes "everything that makes her think about sex". Joe paints out mirrors and removes pictures, and wraps phallic-shaped objects in layers of paper and tape so as to conceal their form.

The notion of the "sick fuck" as represented in these and other films, it is clear, is predicated on at least three crucial conditions. First, that there is in fact such a thing as a "healthy fuck", and second, because the "healthy fuck" takes place within the sexual relationship, there is in fact such a thing as a sexual relationship, and third, that relationship is always already inscribed in such a way that you must renounce your jouissance in favour of a more civilised and hence "guilt-free" enjoyment.

Historically Don Juanism and nymphomania are two names given to "sick fucks" as assigned to gender locations. As pathological destinations they didn't even make it to DSM III. As a trans-historical location for a certain "brand" of masculinity, cinema has depicted the titular Don Juan as a nobleman (in 1926), a great lover hero (in Errol Flynn's take in 1946), and as an adventurer (in 1948). We could say he became rebranded in the 60's and 70's as Don Bond, or James Bond rather, and now has undergone another provisional rebranding as Brand-on in *Shame*, Adam in *Thanks for Sharing*, and obviously, as Jon in *Don Jon*. Once and for all, Don Juan is officially a "sicko". Perhaps we can think of it like this: whereas the Don Juan back in the day if he suffered at all, suffered from his desire, nowadays, he is represented as suffering from his jouissance, which has been re-signified as *de trop* as under the conditions of the push-to-enjoyment society we inhabit.

What then about the jouissance of the nymphomaniac? In particular, Lars Von Trier's one. Towards the end of Volume II of the film Joe has joined a sex addiction group. In the discursive style of the AA model, she announces herself: "My name is Joe and I'm a nymphomaniac." The leader (chair) of the group re-nominates Joe's identity by interjecting the words "Sex addict". Joe repeats: "My name is Joe and I'm a nymphomaniac." Now it is explained by the chair that in this group, "everyone's the same", everyone's a "sex addict". Some three weeks (and five days) later; after following some of the group leader's recommendations, Joe returns to "share". This time she says: "my name is Joe ... and I'm a sex addict." Continuing to address the group she goes on to say: "don't think it's been easy, but I understand now that we are all alike." In Von Trier's film, something a bit different is formulated; Joe has had her shame-free sexual jouissance reconfigured as guilty addiction just like the male sex addicts in the other films, we see her requisite identification with the object of addiction in the group: I am just like you etc., I am a sex addict, I desire just like you. The whole business of the group revealed here as an assemblage of speaking beings grouped according to the fantasmatic belief that they are all caused by the same object *a*, this operation itself one of the natural consequences of the disruption of the social bond (and whose symptoms we see manifested in various ways). But Von Trier has a surprise up his sleeve because just after Joe has begun to open up her pages of notes which she had planned to read aloud to help her to explain how she has managed to not have sex for three weeks and five days she catches sight of herself as a young woman in a mirror; a little bit of cinematic playing with mirrors which allows us to see that Joe is reminded of her singularity, her history. When she speaks again it is to once again dis-identify with the group, underlining the singularity of her surplus jouissance, her filthy dirty lust. "Dear everyone", she begins again, "don't think it's been easy, but I understand now that we're not, and never will be alike." Turning towards one woman she says: "I'm not like you who fucks to be validated". Turning towards another woman, she says, "and I'm not like you [...] all you want is to be filled up and whether it's by a man or by tons of disgusting slop makes no difference." Finally turning towards the Chair, she emphasises: "and I'm *definitely* not like you. [...] I AM A NYMPHOMANIAC and I love myself for being one. But above all, I love my cunt, and my filthy, dirty lust".

Von Trier's nymphomaniac is a subject who is unashamed of her jouissance, but, she takes responsibility for it, cognizant of the desire with which it is cor-related, and hence, betokening something of her own ethical status as such. When Lacan says that it is hardly possible any longer to die of shame, since the gaze that shames us no longer does the trick, he seems to be inspired by the possibility of a recuperative and perhaps in some part ethical operation involved in shame. What psychoanalysis does (whether or not, it reinstates the operation of shame) is to encourage us to get our bearings from our jouissance. For our jouissance we are responsible. What Von Trier's nymphomaniac rejects is a recasting of her filthy, dirty lust as a guilty addiction, which is governed by a disease, and in the way that prevailing discourses around "illness" circu-late in our time, to be ill, is to be without responsibility. And yet ... and yet, what is always on show in this genre of film is the scepticism by most of the un-sex-addicted folk that sex addiction is "even a thing"; the degree to which our symptom – whatever that may be – may be something for which we are responsible and about which we are accountable, is still, mostly, a Freudian idea, and not a very popular one at that.

In any case, not all shamelessness can be seen in the ennobled terms of Von Trier's nymphomaniac. Somewhat exemplifying Lacan's "there is no longer any shame", a leading national newspaper recently ran a column entitled "In the new age of shamelessness, what is the point of blackmail? (O'Toole, 2019)." In fact the subject in question was U.S. President Donald Trump's blackmail-ability. The conclusion is that he is immune to it. Journalist Fintan

O' Toole points out that whereas the threat of political blackmail was long used to persecute and threaten people in political and public positions, when it comes to President Trump, it seems that he is invulnerable to sexual scandal, and hence, any threat of blackmail. When the Access Hollywood tapes emerged in October 2016 with Trump bragging that "you can do anything" to women including "grab them by the pussy", many people in his own campaign and most of the mainstream Republican party assumed his candidacy was effectively dead. However, those assumptions were unfounded. According to O'Toole, Trump has achieved what no liberal ever could, he has raised the level of public tolerance for sexual sleaze (ibid.). The point of course is not to condemn the blackmailer as perhaps we would have done once upon reading such a newspaper column, rather, what we are encouraged to condemn is the lack of shame. We are charting seemingly unnavigable waters at times; whereas we used to know where we were with guilt. As an index of our unconscious ambivalence and of our unconscious desire, we could take our bearings from the affect which let us know when our desire was off track, and we could work through our ambivalences. Shame, that essentially private discomfort, conditioned by the presence of the Other's gaze, finding us in our most intensely extimate jouissance, was an index of our sense of transgression since shame is calibrated to social norms and the social bond. In times of no shame, how might we think about transgressive acts against the social bond?

When the going gets tough, the tough go shoplifting

In August of 2011, a riot started up in North London following a march demonstrating against the police response to the fatal and suspicious shooting of "gangster" criminal Mark Duggan. In the following days, rioting – characterised by rampant looting and arson attacks of unprecedented levels by mainly young and very young people – spread to several parts of London and other areas of England. By the end of August, about 3,000 people had been arrested and an estimated £200 million worth of property damage and theft was incurred (BBC News, 2011a). Another riot, another time, another country: Paris, in May of 1968, there were massive strikes – consisting of up to ten million people – for a period of three weeks, which nearly brought France to a standstill and a threatened state of emergency. Even though there have been many riots and protests in the interim years and more recently of course on Wall Street, exploring a couple of differences between these riots of 1968 and 2011 in particular can allow us to make a couple of remarks about early twenty-first century desire and *jouissance* and consider what kind of acts are involved in transgressions which appear to be full of jouissance and empty of guilt and shame.

One of the slogans written on the walls of the Sorbonne in 1968: *youth isn't just a phase of life, it's a spiritual state!* – incited the notion widely agreed upon that young French students were rejecting the technological age itself along with its bureaucracies, and its narcissism.

In somewhat less revolutionary terms, in August of 2011, one British police constable quoted in the press blamed the computer and playstation game *Grand Theft Auto* for the spread of violence and looting across London neighbourhoods over the previous weekend (Martin, 2011). As dusk fell that evening, people were told to get off the streets for their own safety. "Go home, get a takeaway and watch anything that happens *on TV*," one constable advised.

> These are bad people who did this. Kids out of control. When I was young it was all Packman and board games. Now they're playing *Grand Theft Auto* and want to live it for themselves.
>
> (*London Evening Standard*, 8 August 2011)

Whereas one of the sparks that is argued to have set off the "events" in Paris 1968 was the altercation between the student leader Daniel Cohn-Bendit and the French minister of education over banning male university students from women's dormitories at night.

In both events, it is the modality of enjoyment of the young that is charged as igniting the riot; in Paris it is a sexual enjoyment in response to good old-fashioned prohibition, whereas in London it is a response to the dead satisfaction coordinated with a permanent vegetative state. No longer apparently soothed into submission or titillated by the sham jouissance of virtual transgressive gaming, the young were now wandering the streets "living it for themselves". It is possible to interpret in Paris and in London the whole-scale repositioning of subjects with regard to the law. We also see that the function and target of the violent act is manifested differently. In Paris, it is the university, the factory, and the stock exchange that is attacked; in London and in the British suburbs, it is mainly high street shops. In Paris, the call is to strike, to cease to work, to cease to study and to disrupt the symbol of the market, in London, there is no call: but a rhizomic burning, looting, stealing, destroying. In the absence of any call, Žižek in a short essay about the riots in London came up with the revolutionary – on the nail – slogan: "Shoplifters of the world unite!" (Žižek, 2011b).

The slogans in Paris claiming to be realistic in demanding the impossible, indicate, we may note, a demand addressed to the Other. A perceived loss (or threat of loss of enjoyment) is translated into a militant anti-capitalist plea for enjoyment, freedom, more money (for the workers), more knowledge, more truth, more justice, more equality. On the one hand, this is the very kind of loss and dissatisfaction that we customarily associate with a specific kind of symbolic order, a symbolic authority and law that creates dissatisfied subjects because it forces them to come face to face with the sacrifice of enjoyment required for admission to the symbolic order. Subjects living under the conditions of what we could call a society of prohibition typically rail against this sacrifice of enjoyment that curtails their various freedoms (cf. McGowan, 2004). On the other hand, in Britain in 2011 there are no slogans, no demands, no writings on the walls. Instead, the rioters take to the streets, burning and smashing shop windows and stealing mainly high-end electrical goods, wide-screen, flat-screen, state of the art TVs and laptops, play-stations and Xboxes, iPods and iPads, mobile phones, and other gadgetry. In addition, they burned, apparently just for the fun of it, other shops, office buildings, buses, and cars. What kind of transgression was this? Was it merely, as Žižek might term it, the excessive non-functional cruelty associated with contemporary life and/or the systemic anonymous objective violence of capitalism?

On the 9 August 2011, British Home Secretary Theresa May issued a statement in which she declared that the riots were about *"sheer criminality"*. The UK press were unanimous in arguing that the looters were not politically motivated and called the riots "recreational violence". Some sense of the enjoyment involved is captured in the words of a Manchester rioter: "Every time I go into town I just think how the shops got smashed up by all of us, and I just laugh about it every time" (BBC News, 9 August, 2011b).

Laughing in the face of the Other! We think of this as the logical outcome of the structural changes at the level of the Other that Lacan begins to speak about in the Seminar of 1967–1968 (Lacan, 1967–1968). Now that we live in societies of commanded enjoyment the old-fashioned transgression of symbolic authority, which functioned in the past as a way to *revolt, reform, and ultimately return* to work, to school, et cetera, no longer functions. Instead, there is a paradox at work: symbolic law these days no longer demands that subjects sacrifice what we can think of as their imaginary enjoyment because imaginary enjoyment itself does not threaten the structure of the social order, it supports it! In other words, and as political and cultural theorist Todd McGowan points out, not only is imaginary enjoyment simply not transgressive, it serves the hegemonic requirements of the reigning discourse by allowing people to imagine that they are being subversive (McGowan, 2004, p. 193). Remember that the cop's response to the onlookers of the riots is that (1) the cause of the riot is that young people want to go out on the streets and live their computer games for real and (2) the best thing to do is to go home and watch it all on TV. Watching it all on TV, playing the game instead of living it is imaginary enjoyment legitimated by the social order itself! The nearest thing to a revolutionary act for today's revolting subject is to plug into a device and shoot virtual bullets at virtual state apparatus targets. It is hardly surprising that lighting "real" fires, and stealing real things from real shops is a laugh rather than a crime that carries some symbolic retribution. The final ironic twist is that the very objects that are stolen in vast quantities are the objects that will guarantee continued imaginary satisfaction in the very best manner of commodity fetishism and what Lacan in his 17th seminar calls *lathouses* (Lacan, 2007, pp. 162, 187); objects that function as causes of desire in relation to what we can think of as technological jouissance. Perhaps today's commuter on her netbook, iPhone, and iPad is the kind of subject Lacan may have imagined here. The point though is that the plugged-in subject does not need to flee reality in order to indulge the pleasure principle. In the new technologies of jouissance, where science functions as master's discourse, a world filled with little gadgets (providing the grounds for a "phony" jouissance) substitutes for and militates against any truly transgressive act. Imaginary enjoyment appears to occur in open disdain of symbolic authority, thumbing its nose at that authority. But as McGowan reminds us, symbolic authority depends on imaginary enjoyment because this type of enjoyment renders subjects docile (ibid., pp. 191–196 in particular). It is in this sense that rioting in 2011 whilst resembling a revolt is nothing other than the overflowing of imaginary enjoyment onto the streets, the effect in fact of a docile (lumpen) proletariat.

Look at them enjoying!

In May of 1970, in an interview on the steps of the Pantheon Lacan declared that the proletariat had not been simply exploited, rather, it had been stripped of its function of knowledge. This is one of the functions and consequences of increasingly bureaucratised and digitised (science-led) production. The liberation of the proletarian comes at a cost; it is progressive only in the sense that there is a correlative deprivation at the level of knowledge. In the master discourse the worker/proletariat is stripped of knowledge; in the university discourse, the graduate is as disenfranchised from anything that could count as knowledge as the worker, being in fact produced by the educating operation. Moreover, the student is regarded by the reigning regime which says: look at them enjoying!

What is it that they are supposed to be enjoying? It could be the very *act* of staging a transgression. In Žižek's lecture on the occupation of Wall street, he argues that as a society we miss what he calls the opportunity for collective carnivalesque experiences; the absence and/or prohibition of these events sets up a melancholic staging of a nostalgic hippie protest where what is regained for you is the collective feeling you have been missing in your life (Žižek, 2011a). He argues that today's protesting subject is melancholic and recalls that the Freudian point in melancholia is not that you have necessarily lost the object but rather that you have lost the desire for it. As desire risks becoming lost to the subject, re-installing prohibitions, and staging certain types of transgressions may indeed be functioning as secondary attempts to resuscitate desire.

Of course the other way young people could be said to be enjoying is as a consequence of the capitalist discourse, and in that they move closer to the young people of London of whom it was also said: look at them having a laugh! Look at them obscenely enjoying! About the Londoners we could observe: when the going gets tough, the tough go shopping, or shop-lifting anyway, rather like the survivors in Romero's *Day of the Dead*! In the domain of consumption, the discourse of capitalism takes advantage of desire ensuring that commodity consumption is an infinite domain that can never be satisfied. As Lacan remarked in *Radiophonie*: "Capitalism is the extensive, hence insatiable production of a lack in jouissance" (1970, p. 22). In a society of commanded enjoyment, the superegoic master is heard to yell out: "Young people of the world, enjoy!".

In times of more than one Name-of-the-Father, where the subject is deprived of a universal one-size-fits-all possibility of symbolising authority that regulates jouissance, the social bond is challenged and disrupted. Increasingly, it becomes characterised by "the breakdown of civility, rising belligerence, paranoid delusions, social fragmentation, widespread anomie, and outbreaks of irrational violence (Verhaeghe, 2009, p. 3)". Combined with various hegemonic versions of capitalist ideology tied to neoliberalism, the ferocity of a superego no longer corralled by the ego-ideal is put to very good use as today's subject is hammered into a state of perpetual motion. Between a rock and a hard place, between guilt and shame, between desire and jouissance. And whither ambivalence? Since the social bond is increasingly characterised by fragmentation, rivalry, and violence, the subject's desire remains unrecognised, ambivalence has gone underground, and guilt, once an index of where you stood vis-à-vis your unconscious desire and ambivalence, has itself become transformed. No longer a guide to your ambivalent relation to the Other, guilt now is something to be eradicated, forgiven, or attached to illness, disease, or addiction. Shame, the affect conditioned by the gaze of the Other – at once the embodiment and incarnation of the social bond – which once served to orientate our bearings regarding our unconscious enjoyment, our *plus de jouir*, is also somehow not in its place since the (same) Other (and its gaze) are at the service of the new rules of enjoyment. Enjoy your symptom indeed! We do not have to travel far to find the places where we can see the types of ambivalence that emerge from the tatters of the social bond – where what remains of our social tie as it is strained and stretched – are tied absolutely to an enjoyment that apparently knows no shame, but for all that is endlessly justified.

References

APA. (2013). *Diagnostic and statistical manual of mental disorders*, Fifth Ed. Arlington, VA: American Psychiatric Association.

BBC News. (2011a). England's week of riots. *BBC News*, 15 August 2011. www.bbc.co.uk/news/uk-14532532.

BBC News (9 August 2011b). Rioters revel in thrill of seizing Manchester's streets. *BBC News*. Newsnight. www.News.bbc.uk/2/hi/programmes/newsnight/9572763.stm.

Carnes, P. (1983). *Out of the shadows: Understanding sexual addiction*. Minnesota, MN: Hazelden Publishing.

Critchley, S. (2002). *On humour*. London: Routledge.

Freud, S. (1905e). Jokes and their relation to the unconscious. *The Standard Edition of the Complete Psychological Works of Sigmund Freud, S.E., VIII*.

Freud, S. (1927d). Humour. *The Standard Edition of the Complete Psychological Works of Sigmund Freud, S.E., XXI*, pp. 159–166.

Freud, S. (1930a). Civilization and its Discontents. *The Standard Edition of the Complete Psychological Works of Sigmund Freud, S.E., XXI*, pp. 57–146.

Johnston, A. (2002). The forced choice of enjoyment: Jouissance between expection and actualization. *The Symptom*, 2.

Kafka, M.P. (2010). Hypersexual disorder: A proposed diagnosis for DSM-V. *Archives of Sexual Behaviour*, *39*, pp. 377–400.

Kavanagh, P. (2005). *Collected poems*. London: Penguin Books Ltd.

Lacan, J. (1958). The direction of the treatment and the principles of its power. In Ed. J.-A. Miller, *Écrits: The first complete edition in English* (pp. 489–542). Trans. B. Fink). New York: W.W. Norton & Co., 2006.

Lacan, J. (1967–1968). *The seminar of Jacques Lacan, Book XV. The psychoanalytic act*. Trans. C. Gallagher. www.lacaninireland.com.

Lacan, J. (1970). Radiophonie. *Scilicet*, *2*(3), Paris, Seuil. pp. 55–99. Trans. J. Stone. www.lacantokyo.org/img/Radiophonie_tr_en.pdf.

Lacan, J. (1970–1971). *The seminar of Jacques Lacan, Book XVIII. On a discourse that might not be a semblance*. Trans. C. Gallagher. www.lacaninireland.com.

Lacan, J. (1972). On psychoanalytic discourse. Discourse of Jacques Lacan at the University of Milan, 12 May, 1972. In *Lacan in Italia, 1953–1978* (pp. 32–55). Milan: La Salmandra. Trans. J. Stone.

Lacan, J. (1974/1990). *Television*. Trans. D. Hollier, R. Krauss, and A. Michelson. New York: W.W. Norton & Co.

Lacan, J. (1992). *The seminar of Jacques Lacan, Book VII: The ethics of psychoanalysis, 1959–1960*. Ed. J.-A. Miller. Trans. D. Porter. New York: W.W. Norton & Co.

Lacan, J. (1999). *On feminine sexuality, The limits of love and knowledge, 1972–1973. Encore: The seminar of Jacques Lacan book XX*. Ed. J.-A. Miller. Trans. B. Fink. New York and London: Norton.

Lacan, J. (2007). *The seminar of Jacques Lacan, Book XVII: The other side of psychoanalysis*. Ed. J.-A. Miller. Trans. Russell Grigg. New York: W.W. Norton & Co.

Martin, L. (2011). *"Grand theft Auto" blamed for London riots*. www.digitalspy.com/videogames/a333969/grand-theft-auto-blamed-for-london-riots.

McGowan, T. (2004). *The end of dissatisfaction? Jacques Lacan and the emerging society of enjoyment*. New York: SUNY.

O'Toole, F. (2019). Trump has raised public tolerance for sexual sleaze. *The Irish Times*. 16 February 2019. www.irishtimes.com/opinion/fintan-o-toole/

Owens, C. (2016). Not in the humor: Bulimic dreams. In P. Gherovici & M. Steinkoler (Eds.). *Lacan, psychoanalysis, and comedy* (pp. 113–130). New York: CUNY.

Rothenberg, M.A. (2010). *The excessive subject: A new theory of social change*. Malden, MA: Polity.

Rowling, J.K. (1999). *Harry Potter and the prisoner of Azkaban*. London: Bloomsbury.

Verhaeghe, P. (2009). *New studies of old villains: A radical reconsideration of the Oedipus complex*. New York: Other Press.

Žižek, S. (1992). *Looking awry: An introduction to Lacan through popular culture*. Harvard: M.I.T. Press.

Žižek, S. (2011a). *Occupy wall street speech*. www.scribd.com/document/265500833/Zizek-s-Speech-to-Occupy-Wall-Street.
Žižek, S. (2011b). *Shoplifters of the World Unite!*. www.lrb.co.uk/2011/08/19/shoplifters-of-the-world-unite.
Zupançiç, A. (2000). *Ethics of the real: Kant and Lacan*. London: Verso.

Film references

2011 *Shame*. Dir: Steve McQueen.
2012 *Thanks for Sharing*. Dir. Stuart Blumberg.
2013 *Don Jon*. Dir. Joseph Gordon-Levitt.
2013 *Nymphomaniac* Vols I and II. Dir. Lars Von Trier.

Chapter 7

Extimacy, ambivalence, xenophobia

... what happens when our eyes halt on the words: "hospitality, proximity, enclave, hate, foreigner ..."? Even if for an instant we find some "else-where" in them, they are soon assimilated to a landscape marked by the seal of *our* habitus of thinking and *our* memory.

(Dufourmantelle, in Derrida & Durformentelle, 2000, p. 28)

What kind of a phobia is xenophobia, the fear of strangers, the fear of "the foreigner", and of that unassimilable strangeness in other people that can be located even in our close friends? Psychoanalytically speaking, for a young child who has not yet developed a psychical structure (from a Lacanian differential diagnostics perspective – psychotic, perverse, or neurotic), a phobia can be a path toward becoming a subject. The phobic object is regarded as serving to protect a child since it is a way to symbolize what the Other lacks. Prior to the crystallization of the phobia, a child experiences a kind of free-floating anxiety related to the dangers of being identified with – what Lacan, formulating his thoughts around phobia in his seminar of 1956–1957 designated as – the mOther's "imaginary phallus" *aka* what the mother lacks (Lacan, 1956–1957, lesson of 27 February 1957, p. 222). The phobia thus fixes the child's generalised anxiety onto a specific (and deeply signifier-able) feared object, thereby making up for a deficiency in the paternal metaphor, one that names the mOther's desire/lack, and renders it less menacing. As such, the phobic object is "an all-purpose signifier" (10 June 1959, Session XXIV) "to make up for [*suppléer*] the Other's lack" (1958, p. 610), in fact what Lacan designates as the symbolic phallus, or that which names the Other's desire.

Because of the ... horse

According to how Lacan formulates the development of a phobia in his fourth seminar on the object relation, in the beginning there is a child and another subject (the mOther), one who is already installed in the symbolic order, and hence "castrated"; she is a being who is divided and marked with double lack:

symbolic and imaginary. Because she is a "woman" she is "deprived" of the symbolic phallus. Her *minus* of phallus is at the same time an inscription in the symbolic order as presence. Because she is a "castrated subject", she desires the phallus that she is missing, in Lacanian terms: the imaginary phallus. On account of the imaginary phallus' subjection to the metonymy of desire, this is not a desire that can be sated. But the mother may very well attempt to satisfy her desire with her child. In this way, her own search for the phallus may be calmed somewhat through the child, while at the same time the child cannot match up to the missing phallus, which remains irreducible in the mother. At the precise moment when the subject discovers that this imaginary phallus is lacking to the mother, the subject can find itself engaged in attempting to become a substitute for it.

In so far as the child is engaged with this psychical operation, bringing in her or himself and her/his own lack to fulfil this specific lack in the mother, it dawns on the child that no satisfaction by any real object can match the mother's lack, and the inevitable experience of inadequacy, impotence, and anxiety that will accompany his not measuring up to the task engages him in a game of lure or deception and trickery with the mother. Ultimately he can be led to the shattering conclusion that nothing he has, or is, will be enough for the mother. The horse that bites in the case of little Hans, is – because of regression on the oral-sadistic plane – the *real* mother biting and devouring (Freud, 1909b). As Lacan puts it:

> the horse bites ... that is to say ... since I can no longer satisfy my mother in anything, she will satisfy herself on me the way I satisfy myself on her when she does not satisfy me at all, that is, she will bite me the way I bite her, since it's my last recourse when I am not sure of her love .
>
> (Lacan, 1956–1957, p. 423)

The bite is on the one hand linked to the surging of something that happens each time the mother's love is lacking (ibid., p. 408) but it is also linked to the excitement Hans experiences in his own penis, often described by children with the phrase "it bites me" (Freud, 1909b, p. 30). The phobia thus displaces anxiety from the biting mother (and perhaps indeed away from the biting penis) onto the biting horse. Because of this reasoning Lacan says that all phobic objects in childhood are signifiers belonging to the same genre: lions, tigers, and bears (for example). And it is for this reason that some phobic objects from childhood transmute into fetish objects, having had their origin in a childhood pleasure/jouissance (cf. for example Rene Tostain's most interesting case of Jean in Schneiderman, 1980). Indeed, it is even thinkable that behind the phobia of the biting horse there is the original phobic object as displaced, that is to say, the biting penis, the "widdler", the thing that gives pleasure but becomes a source of anxiety.

As such, it is an accident of development or a kind of historic incident that damages the links of the mother child relation with regard to the phallus, which is what the woman lacks and the child discovers as lacking in the mother. When the harnessing of these three objects is broken, there is more than one solution possible. One of these possible outcomes is that the father intervenes as a fourth term and paves the way towards Oedipus via his menace of castration and second privation of the mother, a symbolic operation that allows the child to renounce being the imaginary phallus for the mother. When this path is not available, as in the case of little Hans whose "*Vatti*" (as regarded by both Freud and Lacan) is too kind to be sufficiently menacing, when as Lacan says later in the seminar – there is no exit from the game of the lure, a phobia constitutes a call to rescue (for more on Lacan's conceptualization of phobia, see our chapters in Owens & Almqvist, 2018). This is why Lacan formulates the phobia as the signifier in the place of the missing father (1956–1957, p. 93).

When an adult – who has already disidentified with the imaginary phallus – has a phobia, it points to something having remained functioning as a kind of inadequately or incompletely nominated lack in the Other, which is psychically threatening although it no longer serves a structural developmental purpose. One patient developed a chronic phobia about her twin sister when she turned 40. The two women had become entirely enmeshed in each other's psychical affairs. The patient had suffered from an unnamed epilepsy since the age of thirteen but only knew it to be epilepsy when she was twenty-one years old. Until then her mother had not wanted to worry her by telling her what was actually causing her to faint, fit, and collapse. But neither had the twin sister ever known what was happening when her sister fell to the ground. In this way, both sisters became nervous and watchful of each other; the non-epileptic twin hyper-vigilantly attending to the epileptic twin, examining her for any trace of trembling, heralding a collapse, while the epileptic twin became hyper-sensitive to being watched by her twin indicative of that twin's anxiety conditioned in turn by her own uncontrollable (and unknowable) tendency to collapse. Double trouble we could say. The original figure in their lives who was prone to collapsing was their father – an alcoholic – who would fall to the ground drunk all throughout their childhood; this had been a cause of great shame for the girls. On the eve of their fortieth birthday, the twins travelled to New York to celebrate with family. Once there, they visited the site of Ground Zero, and at the top of the line the patient collapsed. When she spoke about it in her first session, try as she might, she could not remember the colloquial name of the site where she collapsed. She tried several times; "the place where the two things, whatever they were called crashed down ...", "Ground Zero", "where those two buildings ... the two ... what were they called ... collapsed". What was always repressed was of course, the signifier "twin towers". What was significant was that first one, then the other, collapsed, and moreover that the collapse of the second "twin" retroactively conferred meaning on the collapse of the first. Upon their return from New York, the woman developed a phobia about spending any length of time with her sister, since she felt under constant scrutiny by the sister for signs that she might be about to collapse again. How could it be, the patient despaired, that her sister had escaped the epilepsy, while she had had to suffer all the anxiety and discomfort of it, and the potential shame of having people think that she must be a drunk, collapsed on the ground like that. Avoiding her twin sister and repressing her unconscious desire for her to be the one to fall to the ground produced a hardworking phobic symptom, which via the signifier "collapse" also contains a reference to her identification with the collapsing alcoholic father and her virulent hatred of him for shaming them throughout their childhood. This hatred of the Other's jouissance – the father's drinking, the non-epileptic twin's imagined satisfaction in being unidentified with the father's drinking, shaming, collapsing – crystallised in the production of the phobia.

Another of our patients had a phobia of a man breaking into her home while she was sleeping and then "kidnapping" and raping her. In response to the phobia, she went to great lengths to ensure that someone else was always at the home overnight, feeling that the presence of a third person would protect her from the destructive desire of the man; if her husband and children all happened to be away for some reason, she would spend the night with another family member. The patient's fear, however, belied a kind of unconscious wish. As she wished to be so alluring to a man that he would take her by force, if necessary, unable to resist her. This appealed to her ideal ego, narcissistically, as it transformed her into an object *a*. At the same time, she had repressed her sexual desire, claiming never to have got much pleasure from sexual acts, such that her phobia configured the fearsome lack in the Other as having to do with aggressive sexual desire.

In his sixth seminar, *Desire and its Interpretation*, Lacan remarks that the phobic object is what must be prohibited because it mobilises "a jouissance that is dangerous because it exposes the true abyss of desire to the subject" (1958–1959, p. 504). The following year Lacan went on to formulate for the first time the concept of "extimacy" whereby he claimed that what is most intimate in the subject is inextricably linked with the Other (1992, p. 139). In other words, the Other is *inside* the subject occupying the place of extimacy. The phobic symptom in both of these cases indicates how the phobia allows for a taking flight from one's own lack, and from one's own (extimate) jouissance. As such, extimacy points to the fundamental interconnectedness of subject and Other. Lacan's famous formulation that man's desire is the Other's desire is an early indication of extimacy.

In xenophobia, the alterity of the hated other, that which most gets under one's skin about the other, is at the same time what is already under one's own skin, so to speak. As Jacques-Alain Miller has argued: extimacy is founded upon jouissance, which is what grounds the alterity of the Other in the absence of an Other of the Other since the signifier can never entirely represent difference (Miller, 1994, p. 79). It is jouissance, as the lack in the Other, which is central to xenophobia. However, we argue that since the experiences of ambivalence are increasingly foreclosed in our time and spaces, it is what is hated of the Other's jouissance that has burrowed its way into the most intimate of our spaces, the psyche. Although Lacan claimed that unlike love, hate does not rely on discourse, we see that it makes good use of it all the same. Hate, sutured to the fantasmatic calculations of the jouissance of the Other within the signifiers of alterity finds good purchase in the habitus of xenophobia. Therefore, against Miller we claim that while the alterity of the Other cannot be grounded in one signifier, hate, conditioned by the unbearable extimacy of the jouissance of the Other, it can be grounded in the signifier of the animal invader; the most common human displacement of what is alien and undesirable, albeit fascinating and ultimately phobogenic. We have a signifier for that already: xenophobia.

In *Black Skin, White Masks*, Frantz Fanon argued that the black person was an instance of a "phobogenic object, a stimulus to anxiety" (1967, p. 181). For Fanon, a white individual's perception of a black person's skin threatens him at the level of the ideal ego as it confronts the white individual with the status of his own body as fragmented or lacking. Fanon's argument that the skin of the black person elicits the anxiety of the white person could be said to biologise race and, consequently, to place the stamp of permanence on racial hatred. However, it is our reading of Fanon that in the white person's perception of the black person's skin, the former's jouissance – entering into his awareness as anxiety – has been rejected into the exterior and incarnated as a surplus object in the skin of the black person. In other words, it is via the extimacy of one's own jouissance that the racialised other appears to have the object and, by contrast, the self is revealed as fragmented and lacking. This is precisely our point; xenophobia in its various iterations as a phobia stands in for the *lack in the Other*. Certain features of the xenophobic object represent the Other's desire as well as the Other's jouissance, as these are the two faces of lack.

The concept of extimacy allows us to see that the Other's jouissance is in fact our own jouissance, rejected into the exterior and perceived in the other person. As Miller put it, "There is no other enjoyment but my own. If the Other is in me, occupying the place of extimacy, then the hatred is also my own" ((Miller, cited in Žižek, 1993, p. 203). While others may have a jouissance that differs from ours and other activities and fashions of relating to jouissance, it is impossible to experience another's jouissance in the way that s/he experiences it; as such, our perception of the Other's jouissance is necessarily filtered through our own jouissance, ultimately rendering what we hate of the Other's jouissance into what we hate of our own jouissance. It is our point that although the hatred and fear of our jouissance is the motivating force behind its rejection into the Other, it is also a cherished part of ourselves that we fight against relinquishing – even if it causes us great turmoil. It follows that instead of placing hatred of the Other's jouissance at the core of xenophobia as Miller does, in our view, at the foundation of xenophobia is *ambivalence* about one's own jouissance.

Along these lines, we read a passage from the chapter entitled "Love of one's neighbour" from Lacan's seventh seminar:

> Every time that Freud stops short in horror at the consequences of the commandment to love one's neighbour, we see evoked the presence of that fundamental evil [the neighbour's jouissance] which dwells within this neighbour. But if that is the case, then it also dwells within me. And what is more of a neighbour to me than this heart within which is that of my jouissance and which I don't dare go near?
>
> (1992, p. 186)

As Lacan suggests, we can never ascertain whether jouissance is our own or that of our neighbour. With this fundamental confusion regarding a jouissance from which we flee, ambivalence is inscribed into the concept of jouissance.

We tend to locate this terrifying jouissance in the person of our neighbour or even of our close friend, family member, and so on – as someone does not have to be a stranger to seem strange or alien to us when we are faced with her or his jouissance. In fact, we are experts even at not knowing ourselves. It is our own extimate strangeness, which is operative in xenophobia as a phobia of that which is strange. We see this extimate strangeness functioning as a catalyst for all forms of xenophobia, including xenophobia related to religion, age, sexual preference, gender, race, and so on. Certainly, each type of xenophobia has its own important particularity and situatedness in a cultural and historical context. For example, although we view racism – the subject of the next chapter – as a subtype of xenophobia on account of it too being motivated by ambivalence about one's own extimate jouissance, we take care to elucidate something of its unique structure which cannot be understood without reference to racism's systemic or political-historical nature.

To define xenophobia as ambivalence about our jouissance is to regard the problem of xenophobia from the perspective of the real. We want to emphasise that it is necessary to delineate xenophobia in its various dimensions; that is to say, in the imaginary, symbolic, and the real. Xenophobia in its imaginary component relates to competition and aggression in all forms, while xenophobia in the symbolic is operational at the level of discourse, including ideology, and promotes seeing the other person or group as fundamentally Other. We see the real as running the show, and so we focus on our definition of xenophobia as ambivalence about one's own jouissance.

I am not an animal!

> We have people coming into the country, or trying to come in – we're stopping a lot of them … You wouldn't believe how bad these people are.

These aren't people, these are animals, and we're taking them out of the country at a level and at a rate that's never happened before.

U.S. President Donald Trump (Hirschfeld Davis, 2018)

The earth seemed unearthly. We are accustomed to look upon the shackled form of a conquered monster, but there – there you would look at a thing monstrous and free. It was unearthly, and the men were – No, they were not inhuman. Well you know this was the worst of it – this suspicion of their not being inhuman. [...] they howled, they leaped, they spun, and made horrid faces; but what thrilled you was just the thought of their humanity – like yours ...

(Conrad, 1900, p. 44)

It is interesting to consider how Joseph Conrad's Heart of Darkness is an exemplary support of a Fanonian epidermalised jouissance. In most critiques of *Heart of Darkness*, Conrad is condemned for his racist, white-privileged standpoint, and unreflexive, colonialist gaze. What is of course striking is his riveted encounter with what is arguably an encounter with his own extimate inhumanity. In "Group Psychology and the Analysis of the Ego", Freud (1921c) remarked that the social bond is solidified by its shared hatred of another group, of the outsider; group identification is invested with libido. According to Freud, then, libidinal investment in one's group is increased by comparing "us" with "them". Once we categorise individuals as "us" compared with "them", as social psychologist Henri Tajfel's (1981) research has shown, we subsequently exaggerate the differences between our ingroup and an outgroup. We also tend to perceive our ingroup as comprised of unique individuals whereas we perceive an outgroup's members as all being the same (e.g., looking the same or having the same traits, strengths, and weaknesses) (Tajfel, 1981). In any social group there is an exclusion of the foreign jouissance of another group – an exclusion that strengthens the social bond even if the other group's jouissance is not in actuality much different. We see the fantasmatic work involved in figuring the outgroup's jouissance in political activism too. As Molly Ann Rothenberg has argued, political action is shaped and prompted by the fantasy of transformation conditioned by the notion of the recovery of a lost essence, we could say, jouissance (Rothenberg, 2010, p. 8). In this way, what is belied is the jouissance and defences of each "ingroup" member who participates in political activism. We can read in this light Lacan's formula for the logic of identification and the social bond from "Logical Time and the Assertion of Anticipated Certainty":

1. A man knows what is not a man;
2. Men recognise themselves among themselves;
3. I declare myself to be a man for fear of being convinced by men that I am not a man. (Lacan, 2006a, p. 174)

Notably, in this formula we see that instead of basing the social bond on knowledge about personhood, which allows for identification, the social bond is based on knowledge about who or what is not a person. This could be read as depicting the roots of identity and the social bond as beginning in the deprivation of certain others of the status of human being or, in light of later Lacan, on the rejection of the jouissance of the other. In both cases, a rejection of an alien other is foundational for identity. In the final step, it is fear of being excluded and degraded into this "not-a-man" that solidifies identity and the social bond.

In accordance with this formula, dis-identifying with the "not-a-man", the inhuman, is central to the development of the ego. In this regard, dehumanizing the other is a crucial part of the process of identification. Likewise, it is no accident that denigrating the other is a primary component of xenophobia. It may be, then, that xenophobia is the logical consequence of this mode of identification and the formation of the social bond.

Since at least the inception of philosophy millennia ago, a common way of differentiating oneself from non-persons is to compare oneself to an animal, belying our own extimate savagery. It was animal activist Richard Ryder who first coined the term "speciesism" (Waldau, 2001), which is a form of xenophobia wherein one holds a bias in favour of the rights and interests of one's own species and against those of members of other species; more specifically, speciesism refers to the tendency of human beings to give special status to humans over and above those of other species – a tendency which leads to the denigration and exploitation of animals. Jacques Derrida, in his book *The Animal That Therefore I Am*, criticises Lacan and others (e.g., Kant, Heidegger, and Levinas) for denying the personhood of the animal. In this vein, Derrida speaks of an "immense disavowal, whose logic traverses the whole history of humanity" (2008, p. 14).

What is disavowed? For one thing, as Derrida comments, we tend "to confuse all animal species under the grand category of 'the animal' versus 'man' (without taking into account differences between sexed and non-sexed animals, mammals and nonmammals, without taking into account the infinite diversity of animals …)" (Derrida, ibid., p. 59). This is the characteristic homogenization of the outgroup that we see in forms of xenophobia such as racism (Tajfel, 1981). Perhaps more centrally, humanity has disavowed the agency of each type of animal, disregarding its way of being in the world as lesser than those of humans. Instead, questions are asked such as, "Does the animal think?", "Does the animal produce representations? a self, imagination, a relation to the future as such?" (Derrida, 2008, p. 63), and so on from the point of view of what we value about the human kind of being with an aim to prove that the animal is comparatively insignificant. As Derrida argues, what is disavowed is regarding the animal that we are as a way of answering the question of identity. Swedish director Rubin Ostlund's 2017 film *The Square* wonderfully highlights this disavowal in a scene which depicts a piece of entertainment for invited patrons of the arts seated at a sumptuous banquet hall (none other than the hall of mirrors at the Grand Hotel in Stockholm where the Nobel peace prize ceremony is held). Onto the most elegantly dressed tables of linen, silver, and crystal springs a half-naked gorilla man – played by *Planet of the Apes* animal actor Terry Notary – beating his chest, breaking glasses and grunting at the astonished guests (the majority of whom were actual Swedish glitterati, not extras). Notary's remit was to enter the hall, chase out the alpha male and mate with the prettiest girl in the room. At a certain point, when he has the girl pinned to the floor, a number of male guests charge on him trying to pull him off, but up until that point the couple of hundred or so guests avert their eyes, or smile uncomfortably as Notary's ape man grunts, leers, and pummels his chest, secure in the knowledge that this is but a curious and ironic piece of entertainment, indicating nothing other than humankind's progression; the ape man's behaviour contrasting starkly with the high culture setting, and its most sophisticated inhabitants. Ostlund's quip: "The idea of it basically is that, we're all animals" (Ostlund, 2017) speaks somewhat to the disavowal of the "strange beast" at the core of human subjectivity, that animal that Derrida notes Socrates was not averse to knowing in himself (2008, p. 53).

For it is not merely the animal that suffers on account of this "immense disavowal" (Derrida, 2008, p. 14) at the root of speciesism – and, for that matter, all types of xenophobia – but also the human insofar as something about oneself is hidden from oneself. This is a disavowal, which is bound to have symptomatic consequences. To truly know ourselves – in the Socratic sense – means then to approach and inquire into the part of oneself which is a strange beast, that part occupying the place of extimacy: one's own jouissance.

Speaking of the jouissance of the (racially, religiously, etc.) different neighbour, Derrida finds his own cat a usual exemplar: "… nothing will have ever given me more food for thinking through this absolute alterity of the neighbour […] than these moments when I see myself seen naked under the gaze of a cat" (2008, p. 11). As Derrida points out, as a rule humans tend to discount the gaze of an animal so much that they do not feel shame when naked in front of it and do not investigate the question of "Who am I?" in response to it (although shame at nakedness may be particular to the human kind of being). This is reminiscent of the nurse in David Rosenhan's landmark study, "On Being Sane in Insane Places", who, not seeming to recognise the patients in the ward as fully human, "unbuttoned her uniform to adjust her brassiere in the presence of an entire ward of viewing men" (1973, p. 183) as if the men were not there. Derrida's remark also indicates that to see oneself being seen by an animal is a step toward undoing the "immense disavowal" (2008, p. 14) of which he speaks. Reading Derrida with Lacan, we can say that speciesism is the paradigmatic disavowal upon which human identity is based, and that in order for any type of xenophobia to begin to be overcome by the subject it is necessary to see oneself being seen by the other in her or his absolute alterity. This approach is therefore in opposition with those (often related to empathy) advocating focusing on the similarities one has with a member of an outgroup.

Derrida's remarks on the importance of seeing oneself being seen by the other in her or his absolute alterity are reminiscent of something Lacan said in *Television* in 1973 regarding racism: "Leaving this Other to his own mode of jouissance, that would only be possible by not imposing our own on him, by not thinking of him as underdeveloped" (1990, p. 32). For later Lacan, the absolute alterity of the other is one and the same with the other's different mode of jouissance. As we will continue to argue, there is something deeply disturbing about the Other's jouissance – or, at least, the subject's fantasy of it – and so the typical reaction to it is to attempt to impose one's own sup- posedly superior mode of jouissance on the other who is dehumanised as "animal", "dirty", "vermin", "uncivilised" and so on. This type of xenophobic reaction fills the history books. For example, once settlers arrived in what is now the U.S. – and for centuries thereafter – they viewed the native peoples as "savages" and their ways and customs as uncivilised; correspondingly, Native Americans were systematically killed, stripped of their property, and "reformed" into good, English-speaking Christians. Colonialism in general and the desire to reform individuals, supposedly for their own good, has at its underbelly the hatred side of ambivalence about the Other's jouissance. Indeed, as we have argued in earlier chapters, the prevalence of the figure of the zombie in early twenty-first century film and TV shows testifies to the con- tinuing sense of threat which the migrant or uncolonised subject presents to the social bond, and the unworked-through *hainamoration* of (their) un- reformed jouissance.

In this time, with the increasing lack of orientation in relation to the father, individuals now form their individual and group identifications by rejecting the jouissance of others, whom they dehumanise and extort in the guise of humanitarianism. In this sense, which builds upon Lacan's (2006a) prior for- mula for the logic of the social bond, identity formation in contemporary soci- ety often goes hand in hand with xenophobia.

Borderline jouissance (or, I am not a European)

A couple of operations human beings are fond of organising in our attempts to protect ourselves from the jouissance of the Other are separation and segrega- tion. The zombie, as we have argued, has been used allegorically to speak about a wide variety of contemporary problems, and has most recently been taken up to represent fears of immigration in the film depiction of *World War Z* (2013). In the film, Jerusalem is besieged by hordes of zombies who climb up the walls in great numbers, effectively engulfing the walls of what many consider to be their most sacred city. Unlike the creatures of most previous films, these migrant zombies move quickly and with a sense of purpose, allegorically representing fears of a rapid influx of immigrants should the U.S. open its borders. As Miller (1994) points out, "the Other's proximity exacerbates racism: as soon as there is closeness, there is a confrontation of incompatible modes of jouissance. For it is simple to love one's neighbor when he is distant, but it is a different matter in proximity" (pp. 79–80, italics in original).

Frequently, anti-immigration discourses and their accompanying images are deployed via metaphors of collapsing or destroyed borders. Trump's infamous plan to build a wall between Mexico and the U.S. is a testament to the idea that the U.S. must strengthen and defend its borders against an invasion of foreign criminals. Similarly, images of bombed out buildings in Syria, stripped of their function as containers, can induce anxiety about U.S. borders instead of eliciting empathy and concern for Syrian refugees.

"We want our country back!" and "I am not a European" are recent slogans held high by British citizens during pro-Brexit manifestations. The hotly contested, political and geopolitical minefield that is "Brexit" began when the UK voted to leave the European Union on 23 June 2016 by a 2% majority of voters. At the time of writing, the UK is on course to leave the EU on 31 October 2019. However, the UK's departure from Europe means that Northern Ireland will also be leaving the EU which in turn means that checks may need to be in put in place along the 499 kilometre-long Irish Border, as post Brexit, different trade rules would apply north and south of this border. In November of 2018, agreement was reached by the UK on a "backstop" for the Irish border in order to guarantee that there would be no "hard border" imposed. As the 1998 Belfast Agreement paved the way for the peace process in Northern Ireland, the return of border checks pose a risk to peace since a physical (hard) border would be considered a potential target for paramilitaries. Even though much of the British-received discourse around Brexit consists of rhetoric about trade agreements and tariffs, what supports Brexit for many a Brexiteer is what Irish Taoiseach Leo Varadkar claimed was based on "a feeling, about knowing in their bones, about guts, about getting something 'back'" (Ferriter, 16th March, 2019). This "getting something back", "wanting our country back" and so on is at once a declaration of and support for xenophobia in so far as it mobilises identity reconstitution: "I am not a European"; it is also an index of an extimate (perhaps … ahem … Brextimate) ambivalence at the heart of being. However, xenophobia will fail to be a solution for these Brexiteers as there is no such thing as getting separation from the Other's jouissance, which is ultimately your own jouissance.

The anxiety and hatred that results from metaphors of collapsing structural boundaries (and, as such, can serve to justify the need for building borders) can therefore be seen in the identification of an individual with her or his country, such that the citizen without a border imagines that her or his body can under attack. We think here of Lacan's concept of the mirror stage, whereby the infant libidinally invests in her mirror image, making an imaginary order identification. Having previously only been able to see herself as a collection of fragmented body parts – an arm here, a leg there – the mirror enables the child to see herself as a whole person as if she were beyond her state of "nursling dependence" and could walk around like the others the child has seen thus far in her life. The image in the mirror becomes the template for the child's ideal ego, or narcissistic image, which is forever unattainable. When something threatens the illusory coherence of a bodily border, be it that of the individual's body or of the country with which they identify, it encounters a defense in the form of aggression. As Lacan said, "[a]ggressiveness is the tendency correlated with a mode of identification I call narcissistic, which determines the formal structure of man's ego and of the register of entities characteristic of his world" (2006b, p. 89). The metaphor of collapsing or invaded borders is therefore especially successful at inviting an aggressive response – whether via attitude, thought, or action – against the so-called invaders. Indeed, the metaphor tallies well with Slavoj Žižek's argument about the fundamentally unfathomable abyss of radical Otherness behind the mirror image/the neighbour belying the monstrous "Thing" that cannot be gentrified lurking within (Žižek, 2005, p. 143). What we are calling the extimate ambivalence at the heart of being in its real dimension can be seen from two angles: the side of the subject, in which some cherished aspect of himself is seen to be under threat from an Other, and the side of the Other, who is perceived to possess some offensive jouissance.

Taking a look at the side of the subject, we are reminded of Matt Dillon's character in *Crash* (2004): Sgt. John Ryan. He lives with his retired father who suffers greatly from pain and difficulty urinating. They have an HMO insurance plan, and the father's physician has repeatedly misdiagnosed and discounted the father's symptoms. John visits the local office of the insurance company to try to get permission for his father to see a specialist. He meets with Shaniqua Johnson (played by Loretta Devine), the supervisor, towards whom he had lashed out on the phone the night before, becoming especially aggressive once he learned her name was Shaniqua because he assumed she was black. After John launches into a racist tirade that causes Shaniqua to call security to have him escorted out of the building, John explains to Shaniqua that his father started a waste management company long ago, hired many black individuals and "paid 'em equal wages when no one else was doing that". Then, the city decided only to give their contract to a minority-owned company, and so his father lost his business, lost his wife, lost everything. John's racism was fuelled by his perception that black people stole his father's precious object *a*: his company. Similarly, when Christine and Cameron are pulled over by Sgt. John, Christine believes the provoking cause was that, herself being a light-skinned black person, Sgt. John thought he saw a white woman giving a black man a blow job. In this account, John sees a black man as stealing the rightful property of white men, the white woman as object, and getting off as a result.

In such cases, the object *a* and its associated jouissance is like a kind of property to which one has exclusive rights and must be ardently protected against the threat of being stolen by the racially different other. This object is one, which is felt to be defining, to set someone apart, to render her special and bolster her imaginary identity. In other words, the object is cathected with a great deal of libido, is a symbol of value, and is placed at the centre of identity. Derek Hook has called these objects "libidinal treasures" (2018). Such objects are also at the heart of what bonds social groups together. As Žižek put it,

> The element which holds together a given community cannot be reduced to the point of symbolic identification: the bond linking together its members always implies a shared relationship toward a Thing, toward Enjoyment incarnated. This relationship toward the Thing, structured by means of fantasies, is what is at stake when we speak of the menace to our "way of life" presented by the Other:
>
> (1993, 201)

In 2016 an uproar ensued after American football star Colin Kaepernick began to "take a knee" instead of standing as is customary during the singing of the national anthem. Kaepernick was protesting police brutality against black people and other minorities, but many in the U.S. responded with outrage, insisting that taking a knee was unpatriotic. The national anthem and the U.S. flag serve as treasured objects *a* which stand for the heart of the U.S.; the angry response goes hand in hand with a perception that the cherished cultural ritual or libidinal treasure was being maligned. Of course, Kaepernick's taking a knee, rather than representing aggression toward the U.S., can instead be viewed as calling attention to systemic racism in an attempt to improve the U.S. Nevertheless, racism was brought to the surface of the U.S. cultural imaginary in response to Kaepernick's gesture which brought to mind the destruction of the special quality of U.S. identity.

Castration is at issue with the fear of the loss of the precious object, as that which represents the object *a* for a person or a culture is seen to be a prized possession, the fantasied theft of which would amount to castration. Trump tweeted about such a castration when commenting in June of 2018 on the effects of immigration in Germany. He said,

> The people of Germany are turning against their leadership as migration is rocking the already tenuous Berlin coalition. Crime in Germany is way up. Big mistake made all over Europe in allowing millions of people in who have so strongly and violently changed their culture! 7:02 AM – 18 June 2018.

A few minutes later, Trump tweeted,

> We don't want what is happening with immigration in Europe to happen with us! 7:04 AM – 18 June 2018.

Aside from the fact that crime in Germany was actually down at the time of the tweet (Graham, 2018) Trump's comment was that letting immigrants into a country "strongly and violently" changes something foundational about that country's culture. As Hook has noted,

> the spectre of castration is always evident with such objects. So highly valued are they – both as a medium of enjoyment and as props of symbolic and narcissistic identity – that their anticipated loss cannot but be imagined as catastrophic, as a kind of extinction of being.
>
> (2018, p. 256)

Xenophobic jouissance

One of the reasons why xenophobia is so resistant to change is that xenophobic thoughts, words, and/or deeds themselves produce jouissance. Someone who yells a racial slur is enjoying an embodied excitement. Another person – who might in general consider himself in favour of the equality of the sexes – experiences jouissance when he thinks "bitch!" in response to an interaction with a woman via a misogyny he otherwise disavows. As we have described in Chapter 6, if a person has a shameless relationship with his jouissance and correspondingly believes in the fact that he is being true to himself and to his most authentic drives, then it would seem to him that his xenophobic expression and convictions are entirely justified. U.S. President Donald Trump's description of the animals that need to be taken out of the U.S. were aimed at members of violent gangs such as MS-13, but Trump made use of the hostility mobilised in their direction in order to justify keeping all Mexican immigrants out of the country. Rendering Mexican immigrants as animals who are intent on doing harm to the U.S. is a highly moralised discourse that Trump and others defend with the jouissance that goes along with righteous indignation. Once again we can see the operation of the superego as that which unites the moral law and jouissance. The superego's command to enjoy often goes hand in hand with the jouissance related to xenophobic words and acts.

Those who are in positions of symbolic authority can derive jouissance from meting out punishments, and when the individual being punished is a xenophobic object, the punishment is typically harsher than that delivered to others who have committed similar transgressions. This excessive punishment belies a surplus jouissance connected to the superego and to xenophobia. For example, one recent study (Dovidio et al., 2016) in the field of social psychology informed white student participants that they would give electric shocks to another student, the "learner," who was actually a confederate of the research team. Participants were informed that the purpose of the study was to learn about biofeedback, and that the learner was either white or African American. At first, the white participants administered a lower intensity of electric shock to the African American learners than to the white ones, which may have reflected a desire to demonstrate that they were not racist. Participants subsequently "overheard" the learner making derogatory comments about them, which incited their anger. Upon being given a second opportunity to administer electric shock to the learner, students who were paired with an African American learner administered higher levels of shock than did students paired with a white learner. All participants were angered by a learner who violated ethical norms by making derogatory comments about them. In response, they increased the levels of shock they administered. Notably, racism was a key factor insofar as there was an excess of jouissance in delivering punishments to the African American learners.

We wonder if perhaps this same mechanism is in play with the disproportionate number of minorities who are arrested and prosecuted for crimes. For instance, a higher percentage of white people abuse drugs than do their minority counterparts, but are arrested, prosecuted, and punished much less frequently (Mitchell & Caudy, 2015). As another example, in U.S. schools, black children are suspended nearly three times more often than are white children, even in preschool, but not because of behaving more aggressively or disruptively (U.S. Department of Education, Office of Civil Rights, 2016). The reasons cited for black children's suspensions tend to be less severe and vaguer than those cited for the suspensions of white students. Black students are more likely to be punished for offenses such as having a threatening attitude, making excessive noise, loitering, and being disrespectful. Both black and white students, on the other hand, are equally likely to be suspended for more concrete offenses such as truancy, using drugs, using obscene language, and vandalizing (Skiba et al., 2016, 2002). Those making the racism-motivated suspensions and arrests are deriving jouissance related to the superego. For such individuals, their racism – which may or may not be unconscious – is a moral affair, and one that carries with it great libidinal rewards which are not easily relinquished.

There is also the question of what characterises the offensive ephemeral nature of the minorities in these studies of racist punishment. What, exactly, makes "excessive noise" or "loitering" so threatening in black subjects versus white ones?

Offensive excessive jouissance of the other

Trump's comments about the culture of Germany changing for the worse on account of immigrants calls forth the other side of the object *a* as it manifests in xenophobia. On the side of the Other, what is relevant is *the subject's fantasy about the jouissance of the racially, religiously, or culturally different other.* Today's subject uses the many stereotypes circulating in cultural discourse in order to imagine something that may or may not be true about the other's jouissance. This is often an elusive quality that might in content alter completely but remain an essentially noxious form of jouissance. For example, there is the anti-Semitic portrayal on the one hand of the Jewish person as "dirty" or "vermin" while on the other hand figuring the Jewish person as a mastermind in accumulating wealth (which is, of course, imagined to be "stolen" from non-Jewish people). Then there is the racialised or immigrant other who is either a workaholic stealing our jobs or a lazy idler living off of our charity. In other words, the offensive jouissance of the Other may either seem to result from the lack in the Other or the surplus associated with the Other's perceived possession of the object *a*.

As Žižek put it, we perceive the Other as having

> access to some secret, perverse enjoyment. In short, what gets on our nerves, what really bothers us about the 'other' is the peculiar way he organizes his enjoyment (the smell of his food, his 'noisy' songs and dances, his strange manners, his attitudes to work ...).
>
> (1992, p. 165)

For instance, at a campaign rally in September of 2018, Texas Senator Ted Cruz warned that his opponent Beto O'Rourke would turn Texas into a version of California with "tofu, silicon, and dyed hair" (Papenfuss, 2018). The ridiculous nature of a fear of the likes of tofu – or rather, of those who enjoy eating tofu – makes plain that what is really at stake is an intolerance of the "excessive" jouissance of the other which threatens our libidinal treasures. Claudia Rankine provides an account of the following microaggression in *Citizen*:

> Because of your elite status from a year's worth of travel, you have already settled into your window seat on United Airlines, when the girl and her mother arrive at your row. The girl, looking over at you, tells her mother, these are our seats, but this is not what I expected. The mother's response is barely audible – I see, she says. I'll sit in the middle.
>
> (2014, p. 12)

The girl rejects the jouissance of her racialised seat neighbour, and the mother offers to sit in the middle to "protect" her daughter.

During Trump's presidential campaign, as well as in a speech in 2018, he appeared to enjoy reading the lyrics to a song from the 1960s entitled "The Snake." The lyrics tell a story of a "tender-hearted woman" who takes a half-frozen snake into her home to nurse him back to health. The song ends, of course, with the snake delivering a poisonous and deathly bite to the tender-hearted woman. "The Snake" was actually written by soul singer and social activist Oscar Brown Jr. whose work is decidedly anti-racist. Trump re-appropriated this song such that the tender-hearted woman was the U.S. and the snake is the immigrant. After reciting it, anti-immigrant cheers erupted from the crowd. In Trump's version, it is in the immigrant's nature to bite the hand that feeds. This exemplifies that the fantasy held of the Other's jouissance often posits that jouissance as excessive, as going beyond typical enjoyment. In this case it is an aggressive jouissance, stealing the object from us, which justifies the crowd's anti-immigrant sentiments. The intolerance of the Other's jouissance can often function in this way so as to project aggressive fantasies onto the immigrant, constructing her or him as a threatening oppressor.

The immigrant, then, is imagined to have a kind of unbarred access to the object a, such that anti-immigrant discourses frequently focus on immigrants having "stolen" jobs or food off of the tables of rightful citizens. The idea here being that the immigrant is given a jouissance that s/he does not deserve and – in the case of Trump's allegory of the snake and his accompanying slanders of Mexicans being criminals – a jouissance that is morally reprehensible. Seeing the immigrant's jouissance as excessive corresponds to the experience of the xenophobic individual's "*jealouissance*," a term Lacan coined in Seminar XX (1999) to capture the jouissance involved in the hatred that springs from jealousy. In other words, the xenophobic individual experiences jouissance in her or his jealousy springing from the conviction that the immigrant has the object a and therefore has access to a paradise of full jouissance of which the subject is deprived. This *jealouissance*, as itself enjoyable, is not only highly likely to be repeated, but also strengthens the in-group identity of the xenophobic person. The cheers from the audience after Trump's "Snake" recitation functioned to bind those individuals together in their common *jealouissance* and their common intolerance of their fantasy of the immigrant's jouissance.

To return explicitly to our main argument, xenophobia in essence is fuelled by an ambivalence about one's own jouissance. We understand it to be one's own jouissance – and not that of the racially or culturally different other – which is at issue in xenophobia following the formulations of Lacan and Miller on extimacy (see also Sheldon George, 2016). Extimacy means that what is innermost in the subject is at the same time the stuff of the Other. In Miller's words, "extimacy says that the intimate is Other – like a foreign body, a parasite" (1994, p. 76). Since jouissance – instead of the signifier (being nominated as this or that type of person) – is what grounds alterity, it is because the Other's jouissance intimately concerns the xenophobic person that hatred is elicited. This is why the problem of xenophobia is so intransigent. As Miller puts it (referring to racism in particular), "[i]f no decision, no will, no amount of reasoning is sufficient to wipe out racism, this is indeed because it is founded on the point of extimacy of the Other" (p. 79).

We have been considering the various manifestations of the object *a* as semblance in its role in xenophobia: a libidinal treasure possessed by the subject and an object which fantasmatically causes a fullness, a lack of lack in the Other. Object *a*, or the surplus enjoyment of the Other, arises at the place of one's own castration, one's own lack. Via extimacy, we can see that the object *a* is the subject's own lack even if it is perceived as materialised in an external thing possessed by the Other. In other words, the subject's fantasy of the Other's jouissance – as that which elicits anxiety and hatred, as what makes the Other fundamentally different from the subject – upon which xenophobia as founded – is, in fact, the subject's own enjoyment. As Žižek puts it,

> the other's *jouissance* is insupportable for us because (and insofar as) we cannot find a proper way to relate to our own *jouissance*, which forever remains an ex-timate intruder. It is to resolve this deadlock that the subject projects the core of its *jouissance* onto an Other, attributing to this Other full access to a consistent *jouissance*.

(2016, p. 75)

As such, we argue that ambivalence about our own jouissance is *at the root of xenophobia*. Since the Other is *inside of* the subject occupying the place of extimacy, to hate the jouissance the subject projects into the Other, and to love the jouissance the subject accepts as its own, is ultimately, nothing other than the indexes of the ambivalence about the subject's own jouissance. Hence, xenophobia is linked to an extimate ambivalence at the heart of being.

References

Conrad, J. (1900). *Heart of darkness*. New York: Dover.

Derrida, J. (2008). *The animal that therefore I am*. New York: Fordham University Press.

Derrida, J. & Durformentelle, A. (2000). *Of hospitality. Anne Durformentelle invites Jacques Derrida to respond. Cultural memory in the present*. Stanford: Stanford University Press.

Dovidio, J., Gaertner, S., & Pearson, A. (2016). Racism among the well-intentioned: Bias without awareness. In A.G. Miller (Ed.). *The social psychology of good and evil*, (2nd edition, pp. 95–118. New York: Guilford Press.

Fanon, F. (1967). *Black skin, white masks*. C.L. Markman, Trans.). New York, NY: Grove Weidenfeld Press. (Original work published 1952.

Ferriter, D. (2019). Brexit is really about escaping the emotional ordeal of Europe. *The Irish Times*, 16 Mar, 2019. www.irishtimes.com/opinion/brexit-is-really-about-escaping-the-emotional-ordeal-of-Europe-1.3826059.

Freud, S. (1909b). Analysis of a phobia in a five-year old boy. *The Standard Edition of the Complete Psychological Works of Sigmund Freud. S.E., X*, pp. 1–150.

Freud, S. (1921c). Group psychology and the analysis of the ego. *The Standard Edition of the Complete Psychological Works of Sigmund Freud S.E., XVIII*, pp. 65–144.

George, S. (2016). *Trauma and race: A Lacanian study of African American racial identity.* Waco, TX: Baylor University Press.

Graham, D. (2018). Trump says democrats want immigrants to 'infest' the U.S. *The Atlantic,* 19 June. www.theatlantic.com/politics/archive/2018/06/trump-immigrants-infest/563159/accessed 16 January 2019.

Hirschfeld Davis, J. (2018). Trump calls some unauthorized immigrants 'animals' in rant. *New York Times,* 16 May. www.nytimes.com/2018/05/16/us/politics/trump-undocu mented-immigrants-animals.html accessed 26 January 2019.

Hook, D. (2018). Racism and jouissance: Evaluating the "racism as (the theft of) enjoyment" hypothesis. *Psychoanalysis, Culture & Society, 23*(3), pp. 244–266.

Lacan, J. (1956–1957). *The seminar of Jacques Lacan. Book IV. The object relation.* Trans. A.V. Roche. Unpublished.

Lacan, J. (1958). The direction of the treatment and the principles of its power. In Ed. J.-A. Miller, *Écrits: The first complete edition in English* (pp. 489–542). Trans. B. Fink. New York: W.W. Norton & Co., 2006.

Lacan, J. (1958–1959). *The seminar of Jacques Lacan. Book VI. Desire and its interpretation.* Trans. C. Gallagher. www.lacaninireland.com.

Lacan, J. (1990). *Television.* Trans. D. Hollier, R. Krauss, and A. Michelson. New York: W.W. Norton & Co.

Lacan, J. (1992). *The seminar of Jacques Lacan, Book VII: The ethics of psychoanalysis, 1959–1960.* Ed. J.-A. Miller. Trans. D. Porter. New York: W.W. Norton & Co.

Lacan, J. (1999). *On feminine sexuality, the limits of love and knowledge, 1972–1973. Encore: The seminar of Jacques Lacan Book XX.* Ed. J.-A. Miller. Trans. B. Fink. New York and London: Norton.

Lacan, J. (2006a). Logical time and the assertion of anticipated certainty. In Ed. J.-A. Miller, *Écrits: The first complete edition in English* (pp. 161–175). Trans. B. Fink. New York: W.W. Norton & Co.

Lacan, J. (2006b). The mirror stage as formative of the I function as revealed in psychoanalytic experience. In J.-A. Miller, *Écrits: The first complete edition in English.* Trans. B. Fink. New York: W.W. Norton & Co.

Miller, A. *Extimité,* Paris, November 27, 1985 (unpublished lecture).

Miller, J.A. (1994). Extimité. In M. Bracher, M. Alcorn, R. Corthell & F. Massardier-Kenney (Eds.). *Lacanian theory of discourse: Subject, structure, and society* (pp. 74–87). New York: New York University Press.

Mitchell, O. & Caudy, M. (2015). Examining racial disparities in drug arrests. *Justice Quarterly, 32,* pp. 288–313.

Ostlund, R. (2017). In Fusco, J. Anything can happen in this movie: The sheer satirical brilliance of 'The Square'. *No Film School.* https://nofilmschool.com/2017/10/Rueben-Ostlund-The-Square.

Owens, C. & Almqvist, N. (2018). *Studying Lacan's Seminars IV and V: From lack to desire.* London: Routledge.

Papenfuss, M. (2018). Ted Cruz: Dems want to turn Texas into 'Tofu, Silicon, Dyed-Hair' California. *Huffington Post,* 9 September. www.huffingtonpost.com/entry/ted-cruz-says-dems-trying-to-turn_us_5b959f46e4b0511db3e396fd, accessed 15 September 2018.

Rankine, C. (2014). *Citizen: An American lyric.* Minneapolis, MN: Graywolf Press.

Rosenhan, D. (1973). On being sane in insane places. *Science, 179*(4070), pp. 250–258.

Rothenberg, M.A. (2010). *The excessive subject: A new theory of social change*. Malden, MA: Polity.

Schneiderman, S. (1980). *Returning to Freud: Clinical psychoanalysis in the school of Lacan*. Yale: Yale University Press.

Skiba, R., Arredondo, M., Gray, C., & Rausch, M. (2016). What do we know about discipline disparities? New and emerging research. In R. Skiba & K. Mediratta (Eds.). *Inequality in school discipline* (pp. 21–38). New York: Palgrave Macmillan US.

Skiba, R., Michael, R., Nardo, A., & Peterson, R. (2002). The color of discipline: Sources of racial and gender disproportionality in school punishment. *The Urban Review, 34*, pp. 317–342.

Tajfel, H. (1981). *Human groups and social categories*. Cambridge, MA: Cambridge University Press.

U.S. Department of Education, Office of Civil Rights. (2016). 2013–2014 civil rights data collection: Key data highlights on equity and opportunity gaps in our nation's public schools. www2.ed.gov/about/offices/list/ocr/docs/crdc-2013-14.html. Accessed November 22, 2018.

Waldau, P. (2001). *The specter of speciesism: Buddhist and Christian views of animals*. Oxford: Oxford University Press.

Žižek, S. (1992). *Looking awry: An introduction to Jacques Lacan through popular culture*. Cambridge, M.A.: MIT Press.

Žižek, S. (1993). *Tarrying with the negative: Kant, Hegel and the critique of ideology*. Durham, NC: Duke University Press.

Žižek, S. (2005). *Interrogating the Real*. London: Bloomsbury.

Žižek, S. (2016). *Against the double blackmail: Refugees, terror and other troubles with the neighbours*. London: Allen Lane.

Film reference

2017 *The Square*. Dir: Rubin Ostlund.

Chapter 8

The jouissance of ambivalence

We are not racists, but ...

We have been building an argument throughout this book in order to suggest that what we find intolerable in the Other's way of taking jouissance highlights the acute tensions and enjoyments conditioned by an ambivalence at the very core of being. This ambivalence, we suggest, can be thought of as nothing other than the speaking being's ambivalent relation to its (own) individual real. As such, this ambivalence is quite good at refusing to be humanised, civilised, or modified; indeed, we take our bearings from our *hainamoration* in order to think, to speak, and to act in relation to the small or big other with whom we find ourselves concerned. Then, we (rather stupidly) rely on TV shows, movies and online forums in our inadequate attempts to manage the jouissance (the tensions, and excessive enjoyments) of ambivalence, which is ultimately, intractably extimate. Lacan has remarked that unlike love, hatred does not rely on discourse (Lacan, 1999). Yet, it is precisely the real of what is hated of the Other's jouissance (and hence, of what we hate of our own jouissance) that has found its way into cultural, social, and political spaces, articulated in the discourses and practices organised around the expression of hostile prejudices. The real, per se, is strictly speaking, not wholly representable in the signifying chain but is manifest in our ambivalent, transgressive desire(s), condensed and materialised in our *extreme prejudices*. We do not agree entirely with Miller's claim that we hate our jouissance; rather we believe it is more accurate to propose that we are deeply ambivalent about it, and our extreme prejudices highlight precisely this tortured extimate ambivalence at the heart of our being. It is important to note that extimate ambivalence operates under the (material, ideological, social, and political) conditions of late capitalism. Therefore, the "solutions" offered to the speaking being's ambivalent discontents take place within specific compelling discourses and practices: the promotion of the individual under the ideologies of neoliberalism, the concomitant increasing dehiscence of the subject from the social bond, the fracturing of social identity, and the absence of a singular organizing principle, or signifier, that could or might make sense of what Lacan (speaking about racism in *Television*) referred to as the "melting pot" (Lacan, 1974, p. 32) of contemporary global cultures and social forms. We argue that precise singular arrangements of extreme prejudices find common ground with other singular arrangements via the pathways of identification, and cultural, historical, social, and psychological myth. In this way, racisms – as the most highly organised forms of extreme prejudices – can usefully be thought of as the flypaper upon which a myriad of flying prejudices stick; what they organise in this analogy is the unassimilable jouissance marshalled by the insects' swarming singularities. Since racism offers the most powerful example of the intractable, intransigent aspect of our *hainamoration*, that is, our ambivalent relation to our own individual real, we will examine in this last chapter what solutions are offered up to the speaking being in order to deal with, and to manage the jouissance of ambivalence. Or in other words, how to deal with the fact that "we are not racists, but …".

Contemporary neoliberal capitalism offers particular discourses and rhetorical devices to the speaking being within which they may consciously and unconsciously hide, and hide from, the hostility that they harbour against the one who functions for them as the semblant of their own extimate ambivalent being. The speaking being enculturated in the spaces and times of this epoch adduces these various discourses, mindful – as much as it is possible to be for the subject who is divided by language – of the universal imperative of full tolerance of the neighbor, stranger, semblant, other, racialised other, with whom, under neoliberal capitalism they must compete for a share in the jouissance stakes, but also whom, as a consequence of psychical extimacy they have already identified as an evil twin. We will take a closer look at these various discourses and suggest that they correlate very well with what Freud and later Lacan outlined as the mechanisms of psychical negation: repression, disavowal, and foreclosure.

How to negate ambivalence (not)

At the beginning of this book, we argued that the figure of the zombie on film can be seen to serve as a proxy for the undesirable other whom we regard as too close for comfort; in this way, our thirst for a good zombie apocalypse movie captures something of the tensions of ambivalence which we argue does not find much opportunity to be worked out or worked through in our times and spaces. The individual's relation to what is ambivalent – in his very being – is, because of the extimate nature of this alien jouissance, cast out and identified in an outside figure. The name that is given to the casting out of this alien jouissance is racism. But as racism is the endemic social plague with which humans are infected throughout every single epoch described by the historians; it is safe to say that we have arrived at this late point in our advanced economies with our ambivalence toward our own jouissance, intact. No better, and much worse. In addition, we find at our disposal however, à la carte discursive practices which allow us to tidy up the mess of our hateful ambivalence and furthermore, satisfy ourselves at a much deeper, psychical level that we are good to go.

Repression (on not saying the "n-word" for instance)

Let us consider first of all the operation of repression – in its conscious and unconscious forms – as it functions in the discursive practices of re-signification, nominalist politics, multiculturalism, and intersectionality. The replacement of one "word" by another can be regarded as similar to the (unconscious) neurotic operation involved in the repression of a troubling signifier. Of course, a lot of the business of re-signification is laboriously conscious, and alongside its more commonplace framing as "politically correct speech", re-signification marshals together the powerful belief that saying something differently has effects because words and language are powerful tools that bring about real change.

On 6 December 2015, in the wake of the terrorist attack in San Bernardino, California, in which a Muslim couple shot and killed 14 people and seriously injured another 22, President Barack Obama gave a beautiful speech preaching religious tolerance (2015). In it, he detailed how everyone has a responsibility to "reject discrimination," to realise that "the vast majority of terrorist victims around the world are Muslim," and not to "turn against one another by letting this fight be defined as a war between America and Islam." Stressing that "Muslim Americans are our friends and our neighbours, our co-workers, our sports heroes – and, yes, they are our men and women in uniform who are willing to die in defense of our country" Obama's attempt to resignify the Muslim neighbour as a victim rather than as the attacker failed to change attitudes in the way he might have hoped. Evan Soltas and economist Seth Stephens-Davidowitz found that aggressive and racist Google searches such as "kill Muslims" and "Muslims are evil" actually increased during Obama's speech (2015). However, a subsequent speech Obama gave at the Islamic Society of Baltimore encouraged his audience to see the figure of the Muslim as one among the "generations of Muslim Americans (who) helped to build our nation". Stephens-Davidowitz pointed out that "right after these words were spoken, the angry searches about Muslim Americans actually went down". Seeing the Other as a crucial part of the foundations of the social bond apparently functioned to temporarily reduce the hated aspect of the Other. But it would be difficult to conclude that these are lasting effects. We believe rather that while it is evident that the practice and cultivation of re-signification can sometimes, over time, signify difference differently, typically efforts at re-signification can be seen to fail in the same way that everyone knows that the emperor isn't wearing any clothes; what remains potentially unaltered under resignification therefore is the jouissance of the speaking being who may say something differently in the knowledge that it is a mere saying.

Perhaps one of the most striking examples of this calling out the emperor's state of undress is the rowdy conflict Slavoj Žižek found himself at the centre of, after delivering the concluding lecture at the Left Forum conference in

NYC, May 2016 (Youtube.com, 2016a). During the Q&A session, Taryn Fivek accompanied by Molly Klein heatedly condemned the organisers for funding a lecture by a "racist, misogynist, xenophobe" (ibid.). Apropos of the alleged racism, Fivek referred Žižek to the "joke" he had told on numerous occasions involving the size of a black colleague's penis. In an attempt to manage the proceedings (Chair) Kristen Lawlor claimed that these allegations and in particular the reference to the joke about the size of the black man's penis were "out of context". She argued that Žižek's style involves saying a lot of things that provoke. "Like saying the N-word?" Fivek countered. "In what context is it okay to say the N-word? In what context is it okay to say those things?" Fivek demanded. There followed some minutes of loud argument amongst the assembled audience and some shouting back and forth between Fivek and Klein and members of the audience, before Žižek could respond. Žižek responded to the allegation of racism arguing how – what he regards as-humanistic sentimentalism and right liberalist appropriations of politically correct speech are "stupid" solutions to the concrete material conditions that give rise to the inequalities arising from difference (whether signified as race, gender, or ethnic origin). Agreeing that the joke about the black man's penis was extremely vulgar, he went on to argue that contrary to right liberal opinion, avoiding saying the "N-word" does not solve the problem of racism. In other words, changing the language in which we speak about inequality and oppression does not remove inequality and oppression: in this vein, Žižek argued that soon enough torture will be rephrased as "intense interrogation technique" and rape as "intense seduction technique", but without none-the-less altering those practices. In the same way, the Žižekian moment insists that omitting the "N" ("nigger") word from speech neither re-signifies the object of racism, nor ultimately removes it.

What everyone – not just psychoanalysts - knows about repression is that the problematic signifier always finds a way to return: in dreams, blunders, and slips of speech, and even of the pen. Don King's introduction to Trump in Cleveland in September of 2016 is hilarious precisely because despite all his laboured conscious (and unconscious) attempts to avoid using the "N-word" when talking about Black men, it slips out anyway in front of a huge audience and is captured forever on Youtube (Youtube.com. 2016b). Freud's explanation of repression given to the American audience of scholars at Clark University back in 1909 is still illuminating in this respect (Freud, 1910a, pp. 25–27). He invites his audience to imagine that there is a troublesome and potentially embarrassing person amongst them heckling and causing a disturbance, and that in order to deal with this unwanted presence, he is removed, put outside the door and a "resistance" is put in place to prevent his re-entry. All good and well, but Freud notes that even though the annoying chap has been removed, repressed in fact, he goes on to have an effect from this other place as he continues to shout and hammer on the door. The "other place" is what Freud referred to as der anderer schauplatz, the other stage: the scene of the unconscious, a brilliant metaphor for the indication that the effect of what is repressed continues its business elsewhere. The return of the repressed in the hammering of the blundered action, in the roaring of the slip, was on stage once again when Don King announced:

> I told Michael Jackson … I said if you are poor you are a poor negro … (I would use the 'N-word') … But if you are rich you are a rich negro. If you are intelligent … intellectual, you are an intellectual negro. If you are a dancing and sliding and gliding *nigger* … I mean n-n-negro …
>
> (Youtube.com, 2016b, our emphasis)

This great little example of the "return of the repressed" in fact reveals a double attempt at censorship as well as the failure of re-signification: it shows how King consciously tries to manage not saying "nigger" by saying the word "negro", but as he has already substituted the "N-word" in his spoken remarks for "nigger", it is indeed "nigger" that pops out from under repression. What makes the example even more interesting is that King feels at ease using the "N-word" or the term "nigger" when addressing a black man ("I would use the 'N-word'") but in modulating the term for his address of a different Other (Trump could not possibly be any Whiter) he stumbles and bumbles. We cannot ignore the irony of his addressing Michael Jackson so unproblematically as a "nigger" – "a dancing, sliding, gliding nigger" – given Jackson's own increasing "whiteness" over the last decade or so of his life. But does substituting for the N-word with the word negro remove the signification of that which it so ineffectively covers over? We are reminded of Lacan's claim that the symptom is a metaphor and moreover that it is not a metaphor to say this (Lacan, 1958, p. 439).

In 2017, while co-hosting the NBC network special before the Golden Globes, Jenna Bush Hager (the daughter of former U.S. President George W. Bush) was interviewing singer Pharrell, who had been nominated for best original score for the movie *Hidden Figures*. Hager said, "So, you're nominated for *Hidden Fences*." With this statement, Hager made a slip of the tongue in which she combined *Hidden Figures* (the aforementioned movie centring around three black female NASA employees) with *Fences*, another of the year's Golden Globe-nominated movies featuring a predominantly black cast. Later that same night, while presenting the award for best supporting actress (for which *Fences* Star Viola Davis and *Hidden Figures* star Octavia Spencer were both nominated) Michael Keaton made the same parapraxis as Hager had made! This slip of the tongue, "Hidden Fences", brought to the public's attention an unconscious racist sentiment: that black people and black movies are all the same, interchangeable, whilst also revealing that the business of the return of the repressed insists in a repetition that cannot be effectively regulated.

Nonetheless, the acts of re-signifying (difference) and re-nominating (identity qua different from the "norm") or even nominating en principio (acknowledging new norms) are very much in vogue ideologically and politically speaking. Unsurprisingly, we see this at work on the small and big screen in the efforts to name every single identity as if such an operation will restore parity and equality to everyone. The aforementioned film *Hidden Figures*, set in 1961 segregated Virginia, is based on a true story around three black female employees of the NASA base. One of the women, Katherine Goble (played by the actress Taraji P. Henson), is an extremely capable mathematician and is "promoted" to work in the Space Task Group tasked with helping the group put a man in space. She is the only black person in the group as well as the only woman in a non-secretarial position. The borders in the segregated workplace become clearly defined as Katherine sets foot into the workroom for the Space Task Group. The day after she pours herself a cup of coffee in front of a room full of horrified white men, there appears a small coffee pot labelled "coloured." This is a striking example of Lacan's reversal of Saussure's axiom; where indeed, the signifier "coloured" bears no direct relation to the signified (coffee pot), where, furthermore, its signifierness is revealed as fundamentally arbitrary. Lacan's original riff on this was to call up the image of two doors leading to men and women's toilet facilities with the word "gentlemen" above the men's room and the word "ladies" above the women's (Lacan, 1958, p. 416). One of the several interesting remarks Lacan makes about this is to observe that,

> [T]he point is not merely to silence the nominalist debate with a low blow, but to show how the signifier in fact enters the signified – namely, in a form which, since it is not immaterial, raises the question of its place in reality .
>
> (ibid., p. 417)

As it happens, the whole business of what is signified by toilet doors crops up in *Hidden Figures*; Katherine has to leave the building and run across to another in order to use the ("coloured's") toilet. When subsequently her supervisor marches over to the coloured women's restroom and dramatically knocks down the sign, declaring that from now on restrooms are just restrooms, what is covered over is that Katherine's protestations were necessary for him to notice his whiteness and privilege. But what is also belied, of course, are the signifying effects of the "signs" he removes; our point (following Lacan) is that removing the nomination isn't enough, since the original (arbitrary) signifier – even in its elision/repression – continues to have effects, having entered the signified.

In this light we also want to argue that orange *isn't* the new black. In the massive hit TV show *Orange Is the New Black*, the colour "orange" – the colour of the female characters' prison uniforms – as *the* signifier that organises and condenses all differences in the prison population attempts to carry out the business of representation of transgression and penal servitude. The signifier "orange" is the metaphorical creation of the idea that another sig-nifier of "difference" can substitute for black as signifier of oppression and racist speech. The "impact" of this particular metaphorical production is the one which can therefore be hailed as having an effect upon the signified: that is, upon the American symptom of racism. However, if we take the formula for metaphor with the precision that Lacan intended, we understand that "new black" is already a metaphor, the one that substitutes in fact for "black" itself. In this way, the "big reveal" that *Orange Is the New Black* attempts is to sug-gest that in the prison, all other differences disappear under, and become erased or elided by, the signifier "orange". In this way, "orange" as signifier attempts to represent any single target/object of discrimination/hate: Nigger, Jew, Muslim, Latina, Trans, Lesbian, Hillbilly, Nazi, and so on. At the same time and because of this fantasmatic sense of its own idealism, what is also mobilised is the ideology of full representation of diversity (multiculturalism) and full representation of intersectional stakes (intersectionality).

Here then, is another fly paper, another place where we can be very stuck. For left political theorist Yannis Stavrakakis, identity politics is a quintessentially sticky terrain underwritten by jouissance. Identity, *and its politics*, cannot be shorn of jouissance. These "sticky bonds" of identity polit-ics are also at work in the fantasy of multiculturalism, and its counterpart – the radical fantasy of a thorough-going intersectionality – which is taken up and made use of in all sorts of ways.

Against the notion then, that the element which holds a particular group or community together is only ever a point of symbolic identification, it is worth-while to consider rather how the bond linking together its members also implies a shared relationship towards jouissance (cf. Stavrakakis, 2007, pp. 200–201). In the field of identity politics, a sticky bond of jouissance glues people together, and the fantasy fomented of an imaginarised jouissance stolen by the Other often gives rise to the hatred of the Other. Clearly this argument is most visible in the politics of nationalist identities. However, these "sticky bonds" are also at work in the neoliberal fantasy of multiculturalism, and its counterpart in feminist politics – the radical fantasy of a thorough-going inter-sectionality – which are taken up and made use of in all sorts of ways. In *Orange Is the New Black* for instance, there is the notion immanent in the metaphoric productions of the title of the show that a single signifier represents all women in Litchfield prison. At the same time, in the form of each episode focusing on a particular woman's backstory, there are commensurate attempts therefore to re-signify the manifold object(s) of prejudice and inequitable treat-ment. This "achievement" could not work outside of the ideology of multicul-turalism with its powerfully hegemonic fantasy that full representation of diverse interests/identities is not only desirable but possible. Moreover, because of the transgender character Sophia, whose "triple" identity betokens an "intersectionalist" awareness on the part of *Orange Is the New Black* story writers, the show is regarded as flying the feminist flag of intersectionality.

Netflix's series *Dear White People* (2017-), set at the fictional Ivy League Winchester University, follows five young black people as they navigate the micro and macro-aggressions of racism in one academic year. What unites these young people is their experiences of and protest against racism, but they do not speak out against racism or identify as racialised subjects with a single, unified voice; rather the show offers the solution of nominalist identity and intersectionalist politics for the problem of how racial identity binds to specific narratives. The character, Lionel, for example, is a reporter on a school news-paper who struggles with his homosexual identity as well as with racism. His editor assumes he is gay, surprising Lionel – who was not yet "out" – who says he does not believe in labels. But then, this editor speaks of the import-ance of labels, proclaiming himself a "Mexican-Italian gay verse top otter pup." He advises Lionel, "How can you hope to arrive at a truth when you can't find your own? ... Find your label."

Finding one's label, or self-nomination through defining signifiers, is part and parcel of nominalist identity politics. As one popular strategy to addressing xenophobia of many types, nominalist identity politics binds people with the same labels together in efforts to advocate for their well-being. Poet Audre Lorde, who self-nominates as a "black, dyke, feminist, poet, mother," has said "If I didn't define myself for myself, I would be crunched into other people's fantasies for me and eaten alive" (1982). Although such self-nomination might be an effective solution for certain individuals, nominalism only ever consists of incomplete lists. As Žižek (2017) has commented, the "plus" in LGBTQ+ always exists in nominalist identity politics in the sense that identity can never be completely represented by the signifier. The "plus" is an attempt to repre-sent that which exceeds the level of the signifier. From our point of view, the roots of racism and other types of xenophobia are located at the level of the real, that is, precisely at the level of the unsignifiable. Any attempt to promote the rights of a group using nomination therefore misses something fundamental about the subject who is in question. In the same way, most attempts to "resignify" identity fail because of the same radical impossibility. The push towards intersectionality speaks somewhat to the double imperative of nomin-ating all differences and their intersections as well as to attempts to resignify identity in order to mobilise change and anti-xenophobic movements.

A Lacanian critique of identity politics and its attendant ideologies is mindful of the lure of such motifs as "total representation", especially as they appear to foster and mobilise a naïve multiculturalism and tokenistic intersectionality. This is essentially what concerns us in relation to the themes and narrative arcs in *Dear White People* and *Orange Is the New Black*. Lacan's designation of the Other (or symbolic) as containing its own non-signifiable lack $S(\cancel{A})$ implies one way out of the impasses of the fan-tasy that all lacunae are potentially representable via the signifier (Lacan,

2017, pp. 323–324). But this way out lies not in the endless production of signifiers (or meaning), nor in the promotion of one signifier in the politically and/or ideologically inspired attempt to dissimulate or otherwise elide another signifier; rather, it entails the interrogation of meta-narratives and other approaches to the thinking of subjectivity and identity which – in their sticky bonds of political jouissance – are blinded to, and perhaps sceptical of, the failure of re-signification. Intersectionist dreams and/or multiculturalist hopes risk belying the enduring fact that the concept of race, even the word itself, is deeply problematic and no mere re-signification will suffice to get around the challenges posed by the agency of this particular signifier especially as what is represented by the signifier (the subject) for another signifier is nothing other than the subject's own hated real which is intractable and around which he suffers an unbearable ambivalence; he can neither repress it, nor unglue himself from it. Apropos of his own discussion about attempts to resignify "race", Sheldon George quotes Lacan's pithy remark: "There is nothing more difficult that separating a word from discourse … As soon as you begin at this level, the whole discourse comes running after you" (2017, p. 36).

Disavowal (I am not a racist but ...)

The by now classic statement associated with the disavowal of racism is "I am not a racist, but …" where what follows the "but" is actually a restatement in other terms of what had just been negated. On the surface, this operation looks a lot like the operation (and its vicissitudes) of repression we have just examined, but the mechanism of disavowal is more sophisticated since it allows for an absolute conviction on the one hand as to the truth status of what is negated, while the speaking being continues to behave in just the same way as if it had not been negated. The "I know very well … but nonetheless …" (fetishist) disavowal as framed originally by Octave Mannoni ("*Je sais bien, mais quand meme ...*") has been explicated and made use of in numerous ways and on numerous occasions by Žižek. In this instance Žižek draws attention to the manner in which the disavowal operates in its racist version:

> "The expression I know very well, but nonetheless …" renders perfectly the split of the fetishist disavowal – say, in its racist version: "I know very well that Jews/or Arabs or Blacks … are people like me, but nonetheless … I continue to believe that there is something in them which makes them weird, foreign to our universe".
>
> (Žižek, 2003, p. 125)

We can see disavowal in its racist version in the so-called practice of "colourblind racism", which according to sociologist Eduardo Bonilla-Silva (2002), is the dominant racial ideology of the post-civil rights era. In 2000, Bonilla-Silva and Tyrone Forman had conducted a study of college students in which a number of interviewees used the phrase "I'm not prejudiced, but" as a part of their answers. Here's Rhonda, from their research, a white Jewish woman in her sixties:

> I'm (not) prejudice or racial or whatever. Ah, they've always given the ah, slut … smut jobs … because they would do it. Then they stopped, they stopped doing. Ah, welfare system got to be very, very easy. And I'm not saying all, there's many, many white people on welfare that shouldn't be. But if you take the percentage in the tri-city country area, you will and that the majority are white, but all you see is the black people on welfare …
>
> (Bonilla-Silva, 2002, p. 47)

In Rhonda's speech we can see both the operations of repression and of disavowal. First there is the slip of the tongue – saying "slut" instead of "smut" to describe the jobs of black people – an association of black people with loose sexual morals and perhaps even prostitution (slut jobs). Second, taking up the discourse of neoliberalism over and above social welfare, Rhonda disavows her knowledge about the majority of welfare recipients being white in order to characterise black people as lazy and not doing any better financially because they are content to stay on the dole.

Disavowal is able to function in this way as the psychical operation of the negation of the extreme hate the speaking being holds for herself, extimately, and for the (racialised) other. It is constitutive then as an attitude or standpoint conditioned upon a disavowed knowledge: I know very well that white people claim welfare inappropriately, but all the same, I will reserve that portion of the hate directed at my own jouissance for another whom I regard (like myself) as taking more than his fair share of it. The idea that people are not playing fair is deeply coordinated with neoliberalism and its ideologies. Noam Chomsky remarked on the neoliberal reaction in the 1970s to the civil rights movement in the U.S., which he said escalated "under Reagan and his successors, hit[ting] the poorest and most oppressed sectors of the society even more than the large majority, who have suffered relative stagnation or decline while wealth accumulates in very few hands" (Chomsky, 2017, p. 148). Reagan's drug war, Chomsky continued, "deeply racist in conception and execution, initiated a new Jim Crow, Michelle Alexander's apt term for the revived criminalization of Black life, evident in the shocking incarceration rates and the devastating impact on Black society" (p. 149). This impact included rising unemployment, neoliberal defunding of public schools, services, and welfare benefits, and draconian sentencing for non-violent crimes (Gilligan, 2017). White people, then, through their belief in the fairness of neoliberalist society – that there is equal opportunity for all and hard work will result in financial success – disavow that the game is rigged in their favour. James Baldwin commented in this regard that in "spite of the Puritan-Yankee equation of virtue with well-being, Negroes had excellent reasons for doubting that money was made or kept by any very striking adherence to the Christian virtues; it certainly did not work that way for black Christians" (1993, pp. 22–23). Baldwin's point is that the protestant work ethic (which is associated with neoliberalism in the U.S.) is a white myth inapplicable to minorities and those born in poverty.

The disavowal of the ties of Whiteness with neoliberalism is evident too in those 1980s and 1990s television series with a predominantly black cast that were shown on prime time major network television. Most notably, *The Cosby Show* (1984–1992) featured the Huxtables, headed by Dr. Heathcliff Huxtable (played by the now infamous Bill Cosby) and Clair Huxtable (played by Phylicia Rashad), an obstetrician and an attorney, respectively. On the one hand, *The Cosby Show* helped render possible the subsequent increase in shows with a predominantly black cast (Schwarzbaum, 1992), and enabled black people to be seen as a family living the American dream. On the other hand, as well-educated and firmly upper-middle class, the Huxtables were *white*washed to appeal to a white audience. For African-American studies scholar Henry Louis Gates Jr. *The Cosby Show*'s representation of black Americans implies that black people are themselves solely responsible for their social conditions whilst the constraints operating on black lives goes unacknowledged (Gates, 1989). In other words, the show fell into the neoliberal trap associated with whiteness, "reassuringly throw[ing] the blame for black poverty back onto the impoverished" (ibid., 1989).

In the first decade of the 2000s, *The Wire* (2002–2008), set in Baltimore, Maryland, was one of the first shows to depict in detail the realities of a poor black community. It painted rich portraits of the criminal and non-criminal black residents as well as of black and white police officers and politicians (some of whom engaged in criminal acts without being charged or labelled as criminals). Poverty, drug use, the education system – all of these aspects of the Baltimore community were explored in *The Wire*. In the end, the series showed that although some of the characters accept the harsh realities of their everyday life (selling drugs, getting beaten up and robbed, being incarcerated, etc.) as "all in the game" – as though by agreeing to take part in the drug trade (one of their few clear options) they were freely consenting to a sky-high chance of being murdered or incarcerated along with a chance of making money – the game, as it were, is always already rigged against them.

At present, shows with a predominantly black cast which draw the most amounts of white viewers tend to be those with a healthy dose of whiteness – even if the show does manage to portray something of the realities of particular black lives. For example, a 2017 Nielsen study showed that a whopping 79% of the audience of *Black-ish* were non-black viewers. *Black-ish* features parents who attempt to instil a sense of black identity in their children while living in an affluent, predominantly white neighbourhood. As with *The Cosby Show*, white viewers perhaps find appealing the affluence and success of the *Black-ish* Johnson family, headed by a mother who is an anesthesiologist and a husband who is an advertising executive. Whiteness, then, is closely associated with the neoliberalist values that assist white people in disavowing their (extimate) ambivalence about racialised subjects as well as their culpability in direct and indirect acts of racism.

We also see disavowal at work in so-called acts of "microaggression" where the speaking being is able to convincingly cleave to an idea of themselves as non-racist, non-prejudiced but behave *"quand meme"*. Psychiatrist Chester Pierce first coined the term in 1970 in order to describe everyday discriminatory verbal and nonverbal behaviours that he witnessed non-black Americans inflicting on black Americans (Sommers-Flanagan, 2012, p. 294). Just like the repression of a signifier, the attempt to disavow what is (perversely) known to the subject finds a way to show itself disturbingly. This is even more so the case since the imperative of universal tolerance places greater pressure on the disavowing subject who back in the day only had to worry about avoiding flagrant acts of xenophobia, but nowadays has to be careful not to look at someone "the wrong way" or even not to avoid looking at someone. The two conjoined aspects of so-called "microaggressions" involve on the one hand the disavowal that one speaking being is "being racist", and on the other, its perverse counterpart, that the one who is the recipient of the microaggression is being too sensitive. In the video *Black Analysts Speak* (Winograd, 2014) Kathleen White remarks that microaggressions are commonly encountered by racialised subjects alongside a pressure not to respond to them, not to be seen as "oversensitive". White says, "[t]hey build up and become … rage. And like, oh my god, that was such a small thing. Why did I go off? Well, it's like you've been eating microaggressions for a diet, and the diet is killing you." When the effects of microaggressions are suppressed or repressed over and over again, anger is commonly displaced, and its expression often seems excessive. Psychoanalytically speaking, there is no such thing as an "inappropriate affect", and an excess in a reaction always has its equal source somewhere. In Paul Haggis film *Crash* (2004), Cameron (played by Terrence Howard), a black director, is told by Fred (played by Tony Danza), who appears to have some authority over Cameron, that the scene they just finished shooting in their TV show needs to be redone because a black character failed "to talk like a black person". When Cameron points out something of the fallacy in Fred's thinking, Fred asks if the two of them "have a problem" – as though Cameron's comment were the aggressive one. Cameron says that no, they do not have a problem. Claudia Rankine's "Citizen" is quite simply a masterclass in the discursive operations of the disavowal at work in "microaggression". One bleak example:

> The real estate woman, who didn't fathom she could have made an appointment to show her house to you, spends much of the walk-through

telling your friend, repeatedly, how comfortable she feels around her. Neither you nor your friend bothers to ask who is making her feel uncomfortable.

(Rankine, 2014, p. 51)

In his Netflix comedy special, *Aziz Ansari: RIGHT NOW* (2019), Ansari portrays the other side of white disavowal of racism in the U.S. Ansari draws attention to the ways white people can be seen to be taking up the current superegoic imperative to be aware of their white privilege, enjoying trying to "out-woke" each other and enjoying their moments of moral superiority as well as their failures. Ansari begins by imagining white people gathering together to tally up their scores – as if on a game show – on their actions for equality that day. Imitating a white man engaged in this activity, Ansari says, "Well, I told one of my African-American friends I thought *Black Panther* should have won best picture [in the Oscars]." Ansari then makes a chiming sound – "Blewp!" – indicating his score is going up as he smiles and struts around in self-satisfaction. Sighing happily, he continues, "Then I Instagrammed a little love for Colin Kaepernick. Blewp!" Perhaps paradoxically, the enjoyment of acting supportively to racialised subjects can itself be a way to disavow one's own ambivalence about them. Indeed, the next step in Ansari's account is "But then I crossed the street when I saw a black guy." Finally, in an effort to disavow "his" microaggression, he scored more points by "writing a lengthy Instagram post calling *myself* out for white privilege based on something I did in 2015. Ding ding ding ding!" The white subject's racism and accompanying guilt are disavowed by transforming them to a previous wrongdoing – one that can be self-righteously enjoyed and paraded on social media for others to praise.

Foreclosure (get out!)

The last mechanism of negation we will examine is in fact the first we wrote about in this book; early on we claimed that since 9/11 the zombie on film represents the return of our "foreclosed" ambivalence. In the clinical field, what is understood as foreclosed (in the psychotic structure) "returns" in the form of hallucinated or unchained signifiers. In the social field, we find the same return, but in its racist iteration here, what returns, as Sheldon George has discussed at length in his analysis of racism, is the jouissance of the racialised Other, experienced by the speaking being as what he and other Lacanian scholars think of as *jealouissance*. And this *jealouissance* is glued to the skin of the black man like no other.

In her close reading of Fanon's classic "Look a Negro!" vignette from his *Black Skins, White Masks* (Fanon, 1967), Erica Burman (2019) reflects at considerable length on the multiple interpretations and commentaries from scholars of racism, Lacanian theorists, and other psychoanalytic orientations, of this (by now, infamous) small boy who addresses his mother about Fanon: "look a negro". What in her analysis Burman terms the "traumatogenic child" – is so-named because the child here is the one whose enunciation installs a narrative that "institutes the traumatic subject, Fanon as the black-(ened) man" (ibid., p. 89). Burman establishes that as a "subject position", the child of "Look a Negro!" remains "subjectively inscrutable, unwritten, and perhaps unreadable" (ibid.). For Burman, the problem with this inscrutability is that even though the child's statement is consistent with the voice of the ideology that excises Fanon from the social fabric, it also serves to position the child ambiguously as "neither quite representing nor as separate from the relational and ideational context producing her/him" (ibid.). For us, such an observation indicates how foreclosure as a kind of social solution to the problem of extimate ambivalence has traditionally operated. The excision from the social fabric of what is imagined to be the real cause of extimate troubles becomes inscrutable as a single individual act or as related to psychical context. And acts of racism – whether verbal or non-verbal – indicate compellingly how what is foreclosed (what we could call the colour of extimacy) returns, and returns, and returns. We (sort of) laughed when we read of Liam Neeson's recent troubles when his racist statements of some 17 years ago came to light and spread like wildfire on Twitter. It emerged that in response to hearing about a friend who had been raped by a black man, he declared that he took to the streets with a cosh in the hope that some "black bastard" would come out of a pub and have a go at him so that he would be justified in killing him (BBC News, 2019). What is salient for us is not merely the question of whether Neeson is racist because he says he wants to kill a black man; rather it is Neeson's *jealouissance* in the emphasis of the colour of the man's skin in the first instance. Would he have said, or enjoyed saying the same of a white rapist; "I'd like to kill that white bastard"? Unlikely. As Richard Dyer points out in his book *White* (2017), "[t]his assumption that white people are just people, which is not far off saying that whites are people whereas other colours are something else, is endemic to white culture" (Dyer, 2017, p. 2). Dorothy Holmes, who participated in the video *Black Analysts Speak* (Winograd, 2014), commented on this tendency of white people who do not think of themselves as having a race. She said,

> In a sense, the society is set up that they [white people] don't have to [think of themselves in racial terms]. Even more deep, I think, is they don't dare to. Because if they do, then they would have to acknowledge certain practices, and attitudes, and beliefs. And according to psychoanalytic principles, anything you become really aware of, then it's subject to change. So why would somebody who thinks of themselves in a deep way as holding the power, why are they going to be examining that?
>
> (Winograd, 2014)

Whiteness, then, is seen to function as an invisible carrier of (hidden) privilege. This desire "not to know" about their own racism, or in Neeson's case, about how their own racism is hidden even from their own desire, is from our point of view, the way that foreclosure allows racism to be scotomised from the speaking being's awareness.

However, this type of foreclosure is also hard at work in all the narratives that figure slavery and racism as being things of the past rather than acknowledging that the wealth and privilege of white people in the U.S. is largely based on centuries of the enslavement and dehumanization of black people. Correspondingly, Nancy Fraser (2017) claims that expropriation – which in its various forms strips individuals of their freedom and rights – along with exploitation, is a main feature of capitalism, and that the former has a clear link with racial oppression. Capitalism, then, not unlike the foundation for identity in our times, is built upon dehumanization. The system of capitalism with its expropriative and exploitative distribution of money and power goes hand in hand with whiteness as a desire to hide the operation of what Fraser calls the two "exes" of capitalism. As the 2017 film *Get Out* so chillingly portrays, whiteness goes hand in hand with the notion of *rights* to racialised bodies, whether it is by incarcerating them, beating and killing them, or taking over their bodies. In his comprehensive analysis of capitalism and the unconscious, Samo Tomšič formulates Lacan's critique of capitalist discourse as indicating how capitalism "tends towards the foreclosure of castration" (2015, p. 226). As such, the imperative to jouissance under capitalism strives to heal subjective lack by establishing a univocal relationship between the subject and the object of jouissance. The body of the racialised other as one of these objects has its history in slavery of course, but in its newer formulations, the "behaviour" of the racialised other becomes something that is imagined as a threat to jouissance, especially where that jouissance is regarded as "intolerable".

Sheldon George's analysis of the shooting of Jordan Davis by Michael Dunn in Jacksonville 2012 is tragically illuminating in this respect. Dunn's act of killing is in his words not an act of racism, as he puts it:

> I'm really not prejudiced against race, but I have no use for certain cultures. This gangster-rap, ghetto talking thug "culture" that certain segments of society flock to is intolerable. They espouse violence and disrespect toward women.
>
> (ibid. p. 4)

Dunn thereby evades direct reference to racial difference since he had claimed that it was the boys' "behaviour" – namely, their enjoyment of loud rap music playing in their car and their refusal upon being asked by Dunn to turn it down – that initiated the chain of events that led to his shooting Jordan Davis. George describes how Michael Dunn defends his act of killing Jordan Davis (firing ten bullets into the parked car in which the boy sat along with his friends) as "self-defence" imagining Davis could have been picking up a gun from the floor of the car in order to shoot Dunn. Now, what this achieves for George is the transformation of racial hatred into a more socially acceptable expression of intolerance of violence. As such, hatred of the other extends beyond race towards the other's jouissance – the core around which, George argues otherness articulates itself in order to constitute racial alterity. It is against this jouissance that Dunn's actions must be read, and it is precisely this jouissance that explains the "possibility for hatred in contemporary America to address itself at racial difference without need of acknowledging this difference" (ibid., p.3).

In our clinic, an adolescent boy explained that he had been hanging around a young children's play area with a pal of his and they had been sharing a cigarette. Suddenly an elderly Spanish granny approached them and started to reprimand them for smoking in the area; the boy threw the cigarette away but did not apologise, and he and his friend – engaging in face-saving behaviour – affected a disinterested air. Thereupon, the granny's complaints escalated; she continued to berate them for smoking in the area, for being in the area, and for not responding correctly when reprimanded. The boys continued to look away. And now, the granny shifted discourse. Targeting the main smoking boy, she addressed him as "un moro" and demanded to know why "he was even there". In Spain, "moro" is a term used by Spanish racists when referring to Moroccan people. What is interesting here is the presence of the very twist that George points out in his analysis of Dunn's justification of his "fear-induced" "self defence" shooting of Jordan Davis. First there is the behaviour of the young boy being challenged on account of his jouissance (of smoking in a forbidden zone); when he ignores the effect his jouissance has upon the Spanish granny, she demonstrates a justification for acting in a certain way. Now, she opens fire not with a gun but with the racist slur – Moro! Whereas her racism had been veiled up to a certain point in her use of a reprimanding discourse aimed at his transgressive behavior, it comes out from under its veil as the boy transgresses further by ignoring her frustration.

Acts of *jealouissance* rely on the speaking being's ability to utterly shut out the notion that what they suffer from is their own hateful enjoyment, not in fact, what they have fantasmatically organised in their heads as the (racialised) other's enjoyment. But it is a psychical and social fact that what is foreclosed returns in another form. We are stuck with it. It is stuck to us.

US – loving and dying with ambivalence

It is our argument in this chapter that racisms can be seen to assemble singular prejudices and their jouissances together in a time when the signifier of the Name-of-the-Father has lost its singular, unifying, organizing stickiness. As such, the mobilisation of racist discourses and practices there-fore helps us to understand the psychical, social, political, and ideological forms of satisfaction and compensations for imagined losses that they offer. Lacan was quite right to propose that racism keeps time with social form (Lacan, 1974, p. 32). In other words, as the forms of the social bond undergo change and modification, fantasies concerning the jouissance of the Other escalate in terms of their scope and extremity; as Lacan put it, before the "melting pot" certain fantasies were unheard of (Lacan, ibid.). Psycho-analyst Eric Laurent has remarked that it is not enough to talk about so-called "culture shock" but rather that we should be concerned with what he calls the "shock of different forms of jouissance" since it is this manifold jouissance which splits the social bond apart (Laurent, 2014, p. 5). However, and as Lacan himself argued, there is always, in any human society, a rejection of what counts as an unassimilable jouissance. Ultimately, what is extimate, is, ironically what is also unassimilable!

Jordan Peale's (2019) film *Us* is touted as a "home invasion thriller". But the question for some commentators is about the "social statement" inherent in the film; what would happen if all our shadows were running around in bodies that look exactly like ours but are paradoxically untethered from ourselves (Haubrich, 2019)? This is, quite simply a movie about extimate ambivalence. It is the movie of this book, in a way! The plot twist, is that instead of a white family experiencing the real of their hated jouissance and finding it in their black (or zombie) neighbours, the black family find the real of their hated jouissance in their own uncannily returned (hallucinated) doubles. A twist? Maybe not. Maybe just a touch of Aziz Ansari's proof of Woke; Hollywood is woke, we can rest easy.

We will conclude with Freud's original horrified response to the uncanny intruder:

> I was sitting alone in my wagon-lit compartment when a more than usual violent jolt of the train swung back the door of the adjoining washing-cabinet, and an elderly gentleman in a dressing-gown and a travelling cap came in. I assumed that in leaving the washing-cabinet, which lay between the two compartments, he had taken the wrong direction and come into my compartment by mistake. Jumping up with the intention of putting him right, I at once realised to my dismay that the intruder was nothing but my own reflection in the looking-glass on the open door. I can still recollect that I thoroughly disliked *his* appearance.
>
> (Freud, 1919, p. 248, fn.1, our emphasis)

Even Freud, when he knows it is his own reflection, continues to dislike the look of his intruder, laying bare the extimate ambivalence at the heart of being. We rest our case.

References

Baldwin, J. (1993). *The fire next time*. New York: Vintage.

BBC News. (2019). www.bbc.com/news/entertainment-arts-47117177

Bonilla-Silva, E. (2002). The linguistics of color blind racism: How to talk nasty about blacks without sounding "racist". *Critical Sociology*, *28*(1–2), pp. 41–64.

Burman, E. (2019). *Fanon, education, action: Child as method*. London: Routledge.

Chomsky, N. (2017). Noam Chomsky. In G. Yancy (Ed.). *On race: 34 conversations in a time of crisis* (pp. 147–153). Oxford: Oxford University Press.

Dyer, R. (2017). *White: Twentieth anniversary edition*. New York: Routledge.

Fanon, F. (1967). *Black skin, white masks*. Trans. C.L. Markman. New York, NY: Grove Weidenfeld Press. (Original work published 1952).

Fraser, N. (2017). Nancy Fraser. In G. Yancy (Ed.). *On race: 34 conversations in a time of crisis* (pp. 155–166). Oxford: Oxford University Press.

Freud, S. (1910a). Five lectures on psycho-analysis. In *The Standard Edition of the Complete Psychological Works of Sigmund Freud. S.E., XI*, 1–55.

Freud, S. (1919). The Uncanny. In *The Standard Edition of the Complete Psychological Works of Sigmund Freud. S.E., XVII*, 218–256.

Gates, H.L., Jr (1989). TV's black world turns—But stays unreal. *New York Times*, 12 November. www.nytimes.com/1989/11/12/arts/tv-s-black-world-turns-but-stays-unreal.html. Accessed 13 January 2019.

George, S. (2016). *Trauma and race: A Lacanian study of African American racial identity*. Waco, TX: Baylor University Press.

Gilligan, H. (2017). It's the black working class – not white – that was hit hardest by industrial collapse. *Timeline*, 18 May. https://timeline.com/its-the-black-working-class-not-white-that-was-hit-hardest-by-industrial-collapse-1a6eea50f9f0. Accessed 16 January 2019.

Haubrich, W. (2019). *Us review: What happens when our shadows run free? And what the hell is with the rabbits?* www.thefourohfive.com/film/article/us-review-what-happens-when-our-shadows-run-free-and-what-the-hell-is-with-the-rabbits-155.

Lacan, J. (1958). The direction of the treatment and the principles of its power. In Ed. J.-A. Miller, *Écrits: The first complete edition in English* (pp. 489–542). Trans. B. Fink. London & New York: Norton & Co (2006).

Lacan, J. (1974). *Television*. Translated by D. Hollier, R. Krauss, and A. Michelson. New York: W.W. Norton & Co (1990).

Lacan, J. (1999). *On feminine sexuality, the limits of love and knowledge, 1972–1973. Encore: The seminar of Jacques Lacan, book XX*. Ed. J.-A. Miller. Trans. B. Fink. New York and London: Norton.

Lacan, J. (2017). *Formations of the unconscious. The seminar of Jacques Lacan. Book V.* J.-A. Miller (Ed.). Trans. R. Grigg. London: Polity Press.

Laurent, E. (2014). Racism 2.0. *Lacan Quotidien*, *371*, pp. 1–6. Trans. A. Price.

Lorde, A. (1982). Learning from the 60s. *Blackpast*. www/blackpast.org/African-american-history/1982-audre-lorde-learning-60s/. Accessed 16 January 2019.

Obama, B. (2015). Transcript: President Obama's address to the nation on the San Bernardino terror attack and the war on ISIS. *CNN*, 6 December. www.cnn.com/2015/12/06/politics/transcript-obama-san-bernardino-isis-address/index.html Retrieved January 9, 2019.

Rankine, C. (2014). *Citizen: An American lyric*. Minneapolis, MN: Graywolf Press.

Schwarzbaum, L. (1992). The Cosby Show's last laugh. *Entertainment Weekly*, pp. 20–25.

Soltas, E. & Stephens-Davidowitz, S. (2015). The rise of hate search. *New York Times*, 12 December. www.nytimes.com/2015/12/13/opinion/sunday/the-rise-of-hate-search. html?_r=1 Retrieved January 13, 2019.

Sommers-Flanagan, R. (2012). *Counseling and psychotherapy theories in context and practice: Skills, strategies, and techniques*. Hoboken, NJ: Wiley.

Stavrakakis, Y. (2007). *The Lacanian left. Psychoanalysis, theory, politics*. Edinburgh: Edinburgh University Press.

Tomšič, S. (2015). *The capitalist unconscious*. New York & London: Verso Press.

Winograd, B. (2014). Black psychoanalysts speak. *PEP Video Grants*, *1*(1), pp. 1.

Youtube.com. (2016a). www.youtube.com/controversy-as-slavoj-zizek-talks-at-left-forum.

Youtube.com. (2016b). www.youtube.com/watch?v=Qj_dnpnPfOM.

Žižek S. (2003). *Jacques Lacan Critical Evaluations in Cultural Theory*. Vol. 1. Psycho-analysis Theory and Practice. London and New York: Routledge.

Žižek, S. (2017). Moebius strip, cross cap, Klein bottle: The twisted space of subjectivity. Presentation at LACK conference, October, Colorado Springs, Colorado.

Film references

2019 *RIGHT NOW*. Dir., Spike Jonze.

2019 *Us*. Dir., Jordan Peale.

2017 *Dear White People*. Netflix series.

2013–2019 *Orange is the New Black*. Netflix series.

Afterword

Alas, the TV show *Game of Thrones* (2011–2019) has not ended well (this is not our personal opinion!). No sooner had the series ended when hoards of disgruntled fans posted their disappointment on every form of social media in which they could possibly give vent upon – to date over a million and a half or so of them even signed a petition pressing HBO to do a remake of the final season (Dylan, 2019). Chief among the disappointing features of the last season was the sudden trope twist in which Daenerys ("of the House Targaryen, the First of her Name, the Unburnt, Queen of the Andals, the Rhoynar and the First Men, Queen of Meereen, Khaleesi of the Great Grass Sea, Protector of the Realm, Lady Regent of the Seven Kingdoms, Breaker of Chains and Mother of Dragons") turns out to be just plain bad. Or *mad*. Although demonstrating a penchant throughout the other seven seasons of the show for roasting her enemies alive, the story arc would repeatedly return to her desire to right wrongs and break chains (et cetera). The problem according to those who dedicate themselves to interpreting the (plot) twist of fate for Daenerys (and her victims), is that viewers identified with the character for being fierce, but just, and true (Dockterman, 2019; VanderWerff, 2019), and were thus left with not being able to understand why, in the end, Dany would ride her dragon all over King's Landing roasting soldiers and innocent citizens alike. Here is the rub. While viewers were accustomed to previous series in their entirety setting up a particular character as a would-be liberator or a would-be tyrant, the final season did not adequately set up this particular act of tyranny – what we can think of as Daenerys breaking bad – as her "final solution", despite there being motivation a-plenty for her to "act-out" so to speak (her "bestie" brutally murdered in front of her, her beloved Jon Snow revealed to be not only her nephew, but also her potential rival for the eponymous throne). Unable to process Daenerys's character shift from mostly good to extremely bad, disappointed fans and commentators quickly renamed her in a single new nomination (contrasting bluntly with her multiple nominations hitherto); she became simply, "the *mad* Queen" (following in the footsteps of her father, the mad King). Add to this wide-scale perplexed viewer response the sentiment of hundreds of mortified American parents who – according to the U.S. Social Security Administration – named their daughters Khaleeshi or Daenerys in the last couple of years (Shepherd, 2019) and we have a full-on up to the minute example of the kinds of ambivalent tension fall-out which we have devoted ourselves to examining in this book.

Throughout, we have wanted to identify and explore some of the social and psychical impasses mobilised where experiences of ambivalence are negated, or in Lacanian psychoanalytic terminology: foreclosed, disavowed, and repressed. Commensurately, as psychoanalysts ourselves, we wanted to be able to consider what kinds of symptoms emerge as a result of the negations of the tensions of ambivalence, and/or the very experiences of ambivalence – whether in our social/cultural/political spaces, or in our psychical places (the classical Freudian *der anderer schauplatz*, the Lacanian extimate, amongst others).

We began this investigation into ambivalence with a different game involving thrones, none other than King Henry VIII's escapades with his unfortunate wives in order to consider the function of catharsis and the appetite, ultimately, for zombie killings. Our journey has involved painstaking "research" hours in front of the small, and the big screen, contemplating the conscious and unconscious representational functionalities of vampires, zombie apocalypses, ghosts, and beleaguered Oedipal fathers "breaking bad", as well as sending us tracing and tracking the hidden aspects of ambivalent desires and tensions, on and off the couch, in online forums, in client dreams and associations, and ultimately in every little nook and cranny where we believed we could sniff out the repression of ambivalence and its effects.

Some of these effects we argue are immanent in the persistence and intransigence of hateful prejudices manifest in violent and oppressive acts of xenophobia and racism, in violent and ferocious misogyny such as those carried out by the Blackpill "incel" men and their tribes. Other effects we have been keen to investigate are what we can think of as contemporary *declensions* of the Oedipus complex. Many psychoanalysts today (especially Lacanians) regard Oedipus as a show that has run its final season. We don't agree. As clinicians, we regularly work with iterations of Oedipal guilt, on the one hand in its more classical Freudian iteration as an index of a specifically obsessional brand of neurosis – a guilt of (the idea, or the act of) enjoying too much we could say; on the other hand, we also find a newer form of guilt that we have described as tied to newer forms of ideology such as neoliberalism and late capitalism, with its support of a compulsion to enjoy, in this case the guilt is coordinated with a failure to enjoy enough. Both these forms of guilt hinge upon the desire of the Other and the subject's ambivalent, conflicted relationship to that desire, in particular regarding transgression of that desire and fantasies thereof. In fact, guilt is (as it ever was) itself understandable as a failsafe index of unconscious ambivalence. Ambivalence, intolerable, mobilises us towards all sorts of faulty solutions; and above all, to love, in order to escape guilt (Lacan, 2017, p. 337). But, as such, it is hate that festers in the extimate and *unheimlich* experience of our own disgusting, hateful jouissance, which masquerades as belonging to another. Loving our neighbour when that very neighbour is someone whom, under capitalism, we must compete with, becomes an impossible and stressful task, when we have no place or space within which we can understand why we would rather chew our neighbour's head off.

We did not set out to offer guidelines for the taming, domestication, or management of ambivalence; that would be a very different kind of book. We do however believe that it is smart practice in our affairs with other speaking beings to cultivate understanding and acceptance of both poles of ambivalence – *hainamoration* – as intrinsic to the speaking being's colonisation and overwriting by ideological, political, and cultural discourses, and through psychical operations; the ones we have discussed here are those of twentieth and twenty-first century complexes which are themselves formed, shaped, and conditioned by ideologies bound to the economic system of advanced, global capitalism and the symbolic order coordinates associated with this system.

References

Dockterman, E. (2019). http://time.com/5590729/game-of-thrones-finale-daenerys/.

Dylan, D. (2019). www.change.org/p/hbo-remake-game-of-thrones-season-8-with-competent-writers.

Lacan, J. (2017). *Transference. The seminar of Jacques Lacan. Book VIII. 1960–1961.* Ed. J.-A. Miller. Trans. B. Fink. London: Polity Press.

VanderWerff, E.T. (2019). www.vox.com/culture/2019/5/17/18624767/game-of-thrones-series-finale-season-8-episode-5-the-bells-daenerys-dany-kings-landing-targaryen.

Shepherd, J. (2019). Game of Thrones: parents who named their children Khaleesi respond to Daenerys becoming the Mad Queen. https://www.independent.co.uk/arts-entertainment/tv/news/game-of-thrones-khaleesi-daenerys-children-name-season-8-mad-queen-a8913046.html

Index

Time:

Location: **Cardio Pacemaker Room 31.3.006, Level 3, Out-Patients East, Norfolk & Norwich University Hospital**

If you are arriving by car, at the hospital roundabout, follow the signs for out-patients. You can park in either of the out-patients car parks. Disabled parking is available in all out-patient car-parks and public transport stops directly outside the out-patient entrances.

On arrival, please enter the hospital via the **East Out-patients** entrance, go to **Level 3** and follow the signs to **Pacemaker** and **ICD Service**.

Please note the appointment time given is not necessarily the time you will be seen.

If this appointment is no longer convenient for you, please contact the hospital on **01603 286257**. It is important that you let us know well in advance so that we can use the appointment for someone else.

Please note that if a patient cancels an appointment more than twice, or fails to attend their appointment or admission without giving notice, they will be referred back to the care of their GP for re-referral, if treatment is still required.

Self Check-in

Please bring this letter with you.

health records and although it is not essential to your treatment, it can be helpful if you are able to make a note of the number and give it to NHS staff that need to find your health records.

Yours sincerely

On behalf of
The Cardiology Directorate

Making a Donation
You can support the Trust in its endeavour to provide the highest quality service to its patients. With the restrictions on public funding, voluntary donations can really make a difference in supporting additional medical equipment, medical research and improvements to patient facilities. If you would like to support the Hospital Charity you can do so by donating online at https://www.justgiving.com/nnuhnhs/donate/ or by sending a cheque made payable to NNUH NFT Charitable Fund at Fundraising 6th Floor 20 Rouen Road Norwich NR1 1QQ.

If you were followed up previously at another hospital and this is your first appointment with us please bring your pacemaker/ICD identification card with you and any other information you have regarding your pacemaker/ICD.

If you require hospital transport, please contact **03332 404100** 5-10 days prior to your appointment to arrange this. Please make them aware that you will be ready to go home 30 minutes after the stated appointment time at the time of booking.

If you are allergic to latex gloves or other latex products please advise the doctor or nurse. For the health of our patients, visitors and staff, smoking is not allowed at our hospitals.

The Norfolk and Norwich University Hospital is a teaching hospital and medical students may observe whilst you are being treated. If you would prefer not to have a medical student present, please inform your doctor when you attend the hospital. We are also very active in clinical research. Your doctor may therefore approach you now or in the future to discuss your possible participation in a research project. In both cases, non participation in research studies or a preference not to have medical students present will not affect your care in any way.

Parking at the Norfolk and Norwich University Hospital cannot be guaranteed at peak times. Please try and use the Hospital Shuttle which operates from the Costessey Park and Ride or other bus services wherever possible *'It's less fuss by bus'*. For more information on local bus services contact Traveline: 0871 200 22 33 or www.traveline.org.uk

This letter includes your NHS Number. This number helps healthcare staff to find your

Our Vision
To provide every patient
with the care we want
for those we love the most

Norfolk and Norwich University Hospitals **NHS**

NHS Foundation Trust

Cardiology Directorate

**Norfolk & Norwich University
Hospitals NHS Foundation Trust**
Colney Lane
Norwich
NR4 7UY

16 January, 2020

Hospital Number: **1580199**
NHS Number: **452 039 6271**

Dr Richard Pannett
40 Damgate Lane
Martham
Great Yarmouth
Norfolk
NR29 4PZ

Dear Dr Pannett

The Outpatient appointment previously arranged for you to see **Technician** on Tuesday
24 March 2020 **has been cancelled:**

This is to confirm you have cancelled these arrangements.

A further appointment has been arranged:

Clinic: **Pacemaker Clinic**
Da   Wednesday 18 March 2020